A JOURNAL OF
CONSCIOUSNESS AND TRANSFORMATION

ReVision

http://revisionpublishing.org   P.O. Box 783, Middletown, CA 95461   (707) 987 1967

• Envisioning...Revisioning • *Jürgen W. Kremer, Editor* •

CONTENTS

cover art: *Domestication, Mariana Castro de Ali*

• *Summer & Fall 2008* • *Volume 30* • *Numbers 1 & 2* •

What is ReVision?

For almost thirty years *ReVision* has explored the transformative and consciousness-changing dimensions of leading-edge thinking. Since its inception *Revision* has been a vital forum, especially in the North American context, for the articulation of contemporary spirituality, transpersonal studies, and related new models in such fields as education, medicine, organization, social transformation, work, psychology, ecology, and gender.

With a commitment to the future of humanity and the Earth, *ReVision* emphasizes the transformative dimensions of current and traditional thought and practice. *ReVision* advances inquiry and reflection especially focused on the fields presently identified as philosophy, religion, psychology, social theory, science, anthropology, education, organizational transformation, and the arts. We seek to explore new models of transdisciplinary, interdisciplinary, multicultural, dialogical, socially engaged inquiry, and frontier science, as well as ancient ways of knowing, and to bring such work to bear on what appear to be the fundamental issues of our times through a variety of written and artistic modalities. In the interests of renewal and fresh vision, we strive to engage in conversation a diversity of perspectives and discourses which have often been kept separate, including those identified with terms such as Western and Eastern; indigenous and nonindigenous; Northern and Southern; feminine and masculine; intellectual, practical, and spiritual; local and global; young and old.

Volume 30, Nos. 1 & 2 (ISBN 978-0-9819706-0-8)
ReVision (ISSN 0275-6935) published as part of the
Society for the Study of Shamanism, Healing, and Transformation.

POSTMASTER: Send address changes to
ReVision Publishing, P.O. Box 783, Middletown, CA 95461.

Manuscript Submissions
We welcome manuscript submissions. Manuscript guidelines can be found on our webpage http://revisionpublishing.org.

Mailing Address
ReVision Publishing, P.O. Box 783, Middletown, CA 95461.

Subscriptions
For subscriptions mail a check to above address or go to www.revisionpublishing.org.
Individual Subscriptions
Subscription for one year (vols. 30 & 31): $36 online only, $36 print only, $48 print and online.
Vols. 30 & 31 published beginning March 2009.
Subscription for one year (vol. 32): $36 online only, $36 print only, $48 print and online. *Vol. 32 published toward the end of 2009.*
Subscription for two years (vols. 30 – 32): $60 online only, $60 print only, $79 print and online.
Subscription for three years (vols. 30 – 33): $72 online only, $72 print only, $96 print and online.
Add $21 per subscription year for postage outside the U.S.
International subscriptions via PayPal or bank check in US Dollars
Institutional Subscriptions
Vols. 30 & 31: $98 online only, $118 print and online.
Vol. 32: $98 online only, $118 print and online.
Add $21 for postage outside the U.S.
Please allow six weeks for delivery of first issue.

Revision Abstracts

Vol. 30 Nos. 1 & 2   *Summer & Fall 2008*

Ferrer, J. (2008). Beyond monogamy and polyamory: A new vision of intimate relationships for the twenty-first century. *ReVision, 30*(1 & 2), 53-58.

This paper explores how the extension of contemplative qualities to intimate relationships can transform our sexual/emotional responses and relationship choices. The paper reviews contemporary findings from the field of evolutionary psychology on the twin origins of jealousy and monogamy, argues for the possibility to transform jealousy into sympathetic joy (mudita), addresses the common objections against polyamory (or non-monogamy), and challenges the culturally prevalent belief that the only spiritually correct sexual options are either celibacy or monogamy. To conclude, it is suggested that the cultivation of sympathetic joy (mudita) in intimate bonds can overcome the problematic dichotomy between monogamy and polyamory, grounding individuals in a radical openness to the dynamic unfolding of life that eludes any fixed structure of relationship.

Jackson-Paton, R. J. (2008). Rituals of Inquiry; or, Looking for 'Culture and Truth.' *ReVision, 30*(1 & 2), 13-17.

By using a personal narrative centered on the search for the book 'Culture & Truth,' I address the nexus of issues related to the subject/object split in research, divisions between emotion and rationality, as well as whiteness and decolonization. The implications for research agendas, personal transformation, indigenous epistemologies, and (de)constructions of a White settler identity are also introduced.

Jaenke, K. (2008). Earth, Dream, Body. *ReVision, 30*(1 & 2), 10-12.

We live in a time of unimaginable extinction of life forms and disruption of ecosystems. Coming to terms with the reality of our time as one of demise and extinction, and of our human role in the pervasive destruction of life, calls for a searing search into the depths of the human psyche and our collective human history. In trying to find our way through this initiatory moment, my hope turns not to modern technological solutions arising through the powers of the left brain and logical mind (though these no doubt will play a role), but rather to ancient sources of inspiration, guidance, and knowledge that have perennially assisted humanity in crisis. Dreams, the lifeways of indigenous peoples, and bodily wisdom draw upon an extra-rational, synthetic and soulful intelligence arising from the right brain and offer resources for the challenges and potentials posed by our unique moment.

Kesner, A., & Pritzker, S. (2008). *Therapeutic horseback riding with children placed in the Foster Care System. ReVision, 30*(1 & 2), 77-87.

Studies concerning animal-assisted therapies and therapeutic horseback riding have involved specific populations, including individuals with physical disabilities, developmental disorders, the elderly, and at-risk youth. To date, no studies looked at the effect of therapeutic horseback riding on children in therapeutic foster care (TFC). TFC children have been abused and abandoned so they struggle with trusting others, low self-concept, and forming quality relationships. Case study methodology combined with a quasi-experimental design was utilized to answer the research question: What are the effects of therapeutic horseback riding on abused children placed in the therapeutic foster care system? Each child's case was analyzed and triangulated by converging data sources. Qualitative analysis of the interviews identified themes including improved Acceptance of self and others, positive changes in Behavior, decreased Ambivalence, increased Satisfaction and happiness and greater enjoyment of Socialization. The results of this study clearly support the use of animal-assisted therapy with TFC children participants, as well as some of the TFC parents seemed to experience a paradigm shift in their values from the experience.

Kremer, J. W. (2008). Northern Light Ancestors. *ReVision, 30*(1 & 2), 32-43.

Shamanic practice is explored as endeavor that is not just dedicated to balancing and healing individuals, but that is part of endeavors to decolonize and heal cultures and their ecologies. The first part explores dreams that have guided the author's particular shamanic practice. The second part describes the author's ancestral cultural grounding in a specific culture, the Indo-European peoples of the European north. The final section provides meditative statements that appear to be part of the underlying principles of shamanic practices dedicated to individual and cultural healing as well as and egalitarian exchange among spiritual traditions.

Krippner, S., & Feinstein, D. (2008). A mythological approach to transpersonal psychotherapy. *ReVision, 30*(1 & 2), 18-31.

This paper presents a model of psychotherapy that emphasizes the client's evolving personal mythology, its conflicts, and its transformations. While harmonious with Jungian and other transpersonal psychologies, a mythological formulation also takes the cognitive trend in clinical practice a step further by conceptually embracing the intuitive realm and the spiritual impulse in conceiving of the client's assumptive world. Because personal and cultural myths evolve in tandem, a conceptual link to the social basis of human behavior is also inherent in this model.

Low, A. (2008). Creativity and intention in evolution. *ReVision, 30*(1 & 2), 88-96.

The neo-Darwinian interpretation of the theory of evolution is a distortion of Darwin's original theory because it is based upon a misunderstanding of the struggle for existence, which, together with natural selection, forms the keystone of Darwin's theory. Because of this distortion neo-Darwinian theory is unable to account for intentional activity, which is basic to much of life. The attempt by some neo-Darwinians to remedy this omission by recourse to an explanation that claims organisms are endowed with goal seeking programs is shown to be groundless. A new interpretation of Darwin's theory of the struggle for existence is offered, and this interpretation lays the groundwork for seeing evolution as intentional and creative without the need for an external creator.

Mendenhall, M. (2008). A radical approach to delinquency reform. *ReVision, 30*(1 & 2), 71-76.

This article summarizes a qualitative research study that investigated the lived experience of incarcerated juvenile delinquents who practiced Chuan Fa (a form of Buddhist martial arts) daily for twelve weeks. The particular focus was on the subjective experience of participants who practiced Chuan Fa to help resolve emotional problems, and cultivate a strong moral foundation. Results of the study indicate that participation in a Buddhist martial art training program may be a helpful method of curbing aggressive tendencies, and developing self-awareness in the lives of some incarcerated juvenile delinquents.

Pelicci, G. (2008). Growth and transformation among women healers. *ReVision, 30*(1 & 2), 46-52.

This article presents the findings of a research study about growth and transformation among five women healers. Six themes became evident in the study: a) The Importance of a Support Network; b) Ongoing Learning and Self-Transformation; c) Nature as a Teacher and Tool for Healing; d) Energy as a Universal Language; e) Integral Approach to Healing; and, f) Purpose-driven Life.

Slater, P. (2008). Are boys being trained for obsolescence? *ReVision, 30*(1 & 2), 67-70.

Our shrinking world is changing rapidly in a way that favors the skills that women developed playing traditional gender roles. Women have now expanded their role definition to include a full range of human behavior. Men have not, and are finding themselves ill equipped for a world in which communication and cooperation have become primary. Men are still being raised and psychologically conditioned as if they were to spend their adult years in hand-to-hand combat—skills largely irrelevant even in the military. While women are thriving, men are finding themselves confused, since masculinity has always been defined negatively, as 'not feminine', leaving them faced with a constantly shrinking sense of self.

Watson-Gegeo, K. A. (2008). Children with knives: When theory becomes ideology. *ReVision, 30*(1 & 2), 59-65.

The integrity of academe as a site for knowledge construction is undermined when theory becomes ideology. This article analyzes three cases that illustrate how power is used to enforce ideological positions in research via the privileging of theory over practice, the rejection of systematic observation to protect theory from challenge, and the positioning of counter-argument as outside acceptable boundaries. The examples are drawn from the author's research experience over 25 years on children's socialization and indigenous epistemology in Kwara'ae, Malaita, in Solomon Islands.

Envisioning...Revisioning

A Statement from the Editors:

Matthew Bronson, Robert Jackson-Paton, Karen Jaenke, Jürgen Kremer, Alfonso Montuori, Beverly Rubik

This issue turns a new leaf in *ReVision* history: After Heldref published the journal for over twenty years, it is now under new ownership with the Society for the Study of Shamanism, Healing, and Transformation. With this change comes a renewed editorial board: Jürgen Kremer now functions as editor, with Matthew Bronson, Karen Jaenke, Alfonso Montuori, and Beverly Rubik as executive editors; Robert Jackson-Paton is the new managing editor. Together we represent the sixth generation of *ReVision* editors. The journal has now been published continually in the United States for some thirty years.

Our current mission statement, slightly revised in 2009, continues to build on *ReVision's* work of the last thirty years and points to new horizons:

With a commitment to the future of humanity and the Earth, *ReVision* emphasizes the transformative dimensions of current and traditional thought and practice. *ReVision* advances inquiry and reflection especially focused on the fields presently identified as philosophy, religion, psychology, social theory, science, anthropology, education, organizational transformation, and the arts. We seek to explore new models of transdisciplinary, interdisciplinary, multicultural, dialogical, and socially engaged inquiry, frontier science, as well as ancient ways of knowing, and to bring such work to bear on what appear to be the fundamental issues of our times through a variety of written and artistic modalities. In the interests of renewal and fresh vision, we strive to engage in conversation a diversity of perspectives and discourses which have often been kept separate, including those identified with terms such as Western and Eastern; indigenous

and nonindigenous; Northern and Southern; feminine and masculine; intellectual, practical, and spiritual; local and global; young and old.

We continue to be interested in expanding the kind of articles published in *ReVision.* For example, we intend to cultivate in-depth dialogues by encouraging contributors with different views and experiences to explore a common theme, question, or practical challenge. We believe that rigorous and respectful dialogue is deeply needed both in the world at large, with its often warring groups, and among those who would heal and transform the contemporary world. The 1996 *ReVision* series of conversations around the work of Ken Wilber, and other recent articles, continues to stand as an example of the steps we have taken toward a more dialogical journal (since then published as *Ken Wilber in Dialogue: Conversations with Leading Transpersonal Thinkers* by Quest). Future issues may facilitate similar in-depth dialogue around such issues as spiritual traditions and social engagement.

We are aware of historical tendencies to limit or exclude many voices in the discourses of our culture. We commit *ReVision* to develop inquiries and conversations that are multicultural, international, and interdisciplinary in scope and to bring in contributors who have not been part of *ReVision's* past discussions.

We also seek to open the forms of communication by inviting a spectrum of contributions ranging from more abstract and theoretical writing to poetry, personal narratives, and artistic modalities and by grounding these con-

tributions in our personal, interpersonal, social, ecological, spiritual, and political practices. In more recent years issues have included more images. Mariana Castro de Ali will now regularly contribute her artistic images; this issue contains her art on the cover as well as painting, drawings, woodcuts, and photos throughout. Michael Sheffield is contributing his poetry, some of it in haiku-style. Future issues will continue to contain art and poetry and we hope to include commentary on current affairs or questions from the perspective of our mission. Autobiographical writing as well as other features designed to facilitate engagement, reflection, and dialogue in the spirit of *ReVision* will also be included.

In part all this means that we will often share our questions, vulnerabilities, and "reports along the way" rather than our completed "answers." We believe that the issues of our times often call for more humility and less certainty than is currently brought to the debate.

The present issue explores a wider spectrum of issues, from healing to relationship to polyamory, from delinquency reform to women healers. The subsequent issue on Transformative Leadership is edited by Alfonso Montuori. It includes contributions by Ginger Chih, Rita Durant, Urusa Fahim, Charles Hampden-Turner, Connie Jones, Bradford Keeney, Albert Low, Wendy Mason, Jay Ogilvy, Jack Petranker, and Philip Slater on such topics as spiritual leaders, diversity and leadership, why democracy is taking over global culture, and the N/om of the Kalahari Bushmen and transformative leadership.

At the present moment, individual issues *of ReVision* are generally prepared by a single editor or a team of two editors who focus on a particular theme selected by the editors as a group. All articles are peer reviewed. The issue editor then invites a number of contributors for a given issue. We editors are struggling with how to bring our readers more into *ReVision* dialogues and conversations, to help us to carry out many of the core intentions mentioned above. The current issue, like future ones will, also contains unsolicited papers. We are inviting manuscript submissions that fall in the general area of our mission, with a particular interest in frontier science, earth dreaming, ritual, and intuition. Readers are invited to submit ideas for contributions by submitting a one paragraph description of no more than 500 words together with a curriculum vitae (including a list of publications) and a sample of your writing. Alternatively you may submit an abstract together with the complete manuscript to Jürgen Werner Kremer, Editor, at jkremer@sonic.net. *ReVision* accepts electronic submissions only. Please see our website for author information.

You are invited to be part of these conversations as we continue to explore how *ReVision* can serve as a forum to address some of the most fundamental questions and issues of our times.

EDITORS' STATEMENTS

As a way of introducing ourselves to *ReVision* readers, we present here our individual reflections on the mission statement as it relates to each of our interests:

Jürgen Werner Kremer
In recent years I have been involved in interdisciplinary work with indigenous peoples as part of my practice of socially engaged spirituality. My theoretical work is an attempt to transgress the established boundaries of nature, culture, and gender, and to walk in the spaces between and across disciplinary territories exploring the transformative dimensions of current and traditional thought and practice. My spiritual practices are shamanic in nature and I am involved with the organization of the annual *Annual International Conference on the Study of Shamanism and Alternative Modes of Healing* (founded

by Dr. Ruth-Inge Heinze it is now in its 26th year). Recently I have written about ethnoautobiography, dissociation, healing and cosmology, Ken Wilber, trance, the history of sense alienation in euro-centered cultures, my travels in Sápmi (Lappland), the bear in circumpolar stories, the obligations of a white man, ancestral conversations, the trickster of the transpersonal, altered states, Old Norse mythology, and violence against indigenous peoples.

Growing up in West Germany shortly after World War II, I was painfully aware of the pervasive denials of the Shoah (German genocide against Jews). I observed the profound impact of these silences on education, psychotherapy, and narratives of identity in

> I hope that out of the tears about the grievous things our ancestors have suffered and committed, amidst all the achievements, there will arise shared laughter and appreciation.

general. Similar silences exert a continuing power in this country. Deconstruction of Whiteness, decolonization, confrontation with cultural shadow material - these are among my primary professional interests.

My teaching and writing focuses on a decolonizing discourse of Whiteness, the history of modernist White self-constructions, and the critical reconstruction of European indigenous layers. I hope that out of the tears about the grievous things our ancestors have suffered and committed, amidst all the achievements, there will arise shared laughter and appreciation as the joy of the local truth ceases to be a call for dominance, and as people enjoy and appreciate each other's capacity for cross-cultural learning. Facing collective shadow material, the inclusion of the dark and light seem to prevent us from superficial nostalgia and dissociated romanticism in relation to any culture, and help us to move into the future through our connections with ancestral cultural roots. The remembrance of the web of stories that create who we are; the connection with the

surrounding lands, community, and cultural history; the philosophical reflection upon our cultural premises; the dialogue of the various sciences with local knowledge and narratives, i.e. indigenous science – these seem to be ways to open an avenue for rich multicultural inquiry and learning as well as the resolution of cultural wounds and the exploration of the liberating potential of ethnic constructions. My work is dedicated to diverse learning environments that elicit the teachers' and students' potentials through personal and scholarly inquiry for the sake of the communities to which they will dedicate their professional lives. Autobiographical writing, "ethnoautobiography," is an approach I am using with students to help them navigate the processes of personal and cultural ethnic narratives.

I received my education at the University of Hamburg in Germany. My past positions include, Dean of Faculty and Vice President of Academic Affairs at Saybrook Institute in San Francisco; Academic Dean, of the Integral Studies Program and of the East-West Psychology Program and I was co-director of the PhD program for Traditional Knowledge at the California Institute of Integral Studies. I presently teach at the Santa Rosa Junior College. I have (co)written several books and contributed extensively to journals, handbooks, readers, and more popular venues. "Towards a Person-Centered Resolution of Intercultural Conflicts" (1980) is the title of one of my books. After receiving my doctorate in clinical psy-

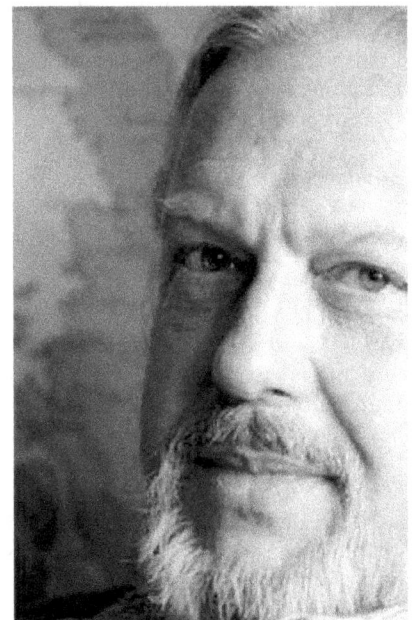

chology at the University of Hamburg, Germany, and working for some years in private practice, I relocated to San Francisco to teach at Saybrook Institute Graduate School.

If there is to be anything like planetary consciousness for us "moderns" (who have grown up with technologies that take us further and further away from the land and increasingly engross us in the cultural life of cities, with dimming memories of roots), I can imagine it only with the inclusion of the denied, suppressed and assaulted parts of humanity and our history—the recovery of our shadow material. This process involves the struggle to overcome sexism, racism, classism, anthropocentrism, colonialism, genocide, biocide, spiritual oppression, and other forces destructive of life. An imagined complete conversation with all our relations, whether human or not, would require that we struggle with the brokenness and the contradictions in human relations. What I see is that as we strive for global awareness the many torn connections seem to reveal themselves ever more vividly.

I have been involved with *ReVision* since 1992, after initially subscribing in 1983. I have edited or co-edited issues on Culture and Ways of Knowing (vols. 14, 4 & 15, 1), Shamanism (vol. 16,4), Indigenous Science (vols. 18, 3 & 19, 3), Transformative Learning (vol. 20, 1), Narrative Explorations of Culture, Roots, and Ancestry (vol. 21, 1), Collective Shadow Work (vol. 22, 1), The New Millennium (vol. 23, 3), Prophecy and Historical Responsibility (vol. 23, 2), Paradigmatic Challenges (vol. 24, 3), Identity and Peace – Transpersonal Perspectives (vol. 26, 2), Dreaming (vol. 28, 4), and Dreams and Place (vol. 29, 1).

Matthew Bronson

Philosophy is grammar writ large.
Dan Moonhawk Alford

My life has been a search for the words to express my awe at the mystery of the world and to help others find the words to do the same. In my never-ending attempt to "eff the ineffable," I began the study of languages at U.C. Berkeley as a young man and came to the stark realization that one could not master twelve languages easily in four years. In linguistics, the systematic investigation of language in all

its manifestations, I found an intellectual home from which to venture forth into the realms of cognitive science, philosophy, anthropology and, most recently, education.

The questions that have guided me through three degrees and anchored my work as a scholar and practitioner have included: How does language influence consciousness and vice versa? How is one's experience of the world different if one is socialized into a different language, culture and worldview? How do the labels we use to frame experience help to construct the meaning of the experience? And more recently as I have worked with social activists and advocates: What do people interested in social change need to know about language and communication to be effective in their work? How can sustained attention to language *qua* language contribute to a deeper understanding of issues of power, identity, gender, class in contemporary settings? What can a critical linguistics contribute to intercultural dialogue and the healing of interpersonal and interethnic conflict?

I have been amazed how my teaching and writing on these topics for more than twenty-five years has touched people and, based on what they tell me, facilitated major breakthroughs and insights on a regular basis. As my students reflect on carefully prepared transcriptions of real-world conversations and contemplate in a sustained way the sea of words in which they swim each day, they cultivate "linguistic mindfulness' that can stay with them for a lifetime. They tell me years after the fact that the work saved marriages, enabled them to handle hecklers more artfully, and gave

them the tools with which to create more effective messages of social change. My work as an academic writing instructor has taught me compassion for the lived struggles of writers to find their voice and to master the rhetoric of power without sacrificing personal vision. As a mentor of future professors in teaching skills, I have attempted to tap the best thinking in educational theory and apply it to the practical situations my students are likely to face.

The trajectory of my professional life has mirrored my shifting focus and increasing sense of responsibility to contribute to a world in crisis. I helped to found one of the first psycho-social intervention programs for people living with HIV in San Francisco in the late 1980s and later took this work to Brazil with a focus on cancer. As a teacher educator at U.C. Davis since 1998, I have struggled to prepare the next generation of high-school teachers to creatively and humanely engage linguistic and cultural diversity. As a professor in a post-colonial anthropology program dedicated to social and environmental

> What can a critical linguistics contribute to intercultural dialogue and the healing of interpersonal and interethnic conflict?

justice, I have helped to prepare scholar-advocates to work on behalf of subaltern communities around the world. As the Director of Academic Assessment at CIIS., I have learned how to bridge the worlds of progressive, integral education and the mainstream requirements for transparency, accreditation and academic quality. My work as an interpreter in South American and Europe is an apt metaphor for my career: once you learn how to say something well in one language, people want you to translate it into another.

My publications and editorial work for *ReVision* thus far has reflected many of these interests. "Rekindling the flutes of fire: Why indigenous languages matter to humanity was my first publication in 2003 when I joined the journal. A special double issue, "The Language of Spirituality" in 2004 showcased ongoing dialogues between native elders and western scientists in search of an ancient future. Another double issue grappled with the attempt to revision higher education in 2005-2006. I am publishing a book in 2009 entitled, "So What? Now What?: The Anthropology of Consciousness Responds to a World in Crisis" with Cambridge Scholar's Press. I am interested in cultivating a continuing dialogue in print on issues related to language and consciousness, cultural and personal healing, indigenous language, spirituality and land rights, higher education reform, assessment, methods and ethics of educational and anthropological research, and intercultural communication. I believe that *ReVision* is uniquely positioned to harness the best thinking of our time to grapple with the pressing issues of our day. I embrace the vision of a more sustainable and just world that the journal embodies and invite you to join more actively in the discussion and community-building possibilities on offer here. May we do good work together in the months and years ahead. The world needs it!

Karen Jaenke

Soul wounding dwells at the heart of my life's work, along with the healing medicine that comes when soul wounding forms the center of inquiry. Personal soul wounding acts as a mirror for unhealed wounds carried in the collective. Unresolved collective issues become pressed into the personal soma-psyche, where they necessitate resolution through unfolding personal destiny.

> Recovering and validating neglected ways of knowing—rooted in human subjectivity, imagination, dreams, the body, subtle perception and the subtle body—guide my engagement with the world.

My adult life has been forged in the crucible of my dreams, where the archetypal wisdom of the human race is funneled into the individual psyche on a nightly basis. During interdisciplinary doctoral studies in consciousness studies, I unearthed my birth trauma through the images of dreams and the

a f-fliction of migraine headaches. Arriving at the origin point of my personal biography opened a vast gateway to transpersonal, ancestral, and indigenous sources of knowledge, dimensions communicated insistently through dreams. My research and writing focus on the recovery of traditional ways of knowing and being of my German ancestors through dreams, and led to heightened awareness of the "somatic understructure" of dreams.

For the last seven years I have taught within a newly coalescing orientation to psychology known as Imaginal Psychology, oriented around the care of the soul, with imagination forming a key portal into soul. Recovering and validating neglected ways of knowing—rooted in human subjectivity, imagination, dreams, the body, subtle perception and the subtle body--guide my engagement with the world.

The planetary ecological crisis frames my understanding of the particular challenges and potentials posed by our zeitgeist. Impending environmental collapse presents humanity with the necessity of a collective initiation, along with renewal of ways of knowing and being attuned to earth mother, matter and the deep feminine. Respect for the natural mind present in the dreaming self and for the deep intelligence within the body offer doorways into respect for the earth body. My editor's essay below gives a more detailed idea of my present concerns.

Alfonso Montuori

I am Professor and Department Chair of the Transformative Studies Ph.D. and Transformative Leadership M.A. at California Institute of Integral Studies. A graduate of the University of London, I was Distinguished Professor in the School of Fine Arts at Miami University of Ohio, and in 1985-1986 was a visiting lecturer at the Central South University in the People's Republic of China.

Born of an Italian father and Dutch mother, I grew up trilingual. I was born in Holland, and grew up in Lebanon, Greece, and England before coming to the United States in 1983. In London I worked as an interpreter for Scotland Yard and as a professional musician on saxophone and flute, making numerous recordings with my own band and as a session-man, and gigging extensively throughout England for several years. Today, I continue my passion for music through the collaboration with my wife, the jazz singer Kitty Margolis, as producer of her award-winning recordings.

My books include *Evolutionary Competence* (Gieben, 1989); *From*

Power to Partnership (co-authored with Isabella Conti, Harper San Francisco, 1993); *Creators on Creating* (co-edited with Barron & Barron, Putnam, 1997); and *Social Creativity, Vols. 1 & 2* (co-edited with Ronald E. Purser, Hampton Press, 1999). I have written articles in publications such as *Academy of Management Review, Human Relations, Journal of Management Education, Pluriverso,* and *Journal of Humanistic Psychology.*

I have consulted on executive and management development and creativity and innovation with numerous international corporations, including Procter & Gamble, Network Appliance, Training Vision (Singapore), Pacific Bell, Stentor Group (Canada), Kaiser Permanente, Interstate Insurance, Omnitel-Olivetti (Italy), ENEL (Italy), U.S. Department of Labor, University of Missouri Kansas City, Nestle Beverage, Pilkington Barnes Hinde, 3Com, Progressive Insurance, and others.

Beverly Rubik

My career has been that of scientist, researcher, educator, and spokesperson, and I've walked the road less traveled. One of my quests is to understand Nature more deeply by participating gently with her, and to hold awe, reverence, and tenderness for every being on this planet. To quote my friend and colleague, Dr. Nick Herbert, physicist, who proposes that we engage with nature differently in what he calls "quantum tantra" that is best expressed in a poem of his, "Jabir's Formula" (Herbert, 2000):

I want to woo Her, not view Her
pet Reality until She purrs
yearning to merge with Dame Nature bodily
longing to mingle my substance with Hers:
and them that's content with merely observing
are nothing but Nature's voyeurs.

I am a female scientist-explorer of the yoga of knowledge and am eager to discover more about the subtlest aspects of life, health, optimal wellness, and healing, recognizing that making life whole happens at all levels of being, from coherence in biomolecules to coherence within the whole person--mind-body-spirit--and beyond, to harmony within the family, community, and the environment. I'm flabbergasted and exasperated at much of the mythology of our times put forth by conventional science and the dominant health care system about what constitutes adequate care, because so much of it is inadequate or dead wrong. I'm also excited about new perspectives; out-of-the-box thinking; alternative and complementary modalities of healing; and novel discoveries in general that challenge the status quo.

To many, my name is synonymous with "frontier science," because for decades I have been a strong proponent of new areas and approaches that challenge mainstream science and medicine. I believe that these are among the richest ones to be mined that will lead to novel breakthroughs. I've contributed to several areas of frontier science myself—in my writings on the interrelationship between mind and matter, and the role of consciousness in science; healer interactions and the nature

of spiritual healing; the biofield in health and healing; and toward truly integrative health care. I'm also committed to connecting new scientific knowledge with indigenous wisdom that reconnects us to our role as planetary stewards and to sustainability of life on earth.

I propose that there may be a vital force or subtle energy that is the quintessence of life and central to the new integrative medicine as well as all indigenous healing. It may be a subtle organizing field within the organism and surrounding it, which I, along with others, refer to as the *biofield*. The biofield is within us and extends from the body into the surrounding space, and may be subject to changes by conscious intent. Energetically and informationally, the biofield entangles each person with one another, the biosphere and the cosmos. The biofield is thought to be at the scientific basis of many types of therapies, including laying-on-

> I propose that there may be a vital force or subtle energy that is the quintessence of life and central to the new integrative medicine as well as all indigenous healing.

of-hands by energy healers, energy psychology, homeopathy, and "energy medicine" devices. Biofield science has been one of my main contributions and most recent interests at the frontier, and I'm intrigued how much wisdom indigenous medicine contributes to our understanding of the human energy field. I wish to facilitate the building of bridges between cutting edge discoveries and indigenous knowing.

I am also a hands-on person who likes to get her hands dirty in the garden and in the kitchen. There is an incredible sense of peace and relaxation that comes from touching and caring for the earth and working with whole foods. I explore how to improve my little corner of the world and its capacity to support life, including mine. I rescued and restored an old orchard that was neglected for decades. I make my own compost and watch how the health of my own biological terrain, the blood, changes with better soil and

sturdier crops that I grow and eat. The taste of homegrown food from the richest, life-giving soil that one can make surpasses that of today's commercial organic foods. I am blessed to live in the San Francisco Bay Area where I can grow many of my own vegetables yearlong. I would like to inspire others to touch the earth, too. I would like to help them learn more about sustaining life from healthier air, soil, and water.

How can we begin anew to take better care of ourselves and one another, to rebuild a sustainable community, and to thrive once again? These are the questions that preoccupy me now in this latest most challenging epoch in which we now find ourselves. Clearly we need many revisions in our lives. My intention is that *ReVision* help us see new perspectives on how to make nourishing change.

Robert Jackson-Paton

Born in Philadelphia, Pennsylvania, in 1968, I am the third son of parents from a long and predominantly Quaker lineage. Just before I was born, my family relocated from Algeria in order to be in the United States for my birth. Yet, I lived in Philadelphia only a short time, as my family continued to move after I was born. The first stop – at six weeks of age – was India, until I was three. Then, Greece until I was about 6 years old. Even after returning to the U.S., moving continued: Utah, New York, California. Continuing this model, I went to college in Oregon, and spent two years in the Philippines, before finally staying put in the Bay Area for the last decade.

Undergraduate work at Lewis & Clark College in Portland, Oregon laid

important foundations. In sociology and education, I was deeply influenced by the work of Paulo Freire. This established a strong basis for cultural criticism, self-reflection and transformative learning. My work of naming and changing the world began there. This early formation also fostered a strong spiritual growth as I questioned aspects of my relationship with formal Christianity, and began to explore nature religions. During this time, I became an environmental activist and Native rights supporter. Again, cross-cultural understanding (and lack thereof!) was a major influence.

Currently an advanced graduate student at Saybrook Graduate School in San Francisco, my research interests include: *Decolonization for Whites*: healing and (re)placing masculine white consciousness; *Other Ways of Knowing, or Knowing Other Ways*: indigenism and alternative inquiries of self/world; and *Cultural Ecology*: ecopsychology and recovering relationship between culture and nature. My dissertation research centers on decolonizing White identity as a prerequisite for indigenous rights, cross-cultural reconciliation and environmental restoration. I will be presenting papers this year on issues of decolonization for Whites at the White Privilege Conference in Memphis, TN (April 2009) and the International Congress for Qualitative Inquiry at University of Illinois, Urbana (May 2009).

I am inspired to teach (at all age levels), write, and do consulting work around reconciliation: between people, as well as between people and nature. I am developing "reality tours" taking various people to natural areas, with Native and non-Native people explaining relationships with those places. I want to support and conduct reconciliation workshops to help White folks account for, deal with, acknowledge and heal from the legacies of guilt, pain and trauma in family and cultural histories. I want to assist young people with finding a way through the cultural and historical confusion through rites of passage.

I currently live on Muwekma Ohlone land, in the San Francisco east bay, with my beloved spouse, teen-age children, and four critters, in a big blended family. I love to cook, listen to music, and be outside, especially swimming in rivers like a salmon! I have worked in elementary education for ten years, and am the production stage manager for the annual December solstice celebration in Oakland, California, the Christmas Revels.

Please see my essay below for a further introduction to my interests.

ReVision History

Since its inception *Revision* has been an important forum, especially in the North American context, for the articulation of contemporary spirituality, transpersonal studies, and related new models in such fields as medicine, organization, social transformation, work, psychology, ecology, and gender. The group of previous editors includes many North Americans who are key contributors in those areas, most notably in the fields of transpersonal psychology and comparative religion.

ReVision was founded by Jack Crittenden in 1978, in part as a successor to the pioneering journal *Main Currents in Modern Thought.* We have been preceded by the founding editor, Ken Wilber (1978-1985); the second generation of editors: Stan Grof, Ralph Metzner, and Huston Smith (1985-1990); and the third generation: Jeanne Achterberg, William Keepin, Robert McDermott, Donald Rothberg, and Richard Tarnas (1991-1994). The fourth and fifth generations consisted of Mary Gomes, Jürgen Werner Kremer, Joan Marler, Jospeh Prabhu, Donald Rothberg, Caroline Bassett, Adam Blatner, Melissa K. Nelson, and Matthew Bronson.

Since 1995 editors have met several times a year for business meetings and periodic retreats. This tradition was interrupted as a result of structural changes implemented by Heldref. After a period without meetings or regular conference calls the present editorial team is resuming regular meetings to expand and implement our editorial vision. As we are learning of each other's perspectives, biographies, stories, and horizons, we are coming to see that we share not only the general vision that has characterized *ReVision* in the past, but also new elaborations and contemporary interpretations of that vision—as well as differences which we honor and wish to explore. We are beginning to embody these new visions and intentions in our upcoming issues. In reviewing the editorial statement from eleven years ago we can comfortably use some of the language developed by the fourth generation of editors, since it also expresses the intentions we carry.

ReVision has an illustrious history that includes contributions by Jeanne Achterberg, Angeles Arrien, Jorge Ferrer, Mary Gomes, Stan Grof, Stanley Krippner, Joan Marler, Ralph Metzner, Melissa Nelson, Donald Rothberg, Huston Smith, Richard Tarnas, Charles Tart, Frances Vaughan, Roger Walsh, Ken Wilber, and numerous other contributors, consulting editors, and executive editors. Articles first published in *ReVision* have become books or part of books and are used regularly as readings in classes and seminars.

In the past *ReVision* has explored a wide spectrum of topics ranging from sustainability, indigenous science, the participatory turn, revisioning higher education, dreams and dreaming, Rudolf Steiner, deep ecology, shamanism, psychological trauma, mysticism, archetypes, entheogens, the language of spirituality, the developmental nature of consciousness, paradigmatic challenges,

Many issues from our thirty year history of publishing are still available in print via our website at www. revisionpublishing.org. Examples: Nonmechanistic Science (ed. Mary Gomes, vol. 21, #4); Connected Knowing (ed. Peggy Wright, vol. 22, #4); Revisioning Higher Education (ed. Matthew C. Bronson, vol. 28, #2 & #3); Dreams, Visions, Places (ed. Jürgen Werner Kremer, vol. 29, #1); The Participatory Turn (ed. Gregg Lahood, vol. 29, #3 & #4). Please see our website for a full listing. There you can also find updates on upcoming issues.

Earth, Dreams, Body

Karen Jaenke

Of all the generations of humans that have walked the surface of the Earth — for 100,000 years, going back to when we first left Africa — the generation now alive is the most important. The generation now alive, the generation that you see, looking around you, for the first time in history, is the generation that controls the destiny of the planet itself.
-Michio Kaku

We are living in a time of unimaginable extinction of life forms and disruption of ecosystems. At this moment, species are perishing at a rate unprecedented in 65 million years. Not since the demise of the dinosaurs has such extinction and disruption occurred so rapidly and so extensively; indeed, the significance and implications of these trends escape our capacity to conceive. In attempting to place our unique moment in evolutionary perspective, it is helpful to consider that since the origins of life on earth, there have been five great extinction spasms, periods in which a rapid extinction of species occurred, when over 65% of all species perished in a very brief period (Leakey, 1995). Our own moment in history

Photo: Mariana Castro de Ali

Karen Jaenke, M. Div., Ph.D., has been teaching at the California Institute of Integral Studies, John F. Kennedy University, and the Institute of Imaginal Studies for the last eight years. Her approach to human development, soul potential, leadership, and the collective dilemmas of our times has focused on the ancient, abiding yet neglected resources found in dreams, deep memory, imagination, and the body. Her publications include: "Water and Stone: All of Nature Participates in Our Remembering," "Ode To The Intelligence of Dreams," and "Dreaming With the Ancestors," all published in *ReVision*. As a member of the executive editorial team of *ReVision*, she is currently preparing issues on "Imaginal Psychology" and "Earth Dreaming." She has a coaching and consulting practice in Pt. Reyes.

marks the sixth extinction (Leakey, 1995). It signals the end of a great cosmic epoch, the close of an era of proliferation and flowering of diverse life forms. Indeed, as a species and as a planetary community, we have reached a dangerous impasse.

The planetary ecological crisis frames the unique challenges and potentials posed by our zeitgeist. For the sixth extinction spasm is unlike the others, as it originates from within a single species—our own. Humanity, ostensibly the apex of creation, has precipitated a threat to all other life forms on earth. Our planet's present plight arises from a dire imbalance within the human species. Thus we must say that

present global desecration has its locus within human consciousness, in a gross maladaptation to reality, to the actual ecological requirements for sustaining life and well-being on planet earth. Certainly the destruction of planetary life is not something we consciously intend. Yet nonetheless we are the ones inflicting it. How can our imaginations come to embrace the destructiveness of our actual situation? How can we account for and face this bitter truth? If not consciously intended, the destruction emanates from us unconsciously, from something unknown or long forgotten.

* * * * * *

The future of Earth's community rests in significant ways upon the decisions to be made by the humans who have inserted themselves so deeply into even the genetic codes of Earth's process. This future will be worked out in the tensions between those committed to the Technozoic, a future of increased exploitation of Earth as a resource, all for the benefit of humans, and those committed to the Ecozoic, a new mode of human-Earth relations, one where the well-being of the entire Earth community is the primary concern. (Swimme & Berry, 1992, p. 14-15)

Our planetary situation calls for a profound questioning and challenging of our most fundamental and cherished paradigms of reality and conceptions of human nature. In a world precariously on the brink of nuclear holocaust, economic collapse and ecological catastrophe, we are being challenged to examine ourselves deeply. Coming to terms with the reality of our time as one of demise and extinction, and of our human role in the pervasive destruction of life, calls for a searing search into the depths of the human psyche and our collective human history. In reckoning with our global plight, humanity as a species desperately needs a collective transformation, a transformation of consciousness that penetrates to the core, addressing our most fundamental ways of perceiving and being in the world. As the earth-body undergoes massive metamorphosis, only a human metamorphosis as radical as the devastation will open a way to the future. According to Ralph Metzner, an essential aspect of the transformation of our species requires a turning inward, toward self—"not in narcissistic self-absorption but in aware self-confrontation" (1986, p. 2).

Impending environmental collapse presents humanity with the necessity of a collective initiation, along with renewal of ways of knowing and being more attuned to nature, the earth, the body, matter, and the deep feminine. In the words of Angeles Arrien, today humanity must undergo "an initiation... At some level all of us, collectively, know we're being initiated into a new world--arising from an ancient remembering of who we are" (1996, p. 23). In trying to find our way through this initiatory moment, my hope turns not to modern technological solutions arising

snake is the embodiment of wisdom, and no mountain still harbors a great demon.... His immediate communication with nature is gone forever, and the emotional energy it generated has sunk into the unconscious.
This enormous loss is compensated by the symbols of our dreams. They bring up our original nature, its instincts and its peculiar thinking.... [T]hey express their contents in the language of nature, which is strange and incomprehensible to us. (Jung, 1968, p. 85)

Carl Jung speaks to the loss of psychic kinship with the natural world in modern times. Our potential for psychic communication and participation with nature is mediated by the human capacity for symbolizing and by particular symbols and images. Yet in the disenchanted, rationally oriented modern era, this communion with nature is largely an unconscious process carried on by the dreaming rather than waking and dreaming self.

The archetypal wisdom of humanity, channeled nightly through our dreams, pushes against the boundaries of known reality, probing for a way through personal and collective challenges. Though our global predicament is beyond the comprehension of our conscious minds, our unconscious faculties are attuned, aware, responsive. Dreams, arising from the natural and whole self, labor in service of restoring the networks of communication and attunement between conscious mind and unconscious body, between human body and earth body. Dreams transport the dreamer outside familiar and habitual identifications into non-human ways of being. They grant access to the interiority of other, non-human forms of existence. Dreams characteristically cross the boundaries constructed and defended in our daylight world, revealing our deep kinship with all aspects of the cosmos.

It is heartening to remember that humanity once knew how to live in balance with the natural world. Traditional peoples of the world still possess this knowledge. The integrity of traditional lifeways is evident in the sustainable ecology that has been preserved across millennia, in the means of accommodating rather than controlling nature. Indigenous knowledge can help reverse the destruction of the planet and recover balance for the human species. In fact, native knowledge and the survival of the human species now appear to be inextricably linked. Coincidentally, these same native cultures, which adopt a right-hemisphere emphasis, have been called *dream cultures* due to the centrality of dreams to their perception, spirituality and lifeways (Irwin, 1994, p.17).

Dreams come to us unbidden, as a fountain of creativity and wisdom, simultaneously the voice of the spirit world and the natural man, and problem-solver par excellence.

through the powers of the left brain and logical mind (though these no doubt will play a role), but rather to ancient sources of inspiration, guidance, and knowledge that have perennially assisted humanity in crisis. Dreams, the lifeways of indigenous peoples, and bodily wisdom draw upon an extra-rational type of intelligence arising from the right brain and rooted in holistic, embodied powers of perception. This synthetic or holistic perception detects invisible realities and registers subtle phenomena, through reliance upon imagery and the human body's extraordinarily refined nervous system.

* * * * * *

Through scientific understanding, our world has become dehumanized. Man feels himself isolated in the cosmos. He is no longer involved in nature and has lost his emotional participation in natural events, which hitherto had a symbolic meaning for him. Thunder is no longer the voice of a god, nor is lightning his avenging missile. No river contains a spirit, no tree means a man's life, no

* * * * * *

The dream is a hidden door to the innermost recesses of the soul, opening into that cosmic night.... All consciousness separates, but in dreams we put on the likeness of that more universal, truer, more eternal man dwelling in the darkness of the eternal night. There he is still whole, and the whole is in him, indistinguishable from nature and bare of all egohood. (Jung, 2002, p. 185.)

Dreams come to us unbidden, as a fountain of creativity and wisdom, expressing simultaneously the voice of the spirit world and the natural man. They are a problem-solver par excellence, by recasting habitual viewpoints into fresh, imaginative frameworks. They offer an unparalleled means for searching our personal and collective depths, for engaging in the aware self-confrontation demanded by our zeitgeist. For dreams swim in a vast reservoir of ancient collective wisdom, arising from the accumulated wisdom of humanity that is coded into the archetypes of the collective unconscious.

* * * * * *

We are awakening a little to the feeling that something is wrong in the world, that our modern prejudice of overestimating the importance of the intellect and conscious mind might be false.... (Jung, 1977, p. 49)

Ironically, our dreams and our global predicament pose a similar challenge to our conscious collective orientation: both defy rational control. Like nature, dreams eschew rational domination. To be in relationship with one's dream life, one must shed the pretense of rational control, the illusion that reality is ultimately rational and controllable.

Forging a conscious relationship to our dreams simultaneously forges a capacity to be in tune with a non-rational, uncontrollable dimension of ourselves and our universe. In learning to relate to our dreams as native peoples have, as allies transmitting vital inspiration, piercing insight and life-renewing energies, we can reclaim some of the sensitivities and perceptions of indigenous peoples. This reclamation includes enhanced capacities for accommodating, as opposed to dominating, the natural world.

* * * * * *

[I]t is in our dreams that the body makes itself aware to our mind.... The dream is the body's best expression, in the best possible symbol it can express.... The dream calls our mind's attention to the body's instinctive feeling. If man doesn't pay attention to these symbolic warnings of his body he pays in other ways.... When whole countries avoid these warnings ... we are in great danger. (Jung, 1977, p. 48)

Cultivating respect for the natural mind present in the dreaming self and for the sensitivities and intelligence suffused within the body offers a doorway into renewed respect for the earth body. Indigenous peoples and esoteric traditions have cultivated and relied upon the knowing accessible through the subtle body—the most subtle and interior perceptions of which humans are capable. Shamans and tribal spiritual leaders obtained powers of seeing and healing through the cultivation subtle body knowing. The ecological balance preserved for millennia through shamanic practices and rooted in subtle body knowing now appears to be essential for humanity to remain attuned and in balance with the dynamic living system of Gaia.

Respecting the body's deep and subtle intelligence offers a doorway into nature. The body presents a neglected yet profound source of knowing that, when actively cultivated, can become responsive and attuned to the planetary necessities of our times. Indeed, a renaissance of intimacy between the human and natural worlds will depend upon counteracting normative cultural patterns that institutionalize dissociation from the body, and upon opening to the profound depth of knowing-potential present in the body. For this body of mine marks a threshold through which consciousness enters

Photo: Mariana Castro de Ali

into the secret wonders and interior workings of nature. One's body constitutes the foundation for every encounter with nature; attitudes held towards my body translate into attitudes held towards other bodies. Disrespect and dissociation from my body transmits disrespect and dissociation from the earth body. Reverence and communion with my body overflows into reverence and communion with the earth body.

* * * * * *

Without [the] entrancement... [that] comes from the immediate communion of the human with the natural world, a capacity to appreciate the ultimate subjectivity and spontaneities within every form of natural being... it is unlikely that the human community will have the psychic energy needed for the renewal of the Earth." (Swimme and Berry, 1992, p 268)

These times require the re-awakening of a subjective sense of communion with the other inhabitants of the Earth community. This subjective communion arises when consciousness descends from its dissociated heights to dwell within the depths of the body's interiority. Within these mysterious incarnate depths, a unifying field of energy quickens and quivers. The subtle body marks a grand gateway into participatory consciousness, into subjective communion with the mysteries of the cosmos. Through the joy of recovering our true nature as participa-

tory beings, reverence for the earth body awakens from its centuries-long slumber.

REFERENCES

Arrien, A. (1996). Through the eight gates. *Noetic Science Review*, Winter, 22-27.

Irwin, L. (1994). *The dream seekers: Native American visionary traditions of the Great Plains.* Norman: University of Oklahoma Press.

Jung, C. G. (Ed.). (1968). *Man and his symbols*. New York: Dell Publishing.

Jung, C.G. (1970). *Civilization in Transition, Collected Works*, Volume 10, 2nd ed. Princeton, NJ: Princeton University Press.

Jung. C.G. (1977). (W. McGuire & R. F. C. Hull, Eds.) *C.G. Jung speaking: Interviews and encounters*. Princeton, NJ: Princeton University Press.

Jung, C.G. (2002). *The nature writings of C.G. Jung,* ed. Meredith Sabini, Berkeley, CA: North Atlantic Books.

Kaku, M. (n.d.). *Lifeboat foundation quotes*. Retrieved December 2, 2008, from http://lifeboat.com/ex/quotes#kaku.

Leakey, R. (1995). *The sixth extinction: Patterns of life and the future of humanity*. New York: Doubleday.

Metzner, R. (1986). *Opening to inner light: The transformation of human nature and consciousness*. Los Angeles: Jeremy P. Tarcher, Inc.

Swimme, B. & Berry, T. (1992). *The universe story: From the primordial flaring forth to the ecozoic era—a celebration of the unfolding of the cosmos*. San Francisco: Harper Collins.

Rituals of Inquiry; or, Looking for *Culture and Truth*[1]

Robert Jackson-Paton

Who I am as a writer, as a person, is someone continuing the conflict, the coming together, of histories, cultures. My education and training as an academic and writer only add voices, inner disputants, to a world of multiple voices. The chorus of intermingling, often conflicting, voices grows, produces new sounds. What I do, then, as a writer, is convey as much as possible the multiple voices that constitute not only me but also what I think and write about. The politics, personae, and different points of view (and narrative styles associated with different points of view) about a given topic…begin to shine through the writing. What I hope to have done is provide a way for us to start talking interculturally and interpersonally about what is in fact intercultural and interpersonal. (Sarris, 1996, pp. 37-8)

* * *

While reluctant to make an explicit statement of my goals for this essay up front—preferring to allow my process to unfold—I will at minimum invite the reader to join me in this process of self-reflection. This essay attempts to bridge personal experience and theoretical implication, and along the way bring both subject and object back together in inquiry. As the title suggests, my agenda is about restoring a respect-

Robert Jackson-Paton is an advanced graduate student at the Saybrook Graduate School in San Francisco, and is Managing Editor of ReVision. His recent paper "Rituals of Reconciliation: Three Gifts Toward Creating Healing Ceremonies in Settler Societies" was presented in August 2008 at the 25th Annual International Conference on the Study of Shamanism and Alternative Modes of Healing in San Rafael, California. He lives on Muwekma Ohlone land in the Bay Area with his partner, his two teenage children, and four critters. His research interests include healing reconciliation between peoples and the land. He can be reached at rjacksonpaton@mac.com.

ful aspect to human science research, as well as addressing the implications for validity and cultural meaning. Such a process is not unique, but my hope is that a chorus of voices continues to shape a vision for inquiry that is holistic, transformative, and healing.

Human science inquiry increasingly accepts reflexivity and subjective voice. My research emphasizes such relationship between the object of study and the researcher. Quantum theory also supports the experience of connection between subject and object (Arntz, Chasse, & Vicente, 2004). However, rather than bridging such false dichotomies, my purpose is to place such potentials for conflict and resolution both within my process and myself. My self-awareness then must include a personal and cultural heritage and all the resultant historical complications.

The validity for such interconnection is heightened when methodologically approaching my studies with indigenous science. Indigenous science acknowledges that all peoples carry a way of being in relationship with the world rooted in a tribal worldview, what Pamela Colorado (1994, p. 2) calls "the good mind." Further, indigenous peoples (as well as peoples of color and all women) have pointed out that Western research methods are rooted in a Western epistemology and must be decolonized (Denzin, Lincoln, & Smith, 2008; Smith, 1999). Decolonizing methodologies not only acknowledges a Eurocentered worldview, it also has the twofold effect of righting research so that it no longer carries out unconscious colonization. As importantly, such inquiry also then fixes the process of research itself. Thus, research is not purportedly objective but acknowledges, initiates and perpetuates healing (Christian, 1993).

A relationship-based way of being-knowing can be restored or remembered by those who have grown up in a

Photo: Mariana Castro de Ali

Eurocentered or Western culture (Kremer 1996a, 1996b). Recovering indigenous science requires that I invite and acknowledge all the research into my process. The informants thus include the natural world, as well as my personal and cultural histories. The presence of the land—and those who speak with it—participating in my research also transforms my relationship with nature and history. Everything is a part of the research process, and my experience of connection is transformed by it. This is the essence of participation.

A participatory context for research has implications well beyond my research in the human sciences. What has long been seen as an insurmountable divide may now be restored. Subject and object reflexivity opens new possibilities that have long been closed in Eurocentered thought. Now by accepting the call for decolonized White research, we can find not only greater access to research but also to ourselves.

Decolonizing research requires a vulnerable researcher increasing the likelihood that research can heal.

A nascent return to an indigenous coming-to-knowing process greatly increases self-awareness (Peat, 1994). In other words, I experience relationship with the inquiry itself. I study a personal process of transformation and then the inquiry becomes an act of transformation simultaneously. Deslauriers (1992) observes that ritual is an embodiment of knowing. Similarly the process of knowing, or coming-to-know, can be a ritual, as well.

Healing, participatory research invokes elements resembling ritual. Ritual narrative must be told with great respect and humility. In telling the story, the act of the journey is recreated. Honko (1984, p. 51) notes how

Ritual brings the creative events of the beginning of time to life and enables them to be repeated here and now, in the present. The ordinary reality of everyday life recedes and is superseded by the reality of ritual drama. What was once possible and operative in the beginning of time becomes possible once more and can exert its influence anew.

Allow me to tell a story.

* * *

In 1993, Slug Woman (Sarris) introduced me to groundbreaking ideas of how a reader interacts with text. This initiated the process of contextualizing myself as reader and researcher. For the first time, I glimpsed how I participate with narrative, including the history I bring. Beyond noting our participation with texts — and with the diverse cultural experiences we read about — Sarris described the shift among social scientists away from objectivity driven research that has plagued modernity. In so doing, Sarris mentioned several authors grappling with issues of voice and subjectivity, among them anthropologist Renato Rosaldo. This began my search for *Culture and Truth* (Rosaldo, 1993) over the next several years.[1] Unfortunately, as I tried to locate the book, I was unable to do so.

As an anthropologist, Rosaldo did his fieldwork among the Ilongot, one of the peoples of the Cordillera Mountains in the northern Philippines. Together with his wife and academic colleague, Michelle Zimbalist Rosaldo,

they published extensively on the Ilongot.[2] My former spouse and I spent nearly a year living in the Philippine Cordillera as well. Though we lived farther north in Mountain Province among the Kankan-ey in Sagada, the relative proximity to the Ilongot made for an intriguing parallel.

In 1997, while living in Sagada, we assisted community members in the organization and care of the research library of the late William Henry Scott—affectionately referred to as Scotty—a scholar on Cordillera and Filipino culture and history.[3] As one might expect, Scotty's library contained numerous titles by the Rosaldos, but not *Culture and Truth*. As another White American living in the Cordil-

lera, I was deeply interested in Scotty's presence in Sagada, and began to research his life there.

Through my conversations with people who knew Scotty, I met one of the last White American priests of the Episcopal Church (before the local Filipino priesthood took over) who had returned to Sagada for a visit. The priest had lived in Sagada for many years, raising his family there. His daughter grew up in Sagada, and had known Scotty from childhood. My ears perked up when he told me she had begun her Ph.D. studies in anthropology at Stanford University with Michelle Rosaldo. "But she quit when Michelle Rosaldo died," he relayed. "She died?" I was shocked. "Michelle died doing fieldwork in the Cordillera." I had not known that part of the story.

Not long after, I came across *The Vulnerable Observer* (Behar, 1996). Behar responds to Rosaldo's work and legacy in her closing, "Anthropology that Breaks Your Heart." In particular, she responds to his essay about the death of his wife: "Grief and a Headhunter's Rage." According to Behar, "Grief" tells how experiencing the loss of Michelle, had enabled Rosaldo to break through ethnographic distance with the Ilongot. She describes Rosaldo's process as a ritual, coming to terms with the grief of losing Michelle. This not only had academic consequences but deeply personal ones. More accurately, the ramifications were interwoven. As I read these words, I was struck by my own presence, too.

* * *

In "Anthropology that Breaks Your Heart," Behar (1996, pp. 168-171) tells of her participation on a panel responding to Rosaldo's "Grief and a Headhunter's Rage." Two other scholars had criticized Rosaldo's attempt to identify with Ilongot headhunting by his personal experience of grief and rage at the death of Michelle. Behar noted that they considered his work nothing more than "sentimental." Further, they alleged that "Grief" was Rosaldo's only opportunity to critique Michelle Rosaldo's work.

Behar rebuked the scholars and defended Rosaldo and his effort to cross-culturally bridge his research through his own experience of loss and pain. She observed that from a feminist position, it seemed that the two young male academics were denouncing an elder male's "vulnerability." The authors also missed Rosaldo's point about the more complex nature of emotions surrounding grief.

Everything finally fell into place in 1998 when I found *Culture and Truth* (Rosaldo, 1993). The introductory essay was none other than "Grief and a Headhunter's Rage." The essay begins with Rosaldo (pp. 1-2) relating the answer he was told by an older Ilongot man of northern Luzon, Philippines, as to why he cuts off human heads. "He says that rage, born of grief, impels him to kill his fellow human beings. He claims that he needs a place 'to carry his anger.' The act of severing and tossing away the victim's head enables him, he says, to vent and, he hopes, throw away the anger of his bereavement." Rosaldo continues that while anthropologists are supposed to make other cultures understandable, for some time he did not grasp this explanation.

In describing his intention and experience through "Grief," Rosaldo (1993) continues:

At the same time, by invoking personal experience as an analytical category one risks easy dismissal. Unsympathetic readers could reduce this introduction to an act of mourning or a mere report on my discovery of the anger possible in bereavement. *Frankly, this introduction is both and more. An act of mourning, a personal report, and a critical analysis of anthropological method, it simultaneously encompasses a number of distinguishable processes, no one of which cancels out the others* [italics added]. Similarly, I argue in what follows that ritual in general and Ilongot headhunting in particular form the intersection of multiple coexisting social processes. Aside from revising the ethnographic record, the paramount claim made here concerns how my own mourning and consequent reflection on Ilongot bereavement, rage, and headhunting raise methodological issues of general concern in anthropology and the human sciences. (pp. 11-12)

Beginning a long and painful separation and divorce in the months before reading 'Grief,' my personal experience resonated deeply. It would be mistaken to make a direct comparison between my pain and Rosaldo's. In a similar way, Rosaldo cautioned readers about his personal experience and his anthropology. Nevertheless, this process requires my transformation and necessitates vulnerability. Vulnerability is the requirement for a deeper and significant healing. I contend that my experience of vulnerability positioned me in a particular place vis-à-vis Rosaldo's work, much as Rosaldo's vulnerability placed him with regards to the Ilongot.

Behar (1996, p. 175) encourages anthropologists and other social scientists to acknowledge vulnerability. In so doing, rather than making a nation of victims, it creates situations that might encourage deeper healing (Wilkinson, 1996). This is especially true for men who find themselves in the borderlands of masculinity and whiteness (Anzaldua, 1987). Furthermore, Behar (1996, p. 177) suggests that a goal for anthropology is to break hearts in order to heal them. Healing is an explicit goal of her research endeavor, as she picks up the story from Rosaldo and makes it her own. I respectfully pick up their work and wish to make it my own, as well.

Rosaldo details for the ethnographic record Ilongot rituals relating to death. Telling his story is a central part of the process. "…[R]itual…form[s] the intersection of multiple coexisting social processes." Rosaldo (1993, pp. 11-12) makes clear that the various tasks he sets out to do in "Grief," including his personal "act of mourning" are among various social processes. Thus, by connecting personal healing and social science research Rosaldo creates a ritual of inquiry. He vulnerably places himself into the research, reminding the reader that such action "risks easy dismissal." Yet, it is how to make research vulnerable and healing.

I retell this story, and in so doing, it becomes a story for my healing as well

(Sarris, 1993, p. 13). Quite literally the day after reading Behar's essay, "Anthropology That Breaks Your Heart," I finally found *Culture and Truth*. "Looking for *Culture and Truth*" becomes a ritual map for my personal and academic process. Rosaldo (and Behar, as well) were transformed by the interaction and relationship with these powerful stories. From the initial experience(s) that Rosaldo went through, including his study among the Ilongot, the death of his wife and the ritual process of writing the story; to the retelling that Behar engages in; to my reading and retelling. These all are separate aspects, separate ritual processes, all intersecting into a crossroads of a larger process of healing. All of our hearts were broken; they are in turn being healed.

Rosaldo's study of Ilongot culture was ritualized in his experience of grief at Michelle's death. Rosaldo's return from his time among the Ilongot, after the shattering experience of Michelle's death, is when he emerges as a Chicano intellectual. The ritual continues as Behar notes the transformative power of "Grief." Inquiry into ritual and then narrating that experience can become ritual, as well. Similarly, my ritual of grief continues as step out of my experiences and acknowledge that I am White. As a reader and researcher I bring whiteness and my history into everything I interact with. This shatters who I am and creates an opportunity for transformation.

Behar (1996, pp. 173-4) realizes the reflexivity and relationship between reader and text, anthropologist and culture, when she writes that Rosaldo's writing is ritual, noting its transformative nature.

"Grief and a Headhunter's Rage" is itself a kind of tomb, a memorial to Michelle Zimbalist Rosaldo, and we must tread on it lightly. That essay, it seems to me, clearly marks the end of Rosaldo's sojourn as an anthropologist in the Philippines. Forced to part with Michelle, he also parts ways with the Ilongot, though he holds on to them both emotionally and intellectually. But that ending also marks a new beginning, a threshold for Renato, and a return home. It is only after "Grief

> Bound up in this ritual process is the historical reality that I am not from this land; I too am a settler, a miracle, Pakeha. So my relationship with the land itself must be healed.

and a Headhunter's Rage" that Renato comes out actively as a Chicano intellectual and develops his position as a theorist of the meaning of citizenship in the United States.

"Grief" maps Rosaldo's journey through an underworld, where he must come to terms with himself in order to heal, bringing him to a "new beginning, a threshold, a return home." This relates simultaneously to his loss of Michelle Rosaldo and his identity vis-à-vis the dominant culture in the US. "Looking for *Culture and Truth*" then is the map of my ritualized process, in the library and along the pathways in my life, spiritual, emotional and intellectual. Following this trail becomes a pilgrimage through soul and spirit, a map interconnecting seemingly disparate processes, and after the underworld of separation and divorce bringing me to a new beginning, a life on the borderlands (Anzaldua, 1987).

This transformative ritual takes on a greater significance than simply personal self-identification. Cultural healing is required. Some Whites are beginning to approach the connection between personal and social "dis-ease" and the legacy of whiteness (D. S. Raymond, personal communication, March 17, 2007). Nearly absent from explorations of whiteness are any rituals of grief (Browne, Kovgan, Ray, Delude-Dix, & Brown, 2008; Jackson-Paton, 2008). Yet, the legacy of whiteness has created a soul wound among the colonizers as much as it has among the colonized (Berry, 1989; DeWolf, 2008; Duran, 2006; Goodman, 2001; Memmi, 1965). There is the necessity to grieve for many losses carried (out) by White settlers. Turner (1999, p. 29) explains that in Aotearoa/New Zealand there is a similar need to grieve among the White settler (Pakeha) community. "Pakeha do not know how to weep for themselves, or their past. The grief of settlement eludes them."

I have much to grieve. However, recovering indigenous science offers support and validation for my process. I am not alone in this underworld journey through the tombs of my personal and cultural history; I have the likes of Behar, Rosaldo, and Sarris to help guide me through my own borderlands. Similarly, the landscape itself offers me both a map of my journey, as well as solace for my troubles (Basso, 1996).

Bound up in this ritual process is the historical reality that I am not from this land; I too am a settler, a miracle, Pakeha (Sarris, 1996, p. 28; see also Consedine, 2001). So my relationship with the land itself must be healed (LaDuke, 1984). This can only occur by recovering indigenous science. Then I am no longer a settler here on Native land, but a visiting resident (L. M. Silko, personal communication, 2 April 1996). My respect for Native land and culture aids me in my healing, and my ability to reclaim an indigenous mind (Nelson, 1994). Such reclaiming places me in the realm of the borderlands of whiteness.

* * *

Hearing a story makes one a part of the story, part of the ritual, whether conscious of such relationship or not. Participation becomes the context and practice for this journey, shaping the way research unfolds before me. The inquiry that I am engaged in has always led me back to myself. First interested in traditional knowledge of Native peoples, I was led to my ancestry and learning their knowledge. When studying the healing role sacred sites have for Whites, they became beacons for me through troubled waters. Finally, captivated by the mythic stories of the underworld journey, the stories led me on a journey of my own, a journey of "be(com)ing" (Bigwood, 1993, p. 261). Such a powerful healing endeavor is about transformation; it is a ritual of inquiry.

NOTES

1. The title acknowledges Rosaldo, 1993; gratitude to Pamela Colorado for this path.
2. Among the Rosaldos' work: M. Rosaldo. (1980). *Knowledge and Passion: Ilongot Notions of Self and Social Life.* New York: Cambridge University Press, and R. Rosaldo. (1980). *Ilongot headhunting, 1883-1974: A study in society and history.* Palo Alto, CA: Stanford University Press.
3. For example, Scott, W. H. (1982). *Cracks in the parchment curtain, and other essays in Philippine history.* Quezon City, Philippines: New Day Publishers. Also, Scott, W. H. (1992). *Looking for the prehispanic Filipino.* Quezon City, Philippines: New Day Publishers.

REFERENCES

Anthony, C. (1995). Ecopsychology and the deconstruction of whiteness. In T. Roszak, M. Gomes & A. Kanner (Eds.), *Ecopsychology: Restoring the earth, healing the mind* (pp. 263-278). San Francisco: Sierra Club Press.

Arntz, W. (Producer/Director/Writer), Chasse, B. (Producer/Director/Writer), & Vicente, M. (Director). (2004). *What the bleep? Down the rabbit hole* [Motion picture]. United States: Lord of the Wind Films.

Anzaldua, G. (1987). *Borderlands/la frontera: The new mestiza.* San Francisco: Spinsters/Aunt Lute.

Basso, K. H. (1996). *Wisdom sits in places: Landscape and language among the Western Apache.* Albuquerque: University of New Mexico Press.

Behar, R. (1996). *The vulnerable observer: Anthropology that breaks your heart.* Boston: Beacon Press.

Berry, W. (1989). *The hidden wound.* San Francisco: North Point Press.

Bigwood, C. (1993). *Earth muse. Feminism, nature, and art.* Philadelphia: Temple University Press.

Browne, K. (Producer/Director/Writer), Kovgan, A. (Co-Director/Writer), Ray, J. (Co-Director), Delude-Dix, E. (Co-Producer), & Brown, J. (Co-Producer). (2008). *Traces of the trade: A story from the Deep North* [Motion picture]. Ebb Pod Productions, LLC. (Available from California Newsreel P.O. Box 2284 South Burlington, VT 05407)

Christian, B. (1993, Spring). Fixing methodologies: Beloved. *Cultural Critique,* 24, 5-15.

Colorado, P. (1994, April). *Indigenous science and Western science: A healing convergence.* Paper presented at World Sciences Dialog I, New York.

Consedine, R. & Consedine, J. (2005). *Healing our history: The challenge of the Treaty of Waitangi* (2nd ed.). Auckland, New Zealand: Penguin.

Denzin, N., Lincoln, Y., & Smith, L. T. (Eds.). (2008). *Handbook of critical and indigenous methodologies.* Thousand Oaks, CA: Sage Publications.

Deslauriers, D. (1992). Dimensions of knowing: Narrative, paradigm and ritual. *ReVision,* 14(4), 187-193.

DeWolf, T. N. (2008). *Inheriting the trade: A northern family confronts its legacy as the largest slave-trading dynasty in U.S. history.* Boston: Beacon Press.

Duran, E. (2006). *Healing the soul wound: Counseling with American Indians and other native peoples.* New York: Teachers College Press.

Goodman, D. (2001). *Promoting diversity and social justice: Educating people from privileged groups.* Thousand Oaks, CA: Sage Publications.

Honko, L. (1984). The problem of defining myth. In Dundes, A. (Ed.) *Sacred Narrative, readings in the theory of myth* (pp. 41-52). Berkeley: University of California Press.

Jackson-Paton, R. (2008, August). *Rituals of reconciliation: Three gifts toward creating healing ceremonies in settler societies*. Paper presented at 25th Annual International Conference on the Study of Shamanism and Alternative Modes of Healing. San Rafael, CA.

Kremer, J. W. (1996a). Introduction-indigenous science. *ReVision*, 18(3), 2-5.

Kremer, J. W. (1996b). The possibility of recovering indigenous European perspectives on Native healing practices: Developing the basis for respectful knowledge exchanges. *Ethnopsychologische Mitteilungen*, 5(2), 149-164.

LaDuke, W. (1983). Natural to Synthetic and Back Again. In Churchill, W. (Ed.), *Marxism and Native Americans* (pp. i - iix). Boston: South End Press.

Memmi, A. (1965). *The colonizer and the colonized*. Boston: Beacon Press.

Nelson, M. (1994, Fall). Reclaiming an indigenous mind. *Ecopsychology Newsletter*, (2), 3-7.

Peat, F. D. (1994). *Lighting the seventh fire: The spiritual ways, healing and science of the Native Americans*. New York: Birch Lane Press.

Rosaldo, R. (1993). *Culture and truth: The remaking of social analysis* (2nd ed.). Boston: Beacon Press.

Roszak, T. (1992). *The voice of the earth: An exploration of ecopsychology*. New York: Simon & Schuster.

Sarris, G. (1993). *Keeping Slug Woman alive: A holistic approach to American Indian texts*. Berkeley: University of California Press.

Sarris, G. (1996). Living with miracles: The politics and poetics of writing American Indian resistance and identity. In S. Lavie and T. Swedenburg, (Eds.), *Displacement, diaspora and geographies of identity* (pp. 27-40). Durham, NC: Duke University Press.

Smith, L. T. (1999). *Decolonizing methodologies: Research and indigenous peoples*. Atlantic Heights, NJ: Zed Press.

Turner, S. (1999). Settlement as forgetting. In K. Neuman, N. Thomas & H. Erickson (Eds.), *Quicksands: Foundational Histories in Australia and Aotearoa New Zealand* (pp. 20-38). Sydney, Australia: University of New South Wales Press.

Wilkinson, T. (1996). *Persephone returns: Victims, heroes and the journey from the underworld*. Berkeley, California: Pagemill Press.

Art by Mariana Castro de Ali

WINTER SOLSTICE

Go you gently into this good night
Into the dark of open loving arms
Earth Mother holding all
In warm embrace.

All creatures sleep and wake and sleep
Enjoying rest from daylight's busyness.
Relax, renew your tired self.
Restore you soul.

And this remember all the year
The mountain needs the valley
To appear
So high.

And so go gently into this good night
This warm embrace
Below the winter white.

-- Michael Sheffield

A Mythological Approach to Transpersonal Psychotherapy

Stanley Krippner & David Feinstein

Personal myths can be as complexes of beliefs, images, somatic impulses, emotions, values, and priorities -- coalesced around a common theme -- that shape perception, understanding, motivation, and ultimately behavior. When elaborated into narrative form, they are often expressed in symbols and metaphor. The roots of one's personal mythology can be traced to biology, personal history, culture, and transcendent experiences. This paper offers suggestions for conducting psychotherapy within a mythologically-informed framework, a perspective that may be useful even for those not closely identified with Jung or with transpersonal psychology. This paper also discusses the principles by which we believe personal myths develop, and it presents our model of intervention into the individual's evolving mythology.

Stanley Krippner, Ph.D., is professor of psychology at Saybrook Graduate School, San Francisco, and co-author of *Personal Mythology* and *Haunted by Combat: Understanding PTSD in War Veterans.* He is co-editor of *Healing Stories: The Use of Narrative in Counseling and Psychotherapy* and *The Psychological Impact of War Trauma on Civilians.* He has authored or co-authored over 1,000 articles, chapters, or book reviews on such topics as hypnosis, dreams, dissociation, shamanism, human sexuality, learning disabilities, and anomalous phenomena, and is a Fellow in four divisions of the American Psychological Association. He can be contacted at skrippner@saybrook.edu.

David Feinstein, Ph.D., a clinical psychologist, has served on the faculties of The Johns Hopkins University School of Medicine and Antioch College. Among his major works are *The Promise of Energy Psychology*, *Rituals for Living and Dying*, and *Personal Mythology*. He has contributed more than 50 articles to the professional literature and five of his eight books have won national awards, including the 2007 *USA Book News* Book of the Year award in the Psychology/Mental Health Category (for *Personal Mythology*). He can reached at www.EnergyPsychEd.com.

I. Mythology in Contemporary Clinical Thought

In the prologue to his autobiography, Jung (1961) announced, "I have now undertaken, in my eighty-third year, to tell my personal myth" (p. 3), a statement that reflected Jung's longstanding recognition that individuals create and maintain mythological belief systems about how, why, and when they act as they do. In addition, every theory of human personality contains its own implicit or explicit set of myths as reflected in its doctrines, mores, values, practices, and the integrative set of dominant assumptions used to prioritize and categorize experience (Maduro & Wheelwright, 1977, p. 84). Depth psychotherapy, as pioneered by Jung, is, according to James Hillman (1975), "today's form of traditional mythology, the great carrier of the oral tradition" (p. 20).

Rollo May (1991) has argued that contemporary psychotherapy "is almost entirely concerned...with the problem of the individual's search for myths" (p. 9). J. D. Frank and J. B. Frank (1991) have pointed out that all schools of psychotherapy bolster clients' sense of mastery and self-efficacy by providing them with a "myth" or conceptual scheme that explains their symptoms. According to Frank and Frank, psychotherapists also engage in "rituals" that combat client demoralization by strengthening the therapeutic relationship, arousing hope, and inspiring expectations of help, arousing their clients emotionally, and affording them opportunities for rehearsal and practice. As a result, a mutually satisfactory story is constructed, one that will have beneficial consequences for a client's ability to function and for his or her sense of well being (p. 72). Frank and Frank propose that to be effective, these stories need to be couched in terms that capture and hold a client's attention. Indeed, they suggest that "much of the therapeutic power of psychoanalysis and of Jung's...psychotherapy lies in their extraordinary evocative imagery" (p. 73).

For many individuals and groups, Jungian psychology does offer, as Hillman (1975) puts it, a contemporary "form of traditional mythology" (p. 20). In a culture left without collectively-sanctioned values and moral absolutes, members of Western industrialized societies are compelled to bring meaning to their existence by buying into a prearranged religious or secular structure, or -- through education, creative work, or psychotherapy -- formulating their own myths. According to Joseph Campbell (1988), who was profoundly influenced by Jung's work, myths are metaphors for what lies behind the visible world. For Campbell, myth explains the "invisible plane" that underlies the visible. For example, Campbell emphasized that myths teach people to identify not with the body but with the consciousness for which the body is a vehicle. At the same time, Campbell also believed that myths emerge from the body, and are created -- in part -- to explain such bodily mysteries as childbirth, puberty, menstruation, menopause, and sickness.

A primary concern of many approaches to psychotherapy involves uncovering the "invisible plane" that propels behavior -- that is, unconscious motivation. The "invisible plane", the unconscious motivation of a man who enters psychotherapy because of lifelong difficulties with authority figures, for example, may be revealed as unresolved anger toward his father. A growing body of literature suggests compelling conceptual advantages for understanding this invisible context of the individual's behavior as a personal mythology (Bagarozzi & Anderson, 1989; Feinstein, 1979; Feinstein, Krippner, & Granger, 1988; Krippner, 1986; Larsen, 1990; McAdams, 1985,

1993). Hence personal myths can be conceptualized as the language of the "invisible plane" that propels behavior (Feinstein, 2007).

A myth addresses existential human concerns through narrative, and whether a myth is within or outside of consciousness, it will affect behavior. Personal myths and cultural myths converge to govern every important sphere of human activity. Jung emphasized "collective" myths that reside in the unconscious of humankind as a whole. At the societal level, myths may be cultural, ethnic, institutional, familial, or personal. June Singer (1988) has commented, "Personal mythology is but the flower on the bush: the family myth is the branch, society's conventions form the stem, and the root is the human condition" (p. xi). Singer (1990) adds, however, that once psychotherapists identify the "parts", they must also understand how they are organized. Otherwise, therapists will "stop with the five-finger exercises and will never play the concerto" (p. 60).

R. B. Edgerton (1992) points out that some societies have acquired religious, hygienic, or sexual customs that are maladaptive and that will, if not altered, destroy the society in which they have taken hold, or at least the well-being of individuals within that social group. Some of these customs were adaptive at one time but, through the force of tradition, survived long after changing circumstances made them maladaptive. Alternatively, these folkways might have become inadequate once the society was exposed to competition from neighbors with more efficient traditions. In a similar manner, personal myths that may have been extraordinarily useful during childhood typically become maladaptive if they do not evolve as the individual matures.

We use the term myth to identify explanatory narratives, both within and outside of awareness, that impact the experience and behavior of a person, a family, an institution, or an entire society. It misses the mark to judge such myths as "true" or "false", but practitioners may evaluate certain elements of their clients' mythology as "functional" and others as "dysfunctional". This evaluation will, however, inevitably be based on the mythology embedded in the psychotherapist's own clinical perspective. An individual's collection of personal myths comprises his or

her personal mythology, "the vibrant infrastructure that informs your life, whether or not you are aware of it" (Singer, 1988, p. xi). Jungians hold that the most useful, functional personal myths are attuned to the mythology of the "collective unconscious", the stratum of the psyche that purportedly has endured throughout the ages, and that a personal myth often changes as one attempts to resolve its disharmony with a "collective myth".

Our students and colleagues have

applied many of our techniques with people interested in self-development, individuals with mild to moderately severe emotional and behavioral disorders, individuals diagnosed as exhibiting post-traumatic stress disorder (Paulson, 1992), and even those with schizophreniform conditions (Sperry, 1981). The primary requirement of our approach is that the client has a capacity for the creation of verbal or nonverbal narrative. We have not personally used our approach with children, but J. W. Rhue and S. J. Lynn (1991), and M. E. Stevens-Guille and F. J. Boersma (1992) are among those who have used storytelling and fairy tales with children in psychotherapeutic settings, claiming salutary results, and Richard Gardner (1971) pioneered a brilliant psychotherapeutic approach for children based on mutual storytelling. However, we have prepared a self-help workbook (Feinstein & Krippner,

1997) that utilizes a series of "personal rituals" which attempt not only to assist individuals in their own development but also to help them bring a renewed mythology back to their family, community, or social group. The personal rituals in our workbook serve as the core of our narrative therapeutic technique, whether someone uses the book privately, works within a group, or uses it as a supplement to psychotherapy.

II. Theoretical Concepts and Principles

Psychotherapy is a process that attempts to modify behavior and experience which clients and / or their social group deem to be dysfunctional, usually because they inhibit personal relationships, stifle competent performance, or block the actualization of one's talents and capacities (Krippner, 1990, p. 179). Thus, psychotherapy, by its nature, is conducted within the context of the culture's broader mythological framework (Feinstein & Krippner, 1989), ideological struggles (Prilleltensky, 1989), and competing visions of reality (Andrews, 1989). Whatever the client's presenting problem, not to understand it within this larger context is to miss important dimensions of his or her existential situation.

For example, one of the great embarrassments for the psychotherapy establishment is the hand it unwittingly lent in suppressing the brewing discontent among women in the late 1950s and 1960s. By reframing the complaints of their female clients as unresolved intrapsychic problems, therapists served as a repressive force in the lives of disaffected women. Such therapists, by focusing on their clients' failure to adjust to existing role expectations, may have been operating within a worldview that was supported by their training, but they were oblivious to the mythic conflict that was about to take center stage in the societal arena. In this manner, the implicit value assumptions of the therapist, and the deep mythology of which they are a part, shape therapeutic outcome.

Estella Lauter and C. S. Rupprecht (1985) observed Jung's "preoccupation with the feminine" (p. 5) that involved an ability to see beyond the culture's patriarchal myths and stereotypes. Among Jung's most controversial concepts are those of the "animus" and "anima"; he believed that the former represents a culturally constructed masculine image that unconsciously presents itself (especially in dreams) to a woman, while the latter represents a stereotypic feminine image that presents itself to a man. These concepts have been formulated differently by Jung's followers, but the implication remains that culturally defined masculine and feminine qualities are equally available for development by either gender.

Even though Jung did not ignore the social milieu, the question that seems to have driven his intellectual quest centered on the behavioral and psychological characteristics that are held in common by humankind as a species. For Jung, there were no fundamental incompatibilities between humankind's biological origins and its spiritual predispositions (Stevens, 1982, p. 21). Jung's pursuit involved his own self-study, his analysis of the problems brought to him by his patients, and his readings in mythology and comparative religion. Most of the ideas in the 18 volumes of his Collected Works revolve around his assertion that the human psyche -- like the human body -- has a definable structure, and that human societies, no matter what their location in space or time, all focus on similar life issues (Stevens, 1982, pp.

22-23). Jung used the term "archetype" when discussing the images humanity has found to address these common concerns, symbolism that inevitably appears in dreams, fantasy, art, and other expressions of the human psyche. As the individual, the family, or the group searches for meaning, archetypes (which are said to reside in the collective unconscious) become the raw material for the narratives that eventually are referred to as "myths".

Anthony Stevens (1982) has taken Jung at his word -- that archetypes are biologically based (although socially canalized) -- and has reformulated them in terms of neuropsychological processes that possess the capacity to initiate, control, and mediate the everyday behavior and experiences of human beings (p. 296). Drawing from research on the brain's sub cortical structures and hemispheric asymmetry, and from investigations of naturally occurring mental imagery (especially nighttime dreaming), Stevens con-

For Jung, there were no fundamental incompatibilities between humankind's biological origins and its spiritual predispositions.

cludes that "from the viewpoint of modern neurology, Jung's work stands as a brilliant vindication of and belief in the value of intuitive knowledge" (pp. 273-274).

Jung spoke of the "ego" as the center of a person's field of consciousness. C. D. Laughlin and his associates (Laughlin, McManus, & d'Aquili, 1990) have reinterpreted Jung's notion of the ego in terms of research data involving "neural networks". When we are consciously aware of one (or more) of these networks, that network joins the set of percepts, concepts, images, and affects that comprise "our empirical ego". Those neural networks that we perceive and cognize as our ego are typically bounded by intensive neurological inhibitions. Other networks drop out of sight only from the standpoint of the conscious networks, yet they continue to function and develop over time, and may exercise unconscious volition to attain their ends (p. 134). We maybe come aware of these additional networks (Jung's other com-

plexes) only after the healthy psyche has reached midlife following a lengthy period of what Jung called "ego consolidation".

Jungian personality theory, therefore, can be understood from several perspectives -- biological, psychodynamic, social, or transpersonal. Psychotherapists need to be mindful of their own underlying beliefs and values, and of the "hermeneutic circle" these deep myths create in conjunction with their clients' myths (Frank & Frank, 1991). We believe it is both a possibility and a requirement during the contemporary period of unprecedented upheaval and cultural ferment that effective psychotherapists, regardless of their theoretical orientation: (1) develop an awareness of the mythology within which they themselves operate; and (2) help clients understand the deeply personal myths that give form to the way they construct their world and shape their behavior. We will next examine the nature of personal myths and the manner by which we believe they evolve, and then introduce a model by which clinicians may bring a more mythological perspective into their own practices. This perspective utilizes narrative as a central tool for navigating one's way through the territory Jung brought forever into the purview of psychotherapy.

Jung's suspiciousness of metaphysical language makes him a precursor of those postmodernists who have attempted to deconstruct metaphysics. Instead, Jung focused on the images and the phenomenology of the psyche, which goes hand-in-hand with many postmodern thinkers. For Jung, psyche is not only expressed in images, but psyche exists in images, both at a personal and collective level. The dismissal of the collective unconscious by "modern" psychologists stands in sharp contrast to those postmodern thinkers who, like Jung, espouse views on language, customs, imagination, etc., that are largely collective in character (Casey, 1990). It should be noted, however, that Jung's emphasis on the universal aspects of psychological functioning places him at odds with postmodernists. His concepts of "animus" and "anima", for instance, focus on presumed essential differences between men and women, thus -- according to some postmodernists -- fostering and perpetuating power-based patterns of domination and exploitation (Clarke, 1993, p. 1231).

Although Jung's notion of a collective unconscious that consists of "archetypes" -- collective myths, symbols, and metaphors -- is one of the most controversial aspects of his work, such writers as Plato and St. Augustine had proposed similar concepts, and these ideas have continually resurfaced, albeit with different names and descriptions. When Jean Piaget (1971) writes of innate schemata, when Claude Levi-Strauss (1966) speaks of binary oppositions in cultural myths, when Noam Chomsky (1965) proposes that rules for transformational grammar in linguistics are "hard-wired" in the brain, concepts echoing Jung's notion of archetypes are being discussed. Indeed, the "transparency and creativity" emphasized by Jung's dream theory is clearly related to the literary exposition of texts (Hobson, 1988, p. 65). These preoccupations with "essences" are at odds with those postmodernists who emphasize local phenomena particular to time and place.

Our framework fits within the emerging area of narrative psychology in that it treats narrative as an organizing metaphor for human activity. It is based on the assumption that individuals impose socially constituted narrative structures on their experience, therefore serving as both the authors and the actors in stories that form their own personal dramas (Lyddon & McLaughlin, 1992, p.96). The narrative expression of myths need not be written; it may be pictorial, oral, or expressed in dance, sculpture, or a variety of other forms that give expression to the imagination. Using narrative in psychotherapy enhances both awareness and responsibility as it teaches clients to redefine themselves and reconstruct their life stories, as well as showing them how to take a hermeneutic, meaning-oriented approach to personal experience (e.g., Mahoney, 1991; Schafer, 1992). It is for these reasons that T. R. Sarbin (1986), in *Narrative Psychology: The Storied Nature of Human Conduct*, nominates narrative as a "root metaphor" for psychology.

The Nature of Personal Myths

Myths often contain potent symbols and metaphors that organize experience and regulate action (Schorer, 1960). The exploration of myths in this context is more useful than to dismiss them as superstitious falsehoods. The latter usage of the term "myth" is a formulation that belies the reductionism of modern technological, industrialized societies. Nor are myths simply values, ethics, attitudes, or beliefs, although each of these may reflect a deeper mythic structure and contribute to a myth's pattern or gestalt. Unlike other psychological and "pop psychology" terms such as "cognitive schemes", "belief systems", or "scripts", the word "myth" more easily embraces those dimensions of human consciousness that often transcend early conditioning and cultural setting. Myth-making, at the individual, familial, cultural, and collective level, is the

ment, provides social direction, and addresses spiritual yearnings in a manner that is analogous to the way cultural myths carry out these functions for entire societies.

By drawing on the historically rich concept of mythology to describe explanatory and guiding schemata at both the individual and cultural levels, the integral relationship between personal and social constructions of reality is emphasized. Each level, in fundamental ways, mirrors the other. There is evidence, for example, that the hero / heroine's journey, a central motif in Western mythology, exists not only in the guiding images provided by societies, but also as an archetype in the primordial recesses of the psyche and the body. Campbell, who described the hero's (or heroine's) journey based on his comparative studies of mythologies throughout history, notes his "amazement" upon reading of psychiatrist John Weir Perry's (1976) studies of psychosis and discovering that some-

Using narrative in psychotherapy enhances both awareness and responsibility as it teaches clients to redefine themselves and reconstruct their life stories.

primary though often unperceived psychological mechanism by which human beings order reality and navigate their way through life. As the human species evolved, mythological thinking -- the ability to symbolically address existential questions -- replaced genetic mutation as the primary vehicle by which individual consciousness and societal innovations were carried forward (Feinstein & Krippner, 1988b).

Personal as well as cultural myths are generally organized around at least one of the core themes that are customarily the concern of cultural mythology. These, according to Campbell (1988), include: (1) the need to comprehend one's world in a meaningful way; (2) the search for a marked pathway through the succeeding epochs of human life; (3) the urgency to establish secure and fulfilling relationships within a community; and (4) the longing to find one's place in the vast wonder and mystery of the cosmos. Personal myths act as a lens that explains the world, guides individual develop-

times "the imagery of schizophrenic fantasy perfectly matches that of the mythological hero journey" as Campbell (1972, p. 208) had outlined it earlier.

According to Campbell (1986), myths are ultimately "motivated from a single psycho physiological source -- namely, the human imagination moved by the conflicting urgencies of the organs" (p. 12). Campbell, in taking this position, follows Jung, who assumed the inseparability of body and psyche (Rupprecht, 1985). Our model also recognizes this inseparability and conceptualizes personal myths as being the product of four interacting sources. The most obvious are biology (the capacities for symbolism and narrative are rooted in the structure of the brain, information and attitudes are neurochemically coded, physiology, temperament and hormones influence belief systems, etc.), culture (the individual's mythology is, to an extent, the culture's mythology in microcosm), and personal history (every emotionally significant event leaves a mark on one's developing mythology). A fourth source is rooted in transpersonal experiences -- those episodes, insights, dreams, and visions that have a numinous quality and that expand a person's perspective in ways described as "spiritual". For Jung, humanity's spiritual life can be seen not as a denial of its evolutionary origins, but as an expression of them (Stevens, 1982, p. 22).

The spiritual dimension of human existence plays a key role in both myth and Jungian psychotherapy. In Philip Wheelwright's (1942) classic definition, "the very essence of myth is that haunting awareness of transcendental forces peering through the cracks of the visible universe" (p. 10). Jung (1928 / 1969) once stated that his goal in psychotherapy was the cure of the soul. He (1958) later wrote that "virtually everything depends on the soul" because the future of humanity "will be decided neither by the attacks of wild animals nor by the danger of worldwide epidemics but simply and solely by the psychic changes in...our rulers' heads because they can plunge the world into blood, fire, and radioactivity" (p. 97). For Jung, mythology was of critical importance because it contained profound psychological truths not present in scientific psychology, truths essential to the art of "soul-making" (Staude, 1981, p. 76).

The Principles by Which Personal Myths Develop

We have formulated seven principles by which we believe personal myths develop. They are presented here as testable propositions:

1. To emerge from the mythic structure in which one has been psychologically embedded, and to move to another integrated set of guiding images and premises, is a natural and periodic phase of individual development. Personal myths exist within a psychological ecology of mutation and selection in which even the "fittest" mythic structures must continually evolve if they are to further the person's optimal adjustment and development. Not only do circumstances unceasingly change, but new developmental tasks also appear throughout adult life. Jung believed that during the first half of a person's life, a "dominant function" will be established that may work quite

well but, later on, what functioned so effectively becomes problematic (Jung, 1921 / 1971).

Personal myths that are appropriate and effective during one period of life or at one level of development may become inappropriate or dysfunctional at another. As myths grow outmoded, they fail to support the individual's psychosocial and spiritual needs and begin to restrict personal development. Psychological growth often requires a shift to more functional mythic structures. The surrounding culture's attitudes regarding such changes, and the rites of passage it provides or fails to provide for supporting them, may promote or inhibit the success of such transitions. Sometimes a superficial mythic structure is revealed by one's "persona", a term Jung adopted from the Greek word for "mask". It feigns individuality, and can sustain someone for a considerable period of time; but the persona is basically a role that is enacted to adapt to the requirements of specific life situations.

2. Personal conflicts -- both in one's inner life and external circumstances -- are natural markers of these times of transition. When the prevailing mythic structure no longer serves the individual's adjustment or developmental needs, it is advantageous to consider the alternative guiding structures the psyche is continually generating. These are typically revealed in dreams and other windows into unconscious processes. Jung believed that dreams are often prospective, assisting the dreamers to glimpse oppositional aspects of themselves as well as what they can become if they shed or alter their dysfunctional myths. Psychological defenses, however, may prevent individuals from recognizing features of their experience that are incompatible with the dominant myth, even as that myth becomes less capable of providing effective guidance. In maintaining a mythology that is failing, people generally experience an increasing degree of conflict that colors their feelings, thoughts, actions, dreams, fantasies, and the circumstances they draw to themselves. To treat such difficulties as markers of transition, rather than simply to resist them, allows a mobilization for understanding and beginning to resolve underlying mythic conflict.

3. On one side of the underlying mythic conflict will be a self-limiting myth,

rooted in past experience, that is best understood in terms of its constructive purposes in the individual's history. In the early phases of our model, an effort is made to connect current difficulties with past experiences. The old myth is examined for the productive role it played at an earlier time. This reveals the functions the new myth will have to serve and brings attention to previous attempts to meet those needs. By understanding how the old myth developed, even while in the process of abandoning it, one becomes more able to embrace the valid lessons it still holds and to affirm strengths and abilities that may have been called into question by the consequences of the myth's shortcomings.

When a dream reveals a mythic struggle, the Jungian technique of "amplification" can be used to understand it better. Amplification differs from free association as it attempts to find parallels to the dream image or activity; Jung compares it to the way philologists learned to read hieroglyphics and cuneiform inscriptions -- by finding a parallel text. Amplification can be attempted on three levels: the dreamer's personal associations, the dreamer's and the therapist's cultural associations, and any cross-cultural or archetypal associations made by the dreamer or therapist (Hall, 1982). This also resembles hermeneutics, the disciplined examination of texts in an attempt to discover their intended meaning. Like some literary texts, an individual's dreams may contain multiple meanings at various levels, hence Jung's injunction to inspect the potential personal, cultural, and archetypal mythic content. In applying the results of this hermeneutic search to one's daily behavior, the dreamer can attempt to compose a more coherent "plot" for their life (Frank & Frank, 1991, p. 72).

4. On the other side of the conflict will be an emerging counter-myth that serves as a force toward expanding the individual's perceptions, self-concept, world-view, and awareness of options in the very areas the old myth was limiting them. Just as the psyche may produce inspiring dreams that point toward new directions for one's development, it also creates new mythic images whose guidance may be in direct conflict with prevailing myths. Latent qualities of the personality not supported by the existing mythology will naturally push toward expression, spearheaded by an emerging "counter-myth". Counter-myths are woven from the accumulation of life experiences, from a developmental readiness to accept the more useful myths of one's culture or from a reservoir of unconscious primal impulses and presumed archetypal materials such as the "shadow" and anima/animus, each of which plays a prominent role in Jung's thought.

The shadow, for instance, personifies everything that a person refuses to acknowledge about himself or herself. In dreams, the shadow is generally the same gender as the dreamer. A shadow character may be judged to be immoral, barbarous, outrageous, or distasteful. The shadow does not typically represent a final resolution of the dreamer's mythic conflict, but recognizing it may be an essential step in facing what has been repressed and ignored. Counter-myths, whether organized around primal impulses or archetypal material, are best understood as creative leaps in the psyche's problem-solving activities, but like some dreams they play a wish-fulfillment function that lacks real-world utility. Still, they serve as a force to recapture aspects of the psyche that have been repressed under the constraints of the old myth and to integrate unrecognized impulses and images into the personality.

5. While this conflict may be emotionally painful and personally disruptive, a natural, though often unconscious, mobilization toward a resolution will also be occurring, ultimately yielding a mythic image with new meaning. A dialectical process naturally unfolds which can be viewed as a subterranean struggle between conflicting myths vying to structure the individual's perceptions, thoughts, feelings, and behaviors (Pasqual-Leone, 1987). Although much of this process will occur outside of awareness, people will tend to identify consciously more fully with one of the myths, or some of its elements, than with the other. By bringing the dialectic into awareness, people have a greater chance of working out the conflict as a drama in their inner life rather than having to play it out on the rack of life. The dialectic occurs naturally and without volition or attention, but an optimum resolution of the conflict may be enhanced through techniques that

attune conscious awareness to this deeper process. Through the use of such methods, symbols of transformation eventually emerge, pointing toward resolution of the mythic conflict and greater personality integration. Jung spoke of the "transcendent function of symbols", whereby an image emerges that has the power to transcend polarities and unite opposites, fostering a transition from psychic conflict to the achievement of greater inner unity.

6. During this process, previously unresolved mythic conflicts will tend to reemerge -- with the potential of either interfering with the resolution of the current developmental task or opening the way to deeper levels of resolution in the person's mythology. When an individual was unable at an earlier age to successfully meet the requirements of a particular developmental task, such as reconciling oneself to having been raised by an abusive parent, that issue will play a thematic role in the resolution of subsequent mythic conflicts. Certain aspects of the person's mythology become fixated at the level of this unresolved issue and interfere with later developmental steps. Taking a cue from Jung's utilization of imagination in psychotherapy, we often guide clients to use imagery and fantasy to enter an earlier period where their development was arrested. There we provide this younger aspect of themselves with an emotionally corrective rite of passage that leads them to the next developmental tier and into an expanded personal mythology.

7. Reconciling newly conceived personal myths with existing beliefs, goals, and life style becomes a vital task in the individual's ongoing development. Historically, rites of passage provided relatively unambiguous direction for regulating people's lives. For a variety of reasons, including the diversity that characterizes modern cultures, this is no longer possible. The need for such direction, however, is ever more pressing as the myths of contemporary culture, which might guide and comfort, are themselves in unprecedented flux.

The model we have developed for helping people move beyond outdated or otherwise dysfunctional personal myths and into a renewed mythology can be used at any point during adult development. It leads to a fresh guiding

mythology that is based on an informed synthesis of the individual's history and character logical leanings with cultural and archetypal images that are pushing for expression. The task of weaving this renewed mythology into the fabric of life can provide new meaning and purpose to the individual's journey as it addresses the vital functions that cultural rites and rituals no longer serve. It echoes Jung's stress on balance and wholeness, as individuals work toward "higher", more transcendental, stages of integration (Staude, 1981, pp. 84-85).

The prototype for this unending process of (1) emerging from the mythic structure in which one has been psychologically embedded; (2) formulating an alternative guiding structure; and (3) reconciling this new structure with one's earlier mythology and life-style can be seen in Margaret Mahler and her associates' (Mahler, Pine, & Berger, 1975) description of the psychological birth of the human infant. In the infant's earliest mythology -- using here the most basic definition of mythology as simply the psychological construction of reality -- representations of self and other are enmeshed. The developmental task involves differentiating oneself from this embeddedness. Analogously, the maturing individual is for a time psychologically embedded in a particular personal mythology. The next developmental step will involve differentiating one's intrapsychic representations from mythic structures that have become rigid, outdated, or otherwise limiting. Through a series of events that parallel Mahler's "practicing" phase of individuation, a new structure is formulated, a counter-myth begins to coalesce. However, because of the repudiation of the old myth that inevitably accompanies the differentiation stage, the counter-myth is generally skewed. While it may compensate for the shortcomings of the prevailing mythology, it is itself often impaired in the very areas that the old myth was the most adequate.

This is often a painfully disorienting period where the person is caught between two realities -- one that is familiar but no longer functional and another that is not yet fully formulated and is thus unable to provide reliable guidance. Jung (1932 / 1972) commented that feelings of alienation and depression often mark an individual's effort to supplant the domination of the ego with a search for the inner Self. A rapprochement between the old structure and the emerging direction is necessitated, ideally consolidating a new structure into which the person's identity can again, for a time, be advantageously embedded. Higher stages of ego development correlate with greater differentiation and better integration among the elements of the personality -- specifically the personal myths that people consciously and unconsciously construct as they formulate their identities (Kegan, 1982; McAdams, 1985). Clinicians may be useful in assisting people to move through periods of transition in their mythologies with such enhanced differentiation and integration. Just as adults reconstruct in their interpersonal relationships developmental tasks they did not successfully complete as children, early problems in constructing reality are also recapitulated in the manner by which adults attempt to evolve from a failing mythic structure to a new guiding mythology.

III. Strategies and Techniques

The seven principles described above are embodied in a model we have developed for helping people understand, evaluate, and orchestrate transformations in their guiding myths. The model permeates five stages which we believe naturally follow one another as personal myths evolve.

A Five-Stage Model for Intervening in the Individual's Evolving Mythology

Singer (1988) has observed that our first three stages echo the Socratic triad of thesis, antithesis, and synthesis. The fourth stage tests and reinforces insights so that the new myth can move from the imaginative realm into the phase of intention and then into action. Stage Five involves a series of practical steps by which the inner transformation can be actualized in the external world. As Singer (1988) has noted, these stages are informed not only by Jungian psychology but by psychoanalysis, cognitive psychology, and behavior therapy (pp. xii-xiii). We suggest various procedures for moving through the five stages. Our workbook (Feinstein & Krippner, 1997), along with an integrated set of audio cassettes, is designed to assist the process, whether the individual has engaged the

help of a psychotherapist or is working privately, with a partner, or a group.

A dilemma of the modern era is that the ability of cultural myths to adapt to new conditions has been outstripped by the rate of social change (Feinstein & Krippner, 1988a). The lack of unity and coherence in the culture's mythology allows and, in fact, forces individuals to think and act for themselves in ways that were unimaginable in the past. As people in contemporary cultures are propelled to formulate distinctively personal mythologies, the culture's emerging mythology is being hammered out on the anvil of individuals' lives. The requirement that people become conscious of and capable of mindfully influencing the mythologies they are living is more urgent than ever before. By understanding the principles that govern their underlying myths, people become able to influence patterns in their lives that once seemed predetermined and went unquestioned, and they become more able to creatively adjust to the bewildering contradictions in today's guiding myths. A well-articulated, carefully examined

cian would normally conceptualize them, into the larger context of the client's evolving mythology; and (2) to evaluate therapeutic interventions and outcomes within this larger context as well as within the more precise formulations of the therapist's particular school of practice.

The Five Stages

In addition to whatever methods the therapist already employs, we introduce a layer of technique designed to show the client how to work experientially with the inner symbolism the psyche is continually generating. We believe that within each individual is a mythological underworld whose content is reminiscent of the great cultural mythologies. This rich foundation of waking life is revealed in the high drama and conspicuous creativity of the individual's dream life and inner visions as they unfold and are appreciated. We also show clinicians how to help their clients develop and access an internalized ego state which we refer to as the "Inner Shaman" (Feinstein,

A dilemma of the modern era is that the ability of cultural myths to adapt to new conditions has been outstripped by the rate of social change.

personal mythology may be one of the most effective devices available for countering the disorienting grip of a world in mythic turmoil.

For many years, we have been searching for ways to bring to the therapeutic process more focus and mastery regarding these subtle and underlying mythic dimensions of clinical practice (Feinstein, 1979, 1987, 1990a, 1990b; Feinstein & Krippner, 1988a, 1988b, 1989, 1997; Feinstein, Krippner & Granger, 1988; Feinstein & Mayo, 1990; Krippner, 1986). Helping people understand how their personal myths evolve increases their ability to meaningfully engage in the fundamental processes associated with their psychological, social, and spiritual development. When offering therapists training in bringing a mythological perspective into their clinical practices, we do not ask them to shift to a different theoretical orientation or methodology, but rather: (1) to place the diagnostic picture and therapeutic goals, as the cli-

1987), something of a cross between the "observing ego" and the "higher self". Finally, based on our observations from intimate contact with the mythologies of over 4,000 people, we provide a framework for understanding the natural stages by which personal myths evolve, and for formulating interventions that are attuned to the requirements for successfully completing each stage. Each stage is described here, and a case history that illustrates all five of the stages is presented.

First Stage: Framing Personal Concerns and Difficulties in Terms of Deeper Mythological Conflict. Identifying areas of conflict in the client's underlying mythology is the starting point of our 5-stage model. Repetitive dysfunctional behavioral patterns such as involvement in abusive relationships or chronic vocational failures, as well as clinical symptoms such as addictions or hypertension, may provide an entry into areas of the person's mythology that are begging for attention. Dream symbols and other productions of the unconscious, such as drawings, sand play, or free association, may also highlight such areas. We attend to our clients' presenting complaints, identify self-defeating behavioral patterns, and remain alert to unconscious symbolism as we help them begin to uncover the mythic proportions of daily life and to understand their difficulties as reflections of deeper conflicts in their guiding mythologies. To illustrate the 5-stage model, we will follow the experience of a Steve, 38-year-old psychotherapist who was receiving training in bringing a mythological perspective to his own clinical practice.

Steve's training included a series of weekly individual counseling sessions over a 4-month period, participation in a 30-hour class for exploring the mythic foundations of thought and behavior, a 3-day vision quest, a role as an assistant leader in a subsequent class, and various home reading, imagery, and journal assignments. The following includes excerpts from both his journal and a transcript of an interview that took place for the purpose of this write-up after the training was completed. Steve focused on an inner conflict that had plagued him throughout his 3-year marriage, and it had also been responsible for his having delayed the marriage for several years prior to that:

> On the one side are the needs of my marriage, which involves directing my sexual passion toward my wife, and on the other side are my strong, incessant and seemingly biological urges toward other women.

Examining the first side of the conflict, Steve traced the mythology that was guiding him regarding loyalty and

fidelity back to images of his parent's marriage: "My father's loyalty was certainly unwavering, but somewhere in the bargain he traded his passion to live life 'on the edge' for a smoldering, if rarely uttered, resentment about all he was required, at least in his mind, to sacrifice. His was a dutiful, passionless love". Steve had probed this territory with considerable depth in previous psychotherapy sessions. He went on to examine the other side of the conflict:

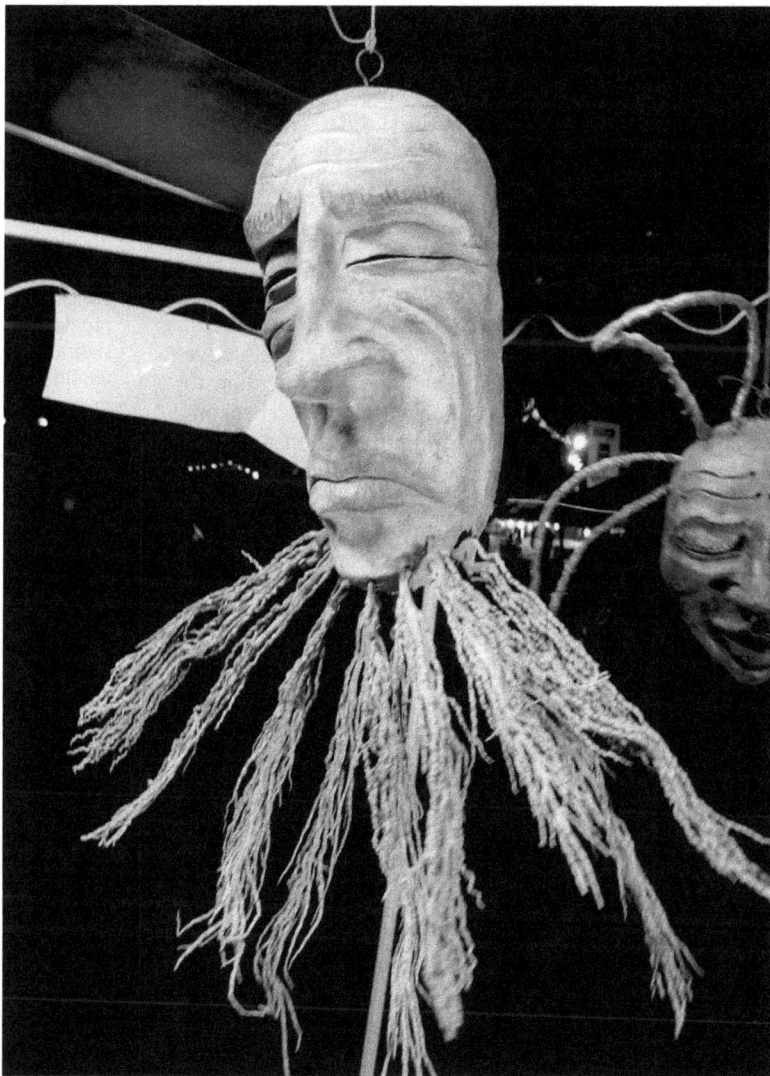

Photo: Mariana Castro de Ali

> This process involved exploring my indiscriminate and unyielding passion for attractive women, always so elusive to analysis but eternally problematic in my relationships. I've tried and tried to understand this attraction in light of the Jungian idea of the anima -- that my obsession is really to find the feminine aspect of my own being. It just doesn't feel that way when I'm confronted with a pretty waitress or bikini-clad bodies on

the beach. A guided imagery journey brought me into a very interesting space. I started by focusing on the nature of my feelings when I see a beautiful woman. It was like putting the experience of arousal under a microscope instead of just being mindlessly turned on, eager for action, and by marriage contract, continually frustrated. I realized that these moments of lust are the most full-bodied experiences I encounter with any frequency -- a rush of sensation in my genitals and chest radiates out to a tingling throughout my body.

As I shifted my attention from the physical experience to sensing its deeper meaning, I had a powerful image of being dwarfed by a very beautiful and sensual goddess, hovering like a genie above me and slightly to my left, with the bottom cone-end of the apparition emanating from the area of my first chakra, attached like a ghostly umbilical cord. Being in her presence was indescribably peaceful and warm. It was as if she could fulfill my innermost longings in a way that was far superior to any satisfaction I could find in the outer world. She told me I could have all I am looking for and more, but in order to receive it, I must be willing to allow my body to be torn apart. That was, literally and terrifyingly, the bargain she offered. At the same time, however, I intuited that she was beckoning me to embrace the feminine principle, and the first gateway through which I would have to pass was to open myself to the total vulnerability of living fully within my body. This led to image after image of the terrible dangers the world holds. Particularly strong were views of gruesome accidents and torture. I settled finally onto a vision of being an ancient warrior reassuring his terrified family as he goes off to protect the village from savage attackers.

The lines from Ann Mortifee's powerful "Beirut Song" ran through my head, of mothers searching skyward, their infants in their arms. "Keep us from harm. Save us from harm!" I came into an awful realization of the vulnerability of the archetypal female, giving birth, rearing children, tending the home fires. I'm aligned with a very different principle. I quickly translate danger -- physical or emotional -- into a mental plan and action. My attention instantly leaves my body and focuses in my mind. It may be a break with reality to leave one's body in the face of danger, but it was suddenly clear that to live fully in the body is to accept the goddess' terrible admonition to me. I've never identified much with ancient warriors, but I was not about to agree to surrender my self into the vulnerable space of just experiencing danger in my body, no matter what rewards this genie-goddess was promising. I said, "No deal", and abruptly found myself roused out of the trance, intuiting that Jung was right: Female images would probably continue to have their elusive enchantment as long as I was unwilling to accept the goddess' bargain. But, if embracing my feminine aspects meant I had to release into that kind of vulnerability, I wasn't interested.

As this inner story unfolded, Steve began to contact dimensions of his original conflict he had never imagined. Starting with an examination of the bodily sensations that were part of his problematic response to the lure of feminine beauty, his associations brought him to both a mythological image of the feminine principle within and a dramatic portrayal of his fear of embracing it.

Second Stage: Bringing the Roots of Each Side of the Conflict Into Focus. Once the mythic conflict that will be examined has been identified, the second stage involves excavating the foundations of the prevailing myth and of the counter-myth that is challenging it. Guiding myths become outmoded as the individual matures and as life circumstances change. The psyche is continually trying on alternative mythic images -- what we have been referring to as counter-myths -- that compensate for the old myth's limitations. Indeed, Jung saw dreams as often "compensating", producing points of view in counterpoint to the stance of the conscious ego (Hall, 1982, p. 136). This reflects Jung's belief that the human psyche is a self-regulating system (Singer, 1972). Thus, counter-myths highlight possibilities and reveal new ways of being, often supporting underdeveloped aspects of the personality. Their imagery is imaginative and inspiring, but like wish-fulfillment dreams, to which they are psychologically akin, they are framed in the logic of magical thinking and immediate gratification. Unlike the prevailing myth, the counter-myth is untried in the real world. The dilemma created when a counter-myth challenges an outmoded prevailing myth is that the person is caught between two worlds -- no longer able to thrive under the guidance of what has been, but not yet having developed guiding images that give practical utility to the new direction that is being intuited. The task in this stage of the work is to bring these opposing internal forces into consciousness, to clarify each, and to trace their roots in the individual's culture, personal history, and psychic depths.

Having reframed his initial conflict as a contest between the urge to embrace the feminine principle within him and his terror of it, Steve was encouraged to maintain in his awareness, through a variation of Jung's active imagination technique and attention to his dreams, both the goddess' beckoning and his cringing response to the terms she offered. He found that the goddess embodied a combination of maternal warmth and voluptuous beauty. In one active imagination session:

> The goddess wept in sorrow that she could not persuade me to come down from my rigid mental structures and into my body where I could dance with her and play with her and make love with her. I just sat there in amazement and watched her weep, but eventually I felt myself coming closer to her and embracing her and I felt myself softening as I held her. Another time, she was furious with me. Face red, nostrils flaring, chest puffed, nipples forming hard outlines under her chiffon robe, she screamed at me for remaining so safe and aloof. I was both afraid of her and excited by her passion. I eventually rose to meet her eye to eye and take in what she was saying. I really wanted her approval, but her demands seemed so capricious and irrational. Soon I was screaming back at her and then realizing that by getting me to lose my cool, she was getting just what she wanted of me. Just as I came to this realization, I again inadvertently opened my eyes and brought myself out of the trance.

Exploring the inner forces that were keeping him from cooperating with the goddess, Steve was brought, through age regression, back to experiences of being ridiculed for crying in public school and humiliated by his parents for having thrown temper tantrums. He remembered in his body how he had learned to fight feelings of fear, anger and emotional pain by tightening his jaw, controlling his breathing, and focusing on something he could do, if not to improve the situation, at least to take his attention away from his feelings. He was encouraged to write a fairy tale to portray this history, and he wrote a story about the primitive warrior he saw in the fantasy in which the goddess first appeared.

> Born, like all children, an innocent, he was effectively and efficiently trained to kill his fears and focus his desires and passions into cunning action. His proficiency with these abilities brought him great success. He was treated with awe and respect by his family and by the other villagers. But one day the gods proclaimed that there could be no more fighting among people. Giant volcanos would erupt all over the world, causing great tidal waves that would wipe out all of humanity, and this holocaust might be ignited by the swing of a single war ax or the tossing of a spear. He believed these reports to be false legends spread by the Evil Empire of the East, but his countrymen believed them and he was forced to destroy his weapons. Dejected, he could no longer be a warrior, and for the first time in his courage-studded adult life, he felt empty and afraid.

Steve's story allegorically portrays both his own upbringing and the way the old models were losing their viability in an age of nuclear weapons and radically new rules for living. As he was later instructed, this tale is but Chapter 1 of a three-part fairy tale. Chapter 2 is designed to explore an emerging counter-myth, and in writing it, Steve had the goddess visit the warrior. In his story, the goddess transported the warrior into an enchanted land where men are so fully open to their hearts that all of life is injected with a loving tint that dissolves fear and greed and anger and makes living a joy. As Steve marveled about the miracle of transformed consciousness that would be needed to cause the world to be so altered, he was told to observe this world carefully for he would soon have to return to his village and bring with him all that he had learned. So ended Chapter 2.

Third Stage: Conceiving a Unifying Mythic Vision. Once both sides of the mythological conflict have been differentiated, the third stage involves integrating the old myth and the counter-myth into a higher order. Promoting such resolution of psychological conflict is a natural function of the psyche, but actively participating in the process can facilitate (1) better life choices at a time when the person is particularly vulnerable to act out unconscious conflict in self-destructive ways; (2) a more rapid resolution of painful inner discord; (3) a greater sense of personal mastery; and, ultimately, (4) a resolution of the mythological conflict that is based on carefully examined beliefs and values as well as the person's deepest intuitive wisdom. The task in this stage is to skillfully mediate and facilitate as the opposing myths push toward a natural synthesis. Having embraced both sides of the conflict, images of integration become more possible. The individual is taught to recognize that facing one's own inconsistencies without a retreat into the old or a flight into the emerging may be as difficult as it is desirable. The objective here is to foster a new mythic image that transcends the old myth and the counter-myth, while embodying the most functional aspects of each. This process represents the self-regulatory attempts of the deepest and most numinous part of the psyche, referred to by Jung as the "Self", which represents a union of opposites, a supraordinate personality that attempts to grow toward wholeness, i.e., to "individuate". Jung (1973) once wrote a friend that one must not linger on the steps of life because the last steps are the loveliest and most precious.

Fourth Stage: Refining the Vision into a Commitment toward a Renewed Mythology. In the fourth stage, the person is called upon to examine the new mythic vision that was synthesized from the processes described above and to refine it to the point where a commitment to that vision may be maturely entered. While it is necessary to allow the natural dialectic between the old myth and the counter-myth to take its course, a time does come when consciously identifying with a judiciously cultivated mythic image both shapes and hastens the resolution. As the old adage has it, "If you don't change your direction, you may wind up where you are headed". Challenging the person to formulate an explicit choice at this point exercises an active participation in the evolution of the guiding mythology and leads to an enhanced sense of mastery in that process. A series of personal rituals is introduced in this stage that attempt to induce changed states of consciousness for accessing deeper sources of awareness to examine and refashion the newly formed mythic image.

Steve orchestrated a dialogue between his inner warrior and his inner goddess. He physically assumed the posture of each as they carried out, at first a heated debate, and, after several sittings, a discussion of their differences. This excerpt is from the middle part of their deliberations:

GODDESS: Look at yourself. Look at how stiff and joyless you have become. I could give you new life. I'm soft and juicy; you're hard and dry. But you don't trust me at all, do you?

WARRIOR: Why should I trust you? After all, you're just another part of Steve''s mind, just like me. I'm not at all certain that you could make me any juicier. And your demand for large pockets of time in which I take my attention off my regular duties to focus on my body and on images of you, all of which would make me feel very vulnerable, is a large ransom for questionable promises of greater happiness.

GODDESS. It's not a ransom. If you will simply slow your pace, tune into your feelings, and keep exploring my image, you will feel juicier. I guarantee it. It won't be as dramatic at first as you would like. And it will probably never be all you are hoping for. But you will feel juicier. Do you have any better offers going than that?

The discussion ended with the warrior reluctantly agreeing to direct his energies in the softer ways that the goddess was inviting. The goddess expressed pleasure in his decision, but skepticism about his ability to wrest his mind away from its traditional ways. The warrior said, "We'll see", and they parted. In another ritual, Steve imagined that the energies of the warrior were on one side of his body and the energies of the goddess on the other. Through a series of processes he was shown how to mingle the energies in his body and then find a new image that incorporated the essential qualities of each:

> Suddenly there was an image of a man and a woman riding together on an open wagon. Two horses were pulling them. It was all very peaceful, a scene from out of the old West. I had a strong sensing that the horses represented my emotions, and there were some situations where they needed to be governed or reined by the man, the male aspect of my personality, and others where they needed to be governed according to the rules by which the goddess was suggesting I live.

During a "vision quest," a 3-day solitary wilderness experience in the Northern California redwoods, Steve chose as his "power object" a tree that guarded the entrance to a glen and seemed to have "a wisdom I could not fathom". Lying at the trunk of the tree and looking skyward at its immense proportions, Steve carefully attuned himself to hear what the tree had to tell him. He felt that he received in images and intuition an entire rendition of history, reflections from this "ageless giant of the forest" on humanity's evolution and his place in it. Later, in his journal, he put into words the essence of what the tree seemed to be conveying:

> I have silently watched humanity's struggle through the centuries. So much of the Paradise I love has been destroyed in your great experiment, your leap from your roots so that you might walk, your leap out of total harmony with the old laws of nature and into the painful situation where you are co-creating the laws at the same time you are living by them.

> Even in your brief lifetime, the laws governing the human story have again changed. The warrior, one of the most sophisticated though most terrible forms you have created, cannot protect his loved ones from nuclear bombs. The disciplines of mind over feelings, action over patience, and suspicion over trust, like the way of the warrior, no longer keep you on a path that will lead to a future for your children.

> Another law has changed. You are a man. Your biological objective is to produce offspring. For aeons of evolution, the best reproductive strategy for the great apes has been for the strongest males to impregnate as many reproductively desirable females as possible. Not so for humans. Your technology has given you unbalanced advantage so Earth is overpopulated with your spe-

cies. The need is not for more humans but for more humane humans. This means humans that come from partnerships of equals, both committed to the needs of the family they are creating, and of one another. It is no longer evolutionarily advantageous to be spreading your seed to every reproductively desirable female who would have you, however much you may still be wired for that response. Your new role in co-creation is to direct that response to eroticize a lifelong partnership, where your age old marriage ceremony promising that two shall become one creates a new form of two souls embracing in their fullness. However much your impulses may keep your energies divided from truly engaging this objective, it is the highest objective, and it is up to you to work out the details.

Another ritual Steve found instructive was to create Chapter 3 of his fairy tale. The warrior was required to return to the village, and Chapter 3, following the motif of the classic hero's journey, is a chronicle of the practical steps the warrior takes to bring back home the insights he gained during his enchanted journey in Chapter 2. The warrior directed his finely honed battlefield disciplines toward developing the new qualities required of him: patience, trust and vulnerability. He opened his heart to his wife in new ways, and his physical passions were drawn toward her. By watching his warrior "work out the details" in the fairy tale, such as when he rephrased the complaints of an angry merchant instead of killing him, Steve gained concrete images that would help him create his own personal rites of passage.

Fifth Stage: Weaving the Renewed Mythology into Daily Life. To prevent individuation from ending up as egocenteredness, Jung stressed the importance of interacting with the world-at-large. The final stage of the model requires clients to become practical and vigilant monitors of their commitment to achieve a harmony between daily life and the renewed guiding mythology they have been formulating. The threads of the new myth now need to be woven into everyday behaviors, thoughts, and actions. The essence of

our 5-stage model is conveyed in an old Hassidic saying that counsels: "We should each carefully observe what way our heart draws us and then choose that way with all our strength". The first four stages are a way of carefully observing what way the heart beckons. By advising that people choose that way with all their strength, the proverb recognizes that old behavioral patterns, conditioning, and character armoring which were associated with the old myth will tend to persist. Choosing the way one's heart beckons with all one's strength is the fifth stage. Focused attention is required for anchoring even an inspiring new myth that has been wisely formulated. In this phase, we draw particularly from the cognitive and behavioral therapies -- using techniques such as behavior rehearsal, visualization, and the monitoring of sub-vocalizations -- in assisting people to integrate the new mythology into their lives.

One of the most effective ongoing tools for Steve was a daily ritual. He

> By coming to understand their own internal mythic processes, individuals become more adept at understanding the mythology of their culture and more able to participate skillfully in its evolution.

spent the first few minutes of his daily morning shower, while enjoying the warm water pounding on his back, closing his eyes, contacting the goddess, and asking her to think through his day with him, showing him where he might approach significant situations in light of her wisdom and teachings. In a technique he came upon during an exercise that helps people use "mental aikido", he used autosuggestion to program himself so that whenever he would be aroused by the sight of a pretty woman, he would draw upon the stimulation to contact his inner goddess. While the bulk of his inner work had explored a theme that was somewhat tangential to his original concern, this technique served to complete the circle by touching directly into the conflict between his marriage and his response to other women.

People move through this 5-stage process at varying rates, and the normal course involves periods of turning back to rework issues from earlier

stages of the model even after embarking upon later stages. There are a number of ways of introducing this 5-stage process into a clinical setting. The clinical practice of one of the authors, for instance, is oriented toward in-depth psychodynamic psychotherapy. Early in the treatment, he introduces to clients capable of self-directed inquiry the self-help workbook that leads them through the 5-stage model via some 30 exercises, or "personal rituals", which are carried out at home. Weekly therapy sessions are informed but not governed by this task; the content of sessions is not dictated by the 5-stage model. Yet this self-study frequently catalyzes feelings and insights that become topics in the therapy. Moreover, simply having the client become familiar with the program frames the therapy within a mythological context. The workbook is completed over a few months, but the personal symbolism and constructs that emerge provide a context for ongoing work and understanding, even long after the therapy has been completed.

In summary, the 5-stage model offers a framework for therapist and client to understand and track the basic tasks that must be accomplished for mindfully transforming an area of one's mythology. We believe it is possible through this model to reliably teach people: (1) to identify outdated or otherwise dysfunctional personal myths that have been operating largely outside of their awareness; (2) to revise these guiding myths based on a balanced integration of deep intuitive sources and an informed cognitive analysis; and (3) to bring this renewed mythology to bear upon their daily lives. In addition, by coming to understand their own internal mythic processes, individuals become more adept at understanding the mythology of their culture and more able to participate skillfully in its evolution.

IV. Research on Personal Mythology

The psychological exemplar of modernity was Freudian psychoanalysis with its claim, "Where id was, there ego shall be". But this "modern" worldview ignores or undervalues what postmodernists consider to be the "other". Specifically, the "other" includes the unconscious, the feminine, racial and oppressed minorities, members of other cultures, and members of other species in the natural environment. In addition, postmodern writers attempt to close the gap between the investigator and the "other", just as they attempt to close other gaps endemic to modernity, e.g., the gap between subject and object, between mind and body, between observable reality and transcendental reality, and between the scientific observer and the phenomena being observed. In their research, postmodern scientists attempt to incorporate intuition and feeling into intellectual knowing, to understand how their attitudes and research procedures become an integral part of the study itself, and to consider the ways in which the identity of a person who serves as a research participant has been socially constructed (Krippner, 1988; Lather, 1990). Through Jung's dialogue with marginalized aspects of Western culture (e.g., the feminine, the occult, fantasy, myth) and his rejection of Western cultural hegemony, he anticipated some perspectives of postmodernism. That certain aspects of Jung's work foreshadowed postmodernism is one reason it is still reaching new audiences and being used in fresh, contemporary contexts.

Using the term "imagoes" (i.e., mythic images), Dan McAdams' (1985) research also falls into this category. He postulated that, beginning in late adolescence, "each of us constructs a self-defining narrative -- a life story that promises to...provide our lives with a sense of inner sameness and continuity" (p. 127). In one study, McAdams asked 20 men and 30 women to take the Thematic Apperception Test (TAT), and, by answering questions in a semi-structured interview, to tell their life stories. From 25 of these accounts, McAdams pieced together the imagoes that represented each person, finding that the most useful taxonomy was one grounded in the mythology of ancient Greece. Each of the major deities...personified a distinctive set of personality traits which were repeatedly manifested in the myths and legends in which his or her behavior can be observed.... We chose 12 major gods and goddesses as our models for imagoes. Taken together, the group

embodies most of the idealized and personified self-images which were observed in the initial 25 cases (p. 187).

Our model, whose origin was an attempt to integrate various psychoanalytic, cognitive, behavioral, and transpersonal trends in contemporary clinical practice, landed squarely within both Jungian and postmodern borders. In Jungian thought, polarity is the result of the differentiation required in the process of ego-development, i.e., the determination of what is "I" and what is "not I". However, the process of individuation requires a transcendence of polarity (Pruitt, 1992, pp. 51-52). In postmodern thought, many pairs of opposites and dualities can be deconstructed. The opposites are seen to interact and may even be interdependent (Levin, 1991). The dialectic which underlies the design of the personal rituals used in our approach leads to a creative synthesis or transcendence that can be appreciated from both the Jungian and the postmodern perspectives.

Jung's preoccupation with myth also has helped to inspire the refinement of personal mythology as a concept open to disciplined inquiry. Ralph Sperry (1981), for instance, worked with three male clients diagnosed as manifesting schizophreniform disorders. Using individual therapy described as "Jungian-existential", Sperry found that his clients' imagery took the form of such myths of renewal as sacral kingships, shamanic initiations, alchemical transformation, and the Greek stories of Dionysis and Orestes. The resulting mythic stories that emerged during psychotherapy appeared to indicate that the clients were reforming their basic mythological assumptions in developing a more productive and integrative existence.

Philip Mengel (1992) adapted McAdams' (1985) *Life Story Questionnaire* for individual interviews with 40 research participants who had engaged in either group shamanistic drumming circles or in the use (six times or more) of MDMA (3, 4-Methylenedioxymethamphetamine), a drug that supposedly enhances empathic experience and self-development. Mengel used a personal mythology framework to explain the catalytic role both groups of respondents claimed their activities had played in enhancing personal development.

Michael Pieracci (1990) asked 20 people who had spent time in psychotherapy to write narratives describing their experiences. These accounts yielded over 100 instances of themes that could be labelled "archetypal". Pieracci used the term "narrative myth" to refer to stories that explained one of these archetypes, finding the most typical narrative myths to focus on "the quest" or "journey", "wisdom", "acceptance", "nurturance", and "intimacy". For James Hillman (1972), the basic mythic psychotherapeutic theme is the story of Psyche and Eros, but only two of Pieracci's respondents mentioned this theme ("a soul in need of love", "a love in search of psychic understanding", p. 102). A more common theme in the psychotherapeutic narratives Pieracci analyzed was "the hero's journey", a metaphor of the psychotherapeutic process often portrayed in Jung's writings.

Pieracci used the term "ontic myth" to identify the basic beliefs that are contained in people's discourses about their reality, i.e., how one understands what is and should be in the world. For example, if someone believes, "Men are strong", this belief will impact the way he or she engages in life activities, as would another ontic myth, "Men must be strong". According to Pieracci, both are ontic myths because they reflect and express a belief about the world, even though neither expresses itself as a narrative as does, "Men must be strong because God made them that way". Pieracci thus constructed a "mythic matrix" so that personal and cultural myths would be the poles of one axis, while narrative and ontic myths would be the poles of the other axis.

Daryl Paulson (1992), conducting intensive interviews with ten Vietnam veterans, reported that reframing their combat experiences in terms of time-dependent personal myths helped them achieve a constructive integration of these events. Paulson also reported that for many veterans, the stage in which the mythic protagonist "returns to the community" never occurred. He commented that this unfulfilled phase of the hero's journey myth holds significant implications, if they are to overcome the traumatic psychological wounds of their experiences in Vietnam.

Bruce Carpenter and Stanley Krippner (1990) explored the dreams of a

Balinese artist who used them as a source of inspiration for his creative work, including his masks of Hindu deities and his woodcarvings of mythological creatures. Three of these dreams also assisted his resolution of personal conflicts, and the interplay of cultural and personal myths could be identified in this dream series. For instance, an encounter with his deceased father crossing a bamboo bridge in one of these dreams illustrated the Balinese emphasis on balance, but this cultural message was delivered in the personalized form of a revered family member. This study also supports Jung's (1959) admonition that dreams be studied as a series; many patterns and themes become evident when examining several dreams that could be missed if only a single dream were considered.

The utility of the personal mythology concept in stimulating original research, with its resulting provocative implications for psychotherapy, altered states of consciousness, and dream interpretation supports those writers who tout narrative psychotherapy as a cardinal example of postmodern therapy (O'Hara & Anderson, 1992). Narrative psychotherapy allows no "expert" to superimpose his or her mythology on a client. Instead, the therapist and client embark on a joint quest, one in which the therapist mindfully brings his or her training, experience, and mythology to each session, but uses these as points of departure for the encounter rather than a template into which each client's mythology must fit. By paving the way for a mythically informed psychotherapy, the ideas of Carl Gustav Jung have been remarkably resilient and flexible over the years, especially in the hands of therapists who see them as compasses for clients who are finding their way toward greater self-realization rather than as road maps by which each client must find his or her predetermined destination.

REFERENCES

Andrews, J. D. W. (1989). Integrating visions of reality: Interpersonal diagnosis and the existential vision. *American Psychologist, 44*, 803-817.

Bagarozzi, D. A., & Anderson, S. A. (1989). *Personal, marital, and family myths: Theoretical formulations and clinical strategies.* New York: Norton.

Campbell, J. (1972). *Myths to live by.* New York: Bantam.

Campbell, J. (1986). *The inner reaches of outer space: Metaphor as myth and as religion).* New York: Alfred van der Marck.

Campbell, J. (1988). *The power of myth.* New York: Doubleday.

Carpenter, B., & Krippner, S. (1990). The interplay of cultural and personal myths in the dreams of a Balinese artist. *The Humanistic Psychologist, 18*, 151-161.

Casey, E. S. (1990). Jung and the postmodern condition. In K. Barnaby & P. D'Acierno (Eds.), *C. G. Jung and the humanities* (pp. 319-324). Princeton: Princeton University Press.

Chomsky, N. (1965). *Aspects of the theory of syntax.* Cambridge, MA: MIT Press.

Clarke, J. J. (1993). Does Jung need rescuing? *Contemporary Psychology, 38,* 1231-1232.

Edgerton, R. B. (1992). *Sick societies.* New York: Free Press.

Feinstein, D. (1979). Personal mythology as a paradigm for a holistic public psychology. *American Journal of Orthopsychiatry, 49*, 198-217.

Feinstein, D. (1987). The shaman within: Cultivating a sacred personal mythology. In S. Nicholson (Ed.), *Shamanism: An expanded view of reality* (pp. 267-279). Wheaton, IL: Quest Books.

Feinstein, D. (1990a). Bringing a mythological perspective to clinical practice. *Psychotherapy, 27*, 388-396.

Feinstein, D. (1990b). Myth-making activity through the window of your dreams. In S. Krippner (Ed.), *Dreamtime and dreamwork* (pp. 21-33). Los Angeles: Tarcher.

Feinstein, D. (2007). Stories from your mythic depth. In S. Krippner, M. Bova, & L. Gray (Eds.), *Healing stories: The use of narrative in counseling and psychotherapy* (pp. 141-159). Charlottesville, VA: Puente Publications.

Feinstein, D., & Krippner, S. (1988a). Bringing a mythological perspective to social change. *ReVision, 11*(1), 23-34.

Feinstein, D., & Krippner, S. (1988b). *Personal mythology: The psychology of your evolving self.* Los Angeles: Tarcher.

Feinstein, D., & Krippner, S. (1989). Personal myths -- In the family way. In S. A. Anderson & D. A. Bagarozzi (Eds.), *Family myths: Psychotherapy implications* (pp. 111-139). New York: Haworth Press.

Feinstein, D., & Krippner, S. (1997). *The mythic path.* New York: Tarcher/Putnam.

Feinstein, D., Krippner, S., & Granger, D. (1988). Myth-making and human development. *Journal of Humanistic Psychology, 28*(3), 23-50.

Feinstein, D, & Mayo, P. E. (1990). *Rituals for living and dying.* San Francisco: HarperCollins.

Frank, J. D., & Frank, J. B. (1991). *Persuasion and healing* (3rd ed.). Baltimore: Johns Hopkins University Press.

Gardner, R. (1971). *Therapeutic communication with children: The mutual-storytelling technique.* New York: Science House.

Hall, J. G. (1982). Dream interpretation in analysis. In M. Stein (Ed.), *Jungian analysis* (pp. 123-156). LaSalle, IL: Open Court.

Hillman, J. (1972). *The myth of analysis: Three essays in archetypal psychology.* New York: Harper & Row.

Hillman, J. (1975). *Re-visioning psychology.* New York: Harper & Row.

Hobson, J. A. (1988). *The dreaming brain.* New York: Basic Books.

Jung, C. G. (1958). *The undiscovered self.* Boston: Little, Brown.

Jung, C. G. (1959). *The archetypes and the collective unconscious.* New York: Pantheon Books.

Jung, C. G. (1961). *Memories, dreams, reflections.* New York: Random House.

Jung, C. G. (1969). Psychoanalysis and the cure of souls. In *Collected works*, Vol. 1. Princeton: Princeton University Press. (Original work published 1928)

Jung, C. G. (1971). Psychological types. In *Collected works*, Vol. 6. Princeton: Princeton University Press. (Original work published 1921)

Jung, C. G. (1972). The stages of life. In *Collected works*, Vol. 8. Princeton: Princeton University Press. (Original work published 1932)

Jung, C. G. (1973). *Letters.* Princeton: Princeton University Press.

Kegan, R. (1982). *The evolving self: Problem and process inhuman development.* Cambridge, MA: Harvard University Press.

Krippner, S. (1986). Dreams and the development of a personal mythology. *Journal of Mind and Behavior, 7*, 449-461.

Krippner, S. (1988). Parapsychology and postmodern science. In D. R. Griffin (Ed.), *The reenchantment of science: Postmodern proposals* (pp. 129-140). Albany: State University of New York Press.

Krippner, S. (1990). Native healing. In J. K. Zeig & W. M. Munion (Eds.), *What is psychotherapy?* (pp. 179-185). San Francisco: Jossey-Bass.

Larsen, S. (1990). *The mythic imagination.* New York: Bantam.

Lather, P. (1990). Postmodernism and the human sciences. *The Humanistic Psychologist, 18*, 64-84.

Laughlin, Jr., C. D., McManus, J., & d'Aquili, E.G. (1990). *Brain, symbol and experience: Toward a neurophenomenology of human consciousness.* Boston: Shambhala.

Lauter, E., & Rupprecht, C. S. (1985). Introduction. In E. Lauter & C. S. Rupprecht (Eds.), *Feminist archetypal theory: Interdisciplinary re-visions of Jungian thought* (pp. 3-22). Knoxville: University of Tennessee Press.

Levi-Strauss, C. (1966). *The savage mind.* Chicago: University of Chicago Press.

Levin, D. M. (1991). Psychology as a discursive formation: The postmodern crisis. *The Humanistic Psychologist, 19,* 250-276.

Lyddon, W. J., & McLaughlin, J. T. (1992). Constructivist psychology: A heuristic framework. *Journal of Mind and Behavior, 13,* 89-108.

Maduro, R. J., & Wheelwright, J. B. (1977). Analytical psychology. In R. J. Corsini (Ed.), *Current personality theories* (pp. 83-123). Itasca, IL: Peacock.

Mahler, M. S., Pine, F., & Berger, A. (1975). *The psychological birth of the human infant.* New York: Basic Books.

Mahoney, M. J. (1991). *Human change processes.* New York: Basic Books.

May, R. (1991). *The cry for myth.* New York: Norton.

McAdams, D. P. (1985). *Power, intimacy, and the life story: Personological inquiries into identity.* Homewood, IL: Dorsey.

McAdams, D. P. (1993). *Stories we live by.* New York: Morrow.

Mengel, P. K. (1992). A retrospective study of alterations in consciousness during shamanistic journeying and MDMA use. Unpublished doctoral dissertation, Saybrook Institute, San Francisco.

O'Hara, M., & Anderson, W. T. (1992, November/September). Welcome to the postmodern world. *Networker,* 19-25.

Pasqual-Leone, J. (1987). Organismic processes for new-Piagetian theories: A dialectical causal account of cognitive development. *International Journal of Psychology, 22,* 531-570.

Paulson, D. S. (1992). *Participation in the Vietnam conflict seen as a male rite of passage.* Unpublished doctoral dissertation, Saybrook Institute, San Francisco.

Perry, J. W. (1976). *Roots of renewal in myth and madness: The meaning of psychotic episodes.* San Francisco: Jossey-Bass.

Piaget, J. (1971). *Biology and knowledge: An essay on the relation between organic regulations and cognitive process.* Chicago: University of Chicago Press.

Pieracci, M. (1990). The mythopoesis of psychotherapy. *The Humanistic Psychologist, 18,* 208-224.

Prilleltensky, I. (1989). Psychology and the status quo. *American Psychologist, 44,* 795-802.

Pruitt, B. (1992). *A theoretical study of projection and the perspectival nature of truth.* Unpublished master's thesis, Saybrook Institute, San Francisco, CA.

Rhue, J. W., & Lynn, S. J. (1991). Storytelling, hypnosis and the treatment of sexually abused children. *International Journal of Clinical and Experimental Hypnosis, 39,* 198-214.

Rupprecht, C. S. (1985). The common language of women's dreams: Colloquy of mind and body. In E. Lauter & C. S. Rupprecht (Eds.), *Feminist archetypal theory: Interdisciplinary re-visions of Jungian thought* (pp. 187-219). Knoxville: University of Tennessee Press.

Sarbin, T. R. (1986). The narrative as a root metaphor for psychology. In T. R. Sarbin (Ed.), *Narrative psychology: The storied nature of human conduct* (pp. 3-21). New York: Praeger.

Schafer, R. (1992). *Retelling a life: Narration and dialogue in psychoanalysis.* New York: Basic Books.

Schorer, M. (1960). The necessity of myth. In H. A. Murray, (Ed.), *Myth and mythmaking* (pp. 354-358). New York: George Braziller.

Singer, J. (1972). *Boundaries of the soul: The practice of Jung's psychology.* Garden City, NY: Doubleday.

Singer, J. (1988) Foreword, D. Feinstein & S. Krippner, *Personal mythology* (pp. xi-xiv). Los Angeles: Tarcher.

Singer, J. (1990). A Jungian approach to dreamwork. In S. Krippner (Ed.), *Dreamtime and dreamwork.* Los Angeles: Tarcher.

Sperry, R. B., Jr. (1981). *Myth and psychological integration inschizophreniform disorders.* Unpublished doctoral dissertation, Saybrook Institute, San Francisco.

Stevens, A. (1982). *Archetypes.* New York: William Morrow.

Staude, J.-R. (1981). *The adult development of C. G. Jung.* London: Routledge & Kegan Paul.

Stevens-Guille, M. E., & Boersma, F. J. (1992). Fairy tales as a trance experience: Possible therapeutic uses. *American Journal of Clinical Hypnosis, 34,* 245-254.

Wheelwright, P. (1942). Poetry, myth, and reality. In A. Tate (Ed.), *The language of poetry.* Princeton, NJ: Princeton University Press.

CHANGE

Change
And time's passing.
How often we are fooled
Thinking a fence will last forever.
Yet frost and thaw
Do their silent work unnoticed
Until one day
The posts are heaved up
Suddenly
Then lie motionless on the ground.

Again we look across the open land,
Look to the sea,
Wondering what tomorrow will bring
Along a path
That not long ago
Seemed familiar.

-- Michael Sheffield

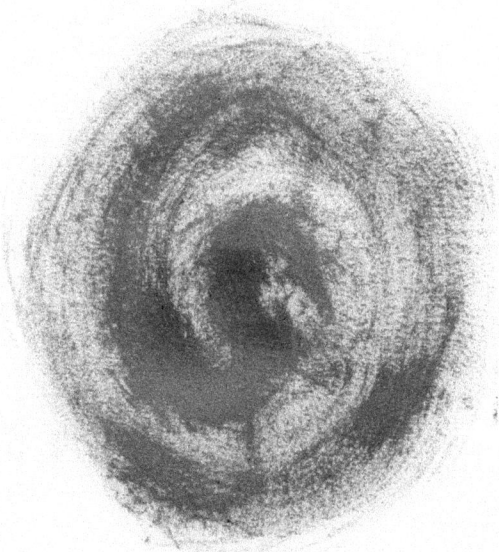

Art by Mariana Castro de Ali

Northern Light Ancestors

Jürgen Werner Kremer

Wunsch, Indianer zu werden
Wenn man doch ein Indianer wäre,
gleich bereit, und auf dem rennenden
Pferde, schief in der Luft, immer wieder
kurz erzitterte über dem zitternden Bo-
den, bis man die Sporen ließ, denn es
gab keine Sporen, bis man die Zügel
wegwarf, denn es gab keine Zügel, und
kaum das Land vor sich als glatt gemäh-
te Heide sah, schon ohne Pferdehals und
Pferdekopf.

Wish to become an Indian
If one were only an Indian, ready at
moment's notice, and on a running
horse, leaning into the air, always once
again trembling briefly above the trembling ground, until letting go of the
spurs, because there are no spurs, until
throwing away the reins, because there
are no reins, and barely seeing the land
in front as smoothly mowed heath, now
without horseneck and horsehead.

Franz Kafka

Islandia
... Fría rosa, isla secreta
que fuiste la memoria de Germania
y salvaste para nosotros
su apagada, enterrada mitología ...

Iceland
... Icy rose, secret island,
you were Germania's memory;
you saved for us
her snuffed-out, buried myths ...

Jorge Luis Borges

Jürgen Werner Kremer is the editor of
ReVision, where he has published recent
articles about the trickster and fundamental issues in the conception of transpersonal psychology, mythic storytelling,
ethnoautobiography, and radical presence.
He is a faculty member at the Santa Rosa
Junior College. He presently is involved
with the preparations for the 26th International Conference on the Study of Shamanism and Alternative Modes of Healing, which convenes annually on Labor
Day outside of San Francisco.

In our nocturnal imaginal theatre, as
we remember it in our reconstructions,
the game of chance and synchronicities
of conscious and unconscious events,
the structures and patterns of our psy-
ches carrying our personal narratives,
and the ancestral, social, and historical
forces, among other factors, open the
opportunity to create our lives as meaningfully embodied visions in place, as
creations responsive and responsible to
not just what meets the eye – surround-
ings, community, weather, etc. – but
what is so easily concealed and forgotten amidst the onslaught of daily trivia
devoid of creative imagination: traumas, personal and collective shadow
material, history, ancestry. The integrative state of consciousness of dreaming, connecting our emotional and rational brain parts in its labor of re-

remedies in the rub between personal
dreaming, ancestral stories of place and
migrations, and a shamanic practice
committed to resolving personal and
collective shadow issues and traumas
into creative and imaginative presences
that heal. Such work addresses historical violations not for the sake of re-
venge but the healing of a restorative
justice for the future. This means bridging our dreams and ancestral stories
into the history of place. For its success
such a practice can never be merely
individualistic, but it needs to welcome, invite, and strive for communal
dialogue and conversation (a dialogue
between multiple communities in one
place). Thus traditions may be renewed
and grounded in deep dreaming with
ancestors and memory of place. Such
shamanic practice supersedes scien-

> Our present collective pathologies may find healing
> remedies in the rub between personal dreaming, ancestral
> stories of place and migrations, and a shamanic practice
> committed to resolving personal and collective traumas
> into creative and imaginative presences that heal.

membering, together with the riches of
traditions and ceremonial or ritual
practices facilitating bridging, affords
opportunities for a re-in-spiriting of
indigenous understandings of humans
living in a particular place. Such re-
inspirations honor traditions in all their
complexity, those of local provenance
and those that have migrated into a
place and those that have blended
peacefully or violently, by confronting
not just needs for personal healing, but
collective shadow material, thus re-
newing traditions in wild (as in: connected to wilderness or nature), creative inspirations and imaginings that
re-member and en-vision for the future
using our "natural reason" (which
Vizenor [2003, p. 36] defines as "an
active sense of presence, the tease of
the natural world in native stories").

Our present collective pathologies –
as manifest in individuals, communities, and ecologies – may find healing

tisms and religious or spiritual funda-
mentalisms by bringing the indigenous
science contained in each tradition into
a life that honors the spirit of inquiry
for the sake of human freedom and
creativity.

This article discusses the personal
embodiment of this abstract philosophical summary. It is designed to
overcome the lethal romance expressed
in the initial Kafka quote and to build
on the ancestral memories Borges refers to. The formulation of this philosophy was guided by indigenous and
non-indigenous teachers, colleagues,
and friends. Dreams are guiding much
of my personal embodiment (Part I).
The specifics of my ancestral culture
define the place of origin of my shamanic practice (Part II), which has
been translated into underlying principles of shamanic healing through decolonization (Part III).

Dreaming with the ancestor

The ephemeral veils of green, red, and blue in the night sky, the northern lights, hold traces of the ancestors in the understanding of the northern Indo-European peoples. Freyja (who will be discussed below) is the primary shaman spirit of old and as such she is part of these magical presences that induce memory and dream. The old ones saw dreams, like birds, as messages from the deities, spirits, and ancestors imparting important knowledge (see, e.g., Grimm, 1966). In the dreams recounted below I am Muninn, the raven of memory, so often a helpful guide in the holarctic realms.

So Muninn remembers.[1]

He remembers a seminal dream.

He is in Hamburg, the Northern German town where he was born. Here he grew up. He is sitting on the threshold in the doorway of an old brick house, one in a row of houses that are considerably older than the First World War. Beside him is a woman. She shares his vista. He overlooks the river Elbe from on high. His threshold perch is atop the ancient ice age rim of the river, once the border of a flow miles wide. Tens of thousands of years ago reindeer herds roamed the tundra of these latitudes. The southernmost border of the thick ice sheet covering much of northern Europe was encroaching then, bringing along boulders and rocks from the north. The reindeer now live much farther north and the river moves in a much narrower bed. It still spreads to considerable widths three hundred or so feet below. Ferries crisscross its course and ocean liners enter and leave the harbor.

Sitting atop this ancient riverbed he is very close to where he went to kindergarten shortly after the Second World War. The heavy wooden doors are high, painted an almost black, dark green, Hooker's green. Inside, a large playroom is warmed by a comforting, white tile stove; its enormous size reaches toward the ceiling. It is the center of this space accommodating a small crowd of children. The room is lambent with light reflected from the wide river. It enters through large windows that allow for a grand vista. Behind the house is a garden with plants and trees inviting a child's playful imaginations. From here the river can
be admired as it stretches below in all its grandeur.

He notices an archaeological excavation in progress behind his old kindergarten. The area is cordoned off with yellow plastic strips, glittering as they twist in the wind. Signs are put up all around: No trespassing! Stay out! *Not to be deterred, his dream allows him to leave the body, his dreambody, at the moment of seeing these signs. There is no pause, no struggle with the prohibitions right in front of him. Assuming a form that permits him to proceed is the natural and immediate dream solution. Invisible now, he enters the forbidden grounds.*

He hovers over the ancient ruins that are clearly visible thanks to the work of the archaeological team. To the right a round, tower-like structure emerges from the underground depths. It appears to extend a good ways into the earth. He recognizes it as an ancestral ceremonial structure. Similar ones are right next to it. The name of the place where this dig into ancient cultural history occurs is Altona, *meaning "all-too-near."*

One legend has it that an orphan was blindfolded when the burghers of Hamburg wanted to expand their overpopulated city. The idea was to place the new town where the orphan would trip and meet the ground. But what happened was unexpected. The boy had barely left the medieval city gates, when he stumbled and fell. The attendant burghers exclaimed in surprise that this was all too near, in the local vernacular: *"All to nah!"* -- thence the name for this part of the city -- *Altona.* This is the story Muninn learned in school.

The place where the dream helps him gain access to the layers below the contemporary city is all too close. Right there with his childhood. Fenced in by signs forbidding entry.

Muninn remembers this dream with the vibrant luminosity common to dreams drawing attention to their meaning. It needs no interpretation. It is all spelled out for him at the end. Lest he deny what he has been shown. He is compelled to pay heed and to take the dream as injunction to trespass across the lines that separate him not just from childhood memories, but also the root memories of his ancestral cultures. He struggles to remember. A dear colleague had reached into these regions during a recent medicine journey,
overcoming his shame stemming from the history of the Third Reich and its abuses of ancestral stories. The memory of their conversation about the recovery of Indigenous roots or Indigenous mind is vivid and now powerfully charged with dreaming. He is ready to trespass.[2]

Not much later he retreats into the desert to fast for raven, the bird that has haunted him since childhood and the bird he feels can help him overcome the shame of Nazi abuse of Germanic mythologies. After asking permission to fast for raven he finds a place in a gorge under a juniper tree to spend four days and nights alone. Right at the beginning of the fast he dreams. *He is in surgery. The surgeons are cutting out the lower parts of his internal organs. They began with the small intestines, now they are on to the large intestines. They also remove his stomach, the spleen, and the gall bladder, then, lastly, his liver. He watches as he is undergoing this surgical procedure. With curiosity, not concern or fear. He now notices that even the lower lobes of both his lungs have just been taken out. He observes the operation with a bird's eye view, but he also feels the increasing emptiness in his body cavity. Then the surgeons perform what seem to be the required cleansing and purification procedures on all his inner organs. They put them in different containers and rinse them with different chemical solutions. All goes well. Even the work on his tiny lung bubbles is successful. He watches in wonderment how skillfully and impeccably the surgeons deal with such complicated organs. Now they put all his body parts back in their proper places and sew him up. He feels good and gets up immediately. Only the lingering effects of the anesthetic make him feel a little unsteady. He staggers slightly for a few moments. Then he walks away without any problem, feeling vigorous and alert.*

At the end of his fast he sits under the Juniper Woman and re-reads the notes of his initial dream. Once again ravens course overhead. *He is in surgery. Ravensurgery. The surgeons are cutting out the lower parts of his internal organs. They begin with the small intestines, then on to the large intestines. They also remove his stomach, the spleen, and the gall bladder, then, lastly, his liver. Raven pecking deeper and deeper. Reaching into his most* essential parts, his soft spots, scraping the flesh on the bone. *He watches as he is undergoing this surgical procedure. With curiosity, not concern or fear.* He trusts the work of the ravensurgeons. He is present to the work of remembering and purification. Aware. *He now notices that even the lower lobes of both his lungs have just been taken out.* Right there. Aware. One of his most vital of organs needs to be cleansed. His breath. The inhalation and exhalation of awareness. His mindful merging with everything around. Needs to be purified. Standstill and pause. Breath coming and going. *He observes the operation from a bird's eye view, but he also feels the increasing emptiness in his body cavity. Then the surgeons perform what seems to be the required cleansing and purification procedures on all his inner organs. They put them in different containers and rinse them with different chemical solutions. All goes well. Even the work on his tiny lung bubbles is successful. He watches in wonderment how skillfully and impeccably the surgeons deal with such complicated organ.* Indeed, this is a sensitive operation. Fraught with pitfalls. Glib explanations that short-circuit. This is cleansing for compassionate ruthlessness. *Now they put all his body parts back in their proper places and sew him up. He feels good and gets up immediately. Only the lingering effects of the anesthetic make him feel a little unsteady. He staggers slightly for a few moments. Then he walks away without any problem feeling vigorous and alert.* Renewal.

Consciousness and intent (symbolized by the raven Huginn in Old Norse) become creative when the memories (symbolized by the raven Muninn) make self true to itSelf. Ravens spread wings, soar, wheel, backflip, stories fly. Huginn directs attention to the memories. Huginn could not soar without Muninn. Muninn would remember in useless turnings without Huginn's intent. The gorge where he fasts is littered with small black rocks, black tourmaline, Raven's rock – hard, dark, harder than most rock, forged by primal forces. Tourmaline holds memory and consciousness from way over

there, where it all started, rock knowing.[3]

Muninn remembers the words of a Diné (Navajo) medicine man: *If you want to understand transformation and healing, then you need to trace yourself backward, through history and stories, through the creation story, to the point of origin. Place yourself there. And then unfold yourself for renewal, for healing. Use the original instructions that come through that place, the visions of old. This is the normal way of creating balance.*[4] In his ancestral traditions this point of origin is called Ginnungagap, the place of arising, a story he will recount in greater detail below.[5] Here we find the elemental

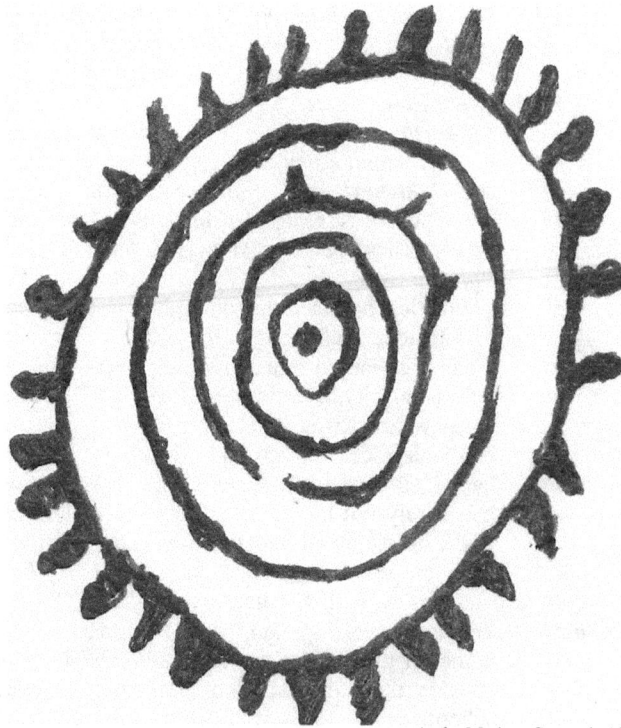

Art by Mariana Castro de Ali

beginnings, the different worlds setting out to work. Then, later, the androgyne, the giants, and the trees found on the beach which became the first humans. This is the fragmented creation story of his people recounting how things came to be. Muninn had placed himself in the gap for his fast, in the gorge, at the root of the tree. He had sought that place of renewal. And what he remembered was Raven. He realizes that, truly, he had not been fasting for Raven -- he had been fasting to *acknowledge* what had been a presence in his life, for a long time. He was slow to catch up. Raven had been his *fylgja*, his familiar and companion. Finally he remembered Raven as who he was, his

relationship to Raven, just as he is getting ready to break his fast. Raven had remembered and accompanied him for ever so long. This was obvious once the veil had been torn. It was his failure of remembrance. He had not reached into the well, had not been taught how to lift its life sustaining riches, its *auður*.[6] Now that he has remembered Raven, he sees that Raven had always remembered him. He sees the story behind the veil. Raven remembers. Muninn. Wings of memory carrying vision.

One night he dreams. *He is standing on the balcony of the apartment where he spent his early childhood. Overlooking the river, the beach. Affording a long vista. The place where his mind would take flight to escape trauma across the vast valley that resulted from an ice age maelstream. The balcony is high up. Now it extends out toward the beach, making the view more wondrous. Still on the balcony, he finds himself above the tan sand strip bordering the river Elbe. Just below he notices several people sleeping on the beach. What looks like a homeless person emerges from the empty lot, created by the Allied bombings during World War Two, next to the house. As he comes closer on the wooden planks Muninn recognizes him as Australian Aborigine. He pushes the shopping cart with his belongings toward the sleepers and glows twice from the inside as he shifts his awareness and his presence crosses worlds. He is an Elder healer. The sleepers begin to wake and talk to each other. They are healers also. Among them are some younger people. Muninn notices that his dream position has shifted: instead of standing atop the balcony he now is perched on the roof of a yurt. Much lower and closer to the people moving about. He observes. The Elder Aborigine begins to perform an initiation ceremony. It is an induction into the next levels of healing, the test and affirmation of capacities acquired. Several other adults are helping the Elder. Several young men awaken, stretch and yawn. They are the ones to be initiated. Two of them run away, try to escape the challenge before them. A couple of adults chase them and immediately return them into the circle. The adult healers are restrained in their reactions, yet visibly agitated. They disapprove of the initiates not taking responsibility for their healing gifts. Muninn looks on from the top of the yurt in fear of discovery. He knows the Elder will pull him down into the ceremony the minute he is discovered.*

While working with this dream Muninn remembers the healing experience he has had in a monastery in Spain, this dream relates to the commitment of what began to unfold that night.

He is in Central Spain to attend a conference together with his wife. It is early in his professional career. Conferences and training workshops play a significant part in their lives. He has driven with few rest stops from Germany to Zaragossa. His nerves are jittery. He only slept in the back of the station wagon for brief periods. Lying wide awake in the bed of a medieval monastery he is jangled into a state of wakefulness he so often experiences after long drives on the autobahn. Thoughts rush through him with the intensity of roller coasters cars. He gets bored with the ceaseless succession of images, reflections, and fragmented remainders of the day. He anticipates tomorrow's events, when he will attend a conference on humanistic and transpersonal psychology. Next to him his partner tosses and turns in fits of discomfort and pain. Her period had started earlier that day. In her sleep she is visibly suffering from menstrual cramps. The tedium of his high-strung mental state prompts him to seek relief in a game of relaxation and imagery. He uses a technique taught to him by a friend during one rainy Christmas in a damp cottage out on the Irish West Coast of Connemara. He prepares for an out-of-body journey. Focusing on relaxing himself he gradually visualizes leaving various parts of his physical self behind. Eventually he ascends through the image of a golden ring he sees hovering above his head. Freed from the usual limitations of embodiment he allows fancy to guide him.

Beside him his partner is still cramping. He decides to use the altered state he has entered to develop images that might help her out. The skeptical part of his mind surrenders under the com-

forting labels of '*play*,' '*as if*,' and '*fantasy*.'

Thus he leaves the vaulted monk's cell. His bodiless being is now sitting atop the roof of a Spanish farmhouse. He can sense the tiles, still warm from the heat of the day, as he ponders how to help his partner. Then a shift occurs: He knows what he needs to do -- with certainty and precision. He has plugged into a program, a stream of

Art by Mariana Castro de Ali

information, a blueprint. The clarity of guidance is a self-evident force not even experienced as clarity. Maybe it is a remembering. He does not see anybody. No lights flitting about. There are no figures in his visual field. Nobody. It is in him. Or maybe on his shoulders. Or behind him. He knows what to do in order to relieve his partner's pain. His mood is experimental, not connected to his analytic mind. The fatigue accumulated during endless hours of driving facilitates this framework. Reflections and second thoughts do not enter. He just follows whatever it is that is leading his disembodied actions.

He moves out to a series of waterfalls cascading down over gentle rock terraces on a nearby slope. He follows the flow of the stream and then glides down to the small human-made lake. On its shore he finds an ancient helmet. It is fashioned Greek or Roman style. A bronze ridge covers the nose. The metal comes down to the cheek on either side of the head. He picks it up and returns to the monastery up above,

swiftly and elegantly sailing in a pleasurable curve through the air. Back in the room he situates himself below his partner's feet. The helmet rests upside down between his legs for use as a vessel. His hands slowly pass over her belly, moving down toward him. They drag along a greenish foul goo from her uterus which then exits through her vagina. He directs the viscous liquid into the helmet. With each pass more

toxins are extracted. When he is finished he transports the vessel, filled with the repulsive substance, down to the lake. There is no question as to what to do with it. He buries the liquid together with the helmet. That done he soars back up and enters the thick-walled cell. He then follows the steps for re-entry taught to him by his Irish friend.

Once he has made himself fully present in his body, he hears his partner give a deep sigh. The sound of relief. With it comes a word: *Dankeschön!* She is American and her German is very limited, far from being her everyday language. They speak English with each other at home. Without waking she moves her body into a comfortable position and falls into relaxed, deep sleep. Next morning she wakes up feeling refreshed, free of cramps. She has no awareness of any of the nocturnal imaginings he engaged in.

The dream of the initiation ceremony, intersecting his childhood years in the place 'all-too-near' with his current process of initiation, the remembrance of his Spanish healing adventure, deepen his commitment to the work of remembrance, healing, and decolonization.

Shortly thereafter, another dream. Bear approaches him. *It is winter. Muninn is camping out in the wilderness. The low mountains are covered in snow. In the distance he sees an emaciated bear cross the unused railroad tracks near where his tent is. The bear changes direction and lumbers toward him, straining as it takes each step. As it approaches it gradually turns into a younger bear. The brown fur then changes to show the markings of a young boar: bright, luminescent stripes run the length of its body. The bear cub continues to move closer. Then it col-*

its sacrifice, each body part changing into the world we now know. The bear is trying to make itself new, puts on special markings, the body painting of renewal. But it has not been provided with proper nurturance, it collapses right in front of him. The sacred bear hunt, a ceremony of many circumpolar peoples, is the story of sacrifice and renewal. Death for life. Maybe this ritual needs to be made new, strengthened.

Not much later Muninn is on his way to the Southwest to seek quiet time and renewal. In this dream *he is in his old office where he worked as academic administrator. A woman is standing in front of him, back to the wall. She is not paying any attention to what is behind her. What he sees glanc-*

meeting with a group of students who are primarily of European ancestries. Their work focuses on the development of a ceremony. He watches with dismay the mental gymnastics and distancing maneuvers they go through. They just don't get it right! He cannot see how all this dilly-dallying will result in ceremonial presence. So he gets up in a huff and proceeds to leave the gathering. A Jewish student, a woman, follows him. They enter the neighboring auditorium, which is alive with people and ongoing religious ceremony. He realizes he has happened into the middle of a seder ceremony. The contrast to what had been going on during the student gathering just before is stunning: Here everything is vibrant. No distancing. Grief is palpable. The memories of bondage, persecution, and suffering permeate the room. Candles are burning all around. Children are putting down memorial tiles they have fashioned. He is deeply affected by the proceedings as he walks through to exit at the other end of the auditorium. Tears well up in him. When Muninn shares this dream with his partner next morning, she points out that this is the day of Passover. Muninn is not Jewish, Muninn has never paid attention to the Jewish calendar. In the remote regions where they are traveling there was no sign of an upcoming Jewish holiday.

Not much later Muninn participates in a Diné (Navajo) crystal gazing ceremony and is told that he has Jewish ancestry. Since then he has discovered ancestral names and places that, by all appearances, are almost certainly Jewish.

So often ancestry is not a simple matter and Muninn's isn't either – German, possibly Jewish, and a family photo suggestive of Sámi connections is what he may be carrying. Out of these the German ancestry, with the shameful woundings it carries, is central to his shamanic work of recovery and healing, the trespassing into the historically forbidden beyond the boundaries of shame, beyond the constructions of whiteness he grew up with, trespassing into the ceremonial dream depths of renewal and healing. These dreams culled from others were part of a pattern of deepening shamanic work.

The dream of the initiation ceremony, intersecting his childhood years in the place 'all-too-near' with his current process of initiation, the remembrance of his Spanish healing adventure, deepen his commitment to the work of remembrance, healing, and decolonization.

lapses and dies.

Bears normally are not out and about in winter. It is their time to hibernate in a den. Something important, maybe some terrible hunger must have brought the bear out of its winter slumber. Maybe it was a physical hunger, he thinks, but maybe it was a different need altogether. *Hibernation, renewal, sustained dreaming,* the words are floating through his waking mind. *Maybe it was a bearmother and she was so very thin because of feeding the young ones in her den. Maybe she had twin cubs.* The bear transformed to look like a boar piglet. He goes to the dictionary and looks up the etymology of the German word for it, *Frischling.* They are the fresh ones, the newly born, but they are also the ones given away as offering, sacrifice. Probably mostly to the female spirit of the north, shaman woman Freyja, she who rides the boar with golden bristles. He begins to think of the dream as renewal, the return of the bear. The bear gives birth out of itself, just as the primal giant Ymir in the Old Norse creation story gives birth to the world through

ing past her is a shrine. Three figures stand in a simple box that opens to the front. They are the three norns. One dressed in black, the next wearing blue, and the third green. Their garments flow shawl-like from head to toe. Muninn cannot believe that the woman is not paying attention to the three figures behind her -- she is quite obviously oblivious to their presence, wrapped up in her own world. She is consumed by the universe of academic administrivia, yet, the radiance of the nornar holds the promise of support.

This anima dream teaches Muninn about the fatefulness of his ancestry, the riches the three nornir hold, and puts him in touch with a central cultural image to be explored below: The three nornir lift the riches of memory from the well. He later carves them in birch he brought from Iceland for his medicine bundle. The imbalance of the masculine and feminine, the distraction of his anima by the bureaucratic and rationalistic mind needs care in this healing process.

One night, during this travel in the Southwest, Muninn dreams. *He is*

Honoring tradition –
renewing tradition

The dreams just recounted are among the ones that have compelled me to investigate the indigenous roots of my ancestral traditions. I have published detailed accounts of some of this scholarly work in other places (Kremer 2000, 2002, 2004a, 2004b, 2008). Rather than summarizing this material in a scholarly fashion I want to present an edited version of a teaching story I developed as part of this work (Bjarnadottir & Kremer, 2000). It explores the place identified by the Diné medicine man, the place of creation and regeneration, the place of healing. In the form of a painted cloth this place is usually present at ceremonies I facilitate (see sample illustration in this article). This story presents what I have recovered through scholarly inquiries as well as ceremonial and shamanic inquiries and what I regard as one version of my ancestral indigenous worldview. (Just as different closely related indigenous peoples hold the same tradition in a slightly different manner, I see it as one telling that attempts to be true to the spirit of its tradition.) This story guides my personal shamanic work and holds me when I work cross-culturally. It represents a renewal of tradition, inspires my work, and gets continually renewed through ceremony, resulting in deepening and widening understanding.

Traditions have always changed, both from the inside (be it through dreams or ritualized experiences) as well as the outside (conquest, tribes merging, borrowing, etc.). In final analysis, tradition is always multiple in origin; it should never be used in the singular and with a capital T. Tradition is a singular as Tradition only in those transient moments when inspirited in its ceremonial life and when the manifestations of traditions connect with the forces of Tradition in wisdom and integrity. The word tradition is truly a conundrum or paradox: in order to be alive it needs the changeful visions of renewal and to be tradition it needs to be true to itself. Honoring tradition requires that we honor the diversity and multiplicity within each tradition (which is different from the license of fantasy unbounded by the knowledge and insight of traditions providing release and burden). The indigenous context of my ancestors is not mine and decolonization into an indigenous process of presence means the renewal of tradition fueled by shadow work confronting the history of Whiteness and colonialism. (What I mean by "indigenous process of presence," radical presence (Kremer, 2002) will be explained in the next section.)

The following describes the place from which you, the reader, can unfold yourself for the sake of healing and renewal. It speaks specifically to those of Indo-European Nordic ancestry. Of course, those of other ancestries are invited to engage with it also following their protocol of cross-cultural honoring. It is a story not told before in this

Art by Mariana Castro de Ali

form. It is a place of healing. The story is told in the voice of a seeress, a *völva*. (All Old Norse terms are explained immediately before or after their first use or in a footnote.)

You ask about healing in the way of your ancestors.[7]

This is the right time and a good place to ask - Venus, the shaman star, the star of the being so important for any healing, is visible and just now high up in the sky. Freyja is the name of this being. And where we are standing here at this tree - it is the center of this community, it is the place which connects us with everything that matters.

There is so much to be said about the time, the star, and this place at the tree. Some of it I will tell today, but other things will have to wait for a later night. So, let me start at the beginning, the place of origins, because there is no healing without going to that place.

One of the völvur,[8] *the seeresses before me, has said: 'In the beginning of time there was nothing: Neither sand nor sea, nor cooling surf; there was no earth, nor upper heaven, no blade of grass - only the Great Void.'*[9] *This void was fertile, it was filled with magical power, the* auður *whence everything arises. This is the place of creation, and without placing ourselves at the source of all there will be no healing. If we seek balance when imbalance threatens us, then we need to start over from the place of balance between the ice of the north and the fire of the south. These are the poles of Ginnungagap, the fertile void, the gap of gaps, out of which our world and we ourselves arose. Where heat and cold meet, the deadly hoarfrost from the rivers of the north is melted by the heat of Muspell, the world of fire. All this would mean nothing, if the richness of* auður *wasn't* örlög, *fated. Without the primal law, without timekeepers, without moonwatchers, without sunwatchers - the world would be nothing, it would be without destinies, örloglaus.*

And then it all starts when the three giant maidens come along. But these women have all kinds of names, and show up in different guises, at times there are even three times three. Sometimes even twelve. Or they number the thirteen months of the moon calendar. When some see them they call them dísir, *protective spirits, others call them* nornir, *fateful spirits, but they also show themselves as* valkyrjur, *bird spirits. Whichever way the maidens are seen, where they are is the power to impart* örlög, *to awaken a being to move in time. They are the measurers of time and their weaving material are moon beams and sun beams. They alone are not subject to it. Whether they awaken giants, or* Vanir *spirits, or* Æsir[10] *spirits, or humans - all these different beings are all subject to the cycles of* örlög *created from the fertile richness of* Ginnungagap.

There is time then, measurement, fate. Out of it emerges a primal force, a

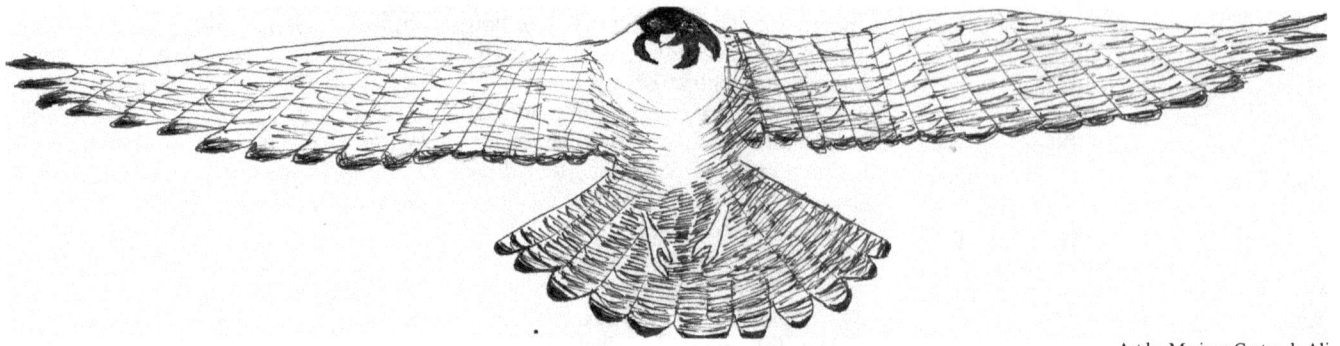

Art by Mariana Castro de Ali

giant by the name of Ymir, a two gendered being, many generations before Freyja and Freyr,[11] the earth beings Njörðr and Nerþuz,[12] and the thunderer Þór[13] dressing as Freyja. Ymir was formed out of the drops at the confluence of the forces streaming out of Niflheimr, the world of ice, and the world of fire, Muspellsheims. He was nurtured by that primal richness in the form of Auðhumla, the nourishing cow of auðr, who is urðr and örlög, the fateful riches of memory. She is the hornless mother of all creation, the matrix which makes life possible. Be patient now, why she is hornless I shall tell you later. At this moment in creation we have nothing but the nourishing matrix of auðr, the riches and the fateful matrix, the örlög, in it administered by the nornir, the fates, and the giants as primal forces.

Not only does the cow Auðhumla nurture the giant Ymir, she also licks Búri, Born, Creator, Father, out of the salty stones over three days. His son Burr - we have forgotten whether he mated with a giant or created out of himself like Ymir - creates with Bestla, the daughter of the giant Bölthorn, the first divine spirits or gods. Some say their names were Óðinn, Vili, will, and Vé, sanctuary, some say Óðinn, Hænir, and Lóður[14] were the first divine spirits. One of them became more and more important, and in recent times many people think first of him when they think of our traditions: The auðr of the primal richness sounds very close in name to Auðun, and we have Óðinn who also shows himself in the form of Óðr, who Freyja cries for - but I am rushing ahead. Yes, yes, as time passed the maleness of creation was the only thing people would see, now a well-known story, but many would say a rather sad story. The first three divine spirits were subject to the örlög, just like everything else, except for the female measurers of time, the nornir.

It was the destiny of the first three divine spirits to create earth, and later human beings, from the primal force which the cow Auðhumla had nurtured in the giant Ymir. They killed - or sacrificed - the two gendered giant and thus formed the earth - the mountains from the bones, the sky from the skull, the seas and lakes from the blood, the trees and vegetation from the hair, middle earth, Miðgarðr, from the brows, the clouds from the brain, the soil from the flesh, and the rocks and scree from the toes and teeth. What remained was food for the maggots, who turned into yet another magical force after feeding on the primal giant: they transformed into dwarfs. One of their duties was to uphold the sky in the four directions, another to dream. Some say that the fire and flames continued to spew out of Muspellsheimr, and these became the stars and planets which the divine spirits ordered to allow humans to measure time.

One day the first three divine spirits wandered the shores and found two tree trunks on the beach. Óðinn or Óðr gave them breath, Atem, Odem, önd; Hænir gave them Óðr, soul or understanding and feeling; and Lóður gave them lá and litu, the bodily fluids which gave them color. These first humans, Askr and Embla, ash and elm, were without fate or örlög, they were örlöglaus, but in the process of becoming human they received örlög, so, somewhere there the fateful nornir must have intervened. The ancestors don't have much to say about that. It may have been much too obvious to them to even mention it. But some people think it was the nornir who gave them the qualities necessary for human life, and not the sons of the giant Burr.

And, you see, there is an interesting thing here: The first divine spirits killed the giant Ymir to create earth and with it the trees. And out of two of the trees they created the first humans. But there was one more special tree

that was created in this process: its roots reach deep down, so far that they even reach Ginnungagap, the gap of gap filled with magic, and its trunk and branches reach way up into the sky, so far that it touches the pole star at the top. In fact, it covers our world. This is the Tree of Life, and the Tree of the World, it holds auðr, riches, and Urðarbrunnur, the well of memory, and the fateful nornir; it is the process of life for us here, and you can even say that is the humans. While our ancestors have handed down many stories about the life of this tree, somewhere along the way the story of its creation got lost. Or maybe it didn't, since the Tree of Life is also us humans. Much more needs to be said about this tree.

There is another way in which the first humans were created: Ymir sweated in his sleep, and under his left armpit developed first woman and first man. And one of his feet created a son with the other foot. Since he was two gendered that seems quite possible.

So, the fertile void has transformed into riches, auðr, who developed örlög, fate. The first giant was the building material for our world, and the tree became the center of this world. So, what is this tree?

The tree comes with many names and under different guises. There is Yggdrasill, there is Irminsul, the sacred tree cut down by Charlesmagne, there is Mjötuðr, the measurer, there is the mysterious Sampo, tree of shamans, and there are many other names for it. At times it is an ash, at times a larch, and it has been and continues to make its appearance as different trees in different places. As you will travel and learn about the different names and the different kinds of trees who have become the holder of life, you will learn about the knowledge and gifts of the people in different regions. This tree is the center of the world, when you look up it reaches into the stars, and connects us with the milky way and the different regions where ancestral spirits go to and come from. The roots of the tree reach into the depths of memory, and the fateful örlög which brought us here. There is one important and crucial name for the tree I have not mentioned yet: Heimdallr, which may mean 'the one who illuminates the world.' The nornir created Heimdallr early on, the nine of them. Although his function has changed over the millennia, I see that he was one of the early divine spirits. He is not only the guardian of Bilröst, the spirit bridge, but also one of the measurers; while the nornir are the movement as they keep count scoring the moon cycles in particular, the tree Heimdallr is the rod who helps them do so (and if you are no prude, and your sexual imagination gets sparked, then I shall not be a woman who inhibits the way you feel). Heimdallr holds the horn of the moon honoring this cycle. He was born from the seas, and he easily changes into a seal. He helps making the örlög real for us humans.

You may wonder what Heimdallr is to do as the guardian of the spirit bridge Bilröst. This spirit bridge appears during the day to us as the rainbow, but at night it shines as the milky way. It is not for everybody. Humans have to be in a special place of wholeness to be permitted onto this special path to the ancestors and other spirits. I shall talk about that in a while, but, in short, you have to be the tree in order to be permitted across Bilröst. Let me explain.

The tree is our life, is us. So I could talk about it all night, and I am glad that the night is young, even though Freyja's star Venus has set by now. Let me say this much: The tree is birth and death, becoming and decaying, generation and regeneration. At its root are the nornir, three of them are well known to us by their name: Urðr, the one who holds the memory from which Verðandi creates what is coming to be present; and then there is Skuld, Schuld, karma, she knows what is owed to the ages, what their meaning is. They keep track of the lunar cycles of time, they score the records as humans have taken the clue from them and

scored the movements of the moon for many thousands of years. Then there are the other nornir who connect with different divine spirits, the Æsir and the Vanir, others connect with the giants, the elves, and the dwarves - we don't remember all their names. What each of these women creates has been seen in the form of white clay, aurr, and with this feminine fluid they spatter the tree of life, they cover it with the riches they lift from Urðarbrunnur. And yes, if you are not afraid to lie at the Ginnungagap of woman, whether you are man or woman, then you see this richness formed out of the moisture created from her heat. But their work has also been seen as the weave they create from the threads the sun woman has spun for them.

Thus the tree of life is nourished by the women who live at her roots and ladle the fluids from Urðarbrunnur and other sources. As the tree receives she gives nourishment to others: At her roots snakes gnaw away, and deer eat her leaves. She gives protection to the eagles and hawks in her top. Squirrels run up and down as messengers between the different parts of the world. Because the nornir never cease to spatter the tree with aurr the tree stays green year round. She stretches into all nine worlds, into all nine aspects of being, she connects us with them, and she is all these, she is the above, the below, and the middle.

There is one other thing you need to know now: When you look at all this you see how much knowledge the tree has, how much knowledge Heimdallr has as the measurer, as Vindlér, the borer, the turner, the spiraling one, the ram. The tree is living knowledge, including the deepest knowledge of the cycles which is created with aurr from örlög. Of course, this drum here, which

I use in ceremony is partly made from a special tree, a tree which also is the world tree, and in the center you see the drawing of the tree. This way the drum is Sampo, the mill, and Yggdrasill, the horse which can take us into other worlds; and it is all the others; this way the drum is knowledge, one way to knowledge. But there is another, actually: there are many others, but an important one is the sacrifice on the tree. We are trees, and to honor our origins and in order to journey across the spirit bridge we can sacrifice our self to spirit on the tree by fasting. On this occasion Heimdallr lets us pass. Even the one who was Óðr in the earliest times of this cycle (who later became Óðinn) did this, and he taught us how to do this. As he hung from the tree for nine days, honoring the nornir, and all the cycles which come from woman, and as he traveled across Bilröst, he used the drum made from a sacred tree to journey. Myself, at times I wonder about that Óðr, since he was also Auður - so: a man? a woman? both?

But now I need to talk about the one who cried for this Óðr, she of the star which governs our cycles of shamanizing, she who lies with the dwarves in the depth of the earth, and she who all the giants yearn for, she who carries the most magic of all divine spirits. She is the owner of the necklace Brisingamen, which holds such great power of healing and auður that the male divine spirits always scheme to steal it from her. And, yes, the dwarves gifted her with it after she had lain with them for four nights. Of course, you know that I am talking about Freyja. She is also known by many other names - Gullveig, Syr, Sjöfn, and many more. Whenever I ponder the names of these divine spirits I see not only how they and their meaning has changed over the generations, I also see their close connection, how their energies melt and merge, and at times I get very confused who is who. There are the siblings Freyr and Freyja, very close they are indeed. At that time among the Vanir there was an understanding of the sacred marriage between sister and brother. There is Dellingur, *the shining one, who is* Heimdallr, *and* Mardöll, *who is* Freyja, *the shining sea. And the thunderer* Þór *dresses up as* Freyja. *The creative forces seem to mix and blend in a fashion which we late borns of this cycle barely understand anymore. But I tell you: when you enter the magic of* seiðr, *our ceremony of seeing and visioning, deeply enough, then you will see and understand.*

Freyja *is* Vanadís, *a divine woman of the* Vanir. *But her name also connects her with the* dísir, *the protective spirits who travel with all humans. And as I have told you: the spirits who are connected with* örlög *seem to be able to shapeshift into each other: now they appear as* nornir *as needed for imparting destinies, then as* dísir *to protect, guide, and carry out destinies, now* nornir, *fates, and* dísir, *protective spirits, being two words for the same; and then finally they appear as the birdgoddesses by the name of* valkyrjur, *divine lovers also; they help humans with the final destinies on their paths as they are entering the realms of the ancestors and merge with what has gone before in* Urðarbrunnur, *the well of memory, up in the sky. You see, talking about one thing leads us in circles around and around until we return where we started - returning with a deepening understanding. And I have barely started to talk about this divine spirit woman, who some call a goddess or the great goddess, she who has brought us everything we know about magic. I see you want to object and talk to me about* Óðinn - *but what would* Óðr *have been without* Freyja? *What would* Óðinn *be without the* valkyrjur, *the bird spirits?*

Freyja *is the holder of magic, at times she flies as the falcon; the* valkyrjur, *the cats are with her. Her sexuality is healing as much as it is fertility; she knows how to tease knowledge out of the white clay of* aurr. *Without her there is no healing. Without her* völvur *and* vitkar *cannot see. She knows how to water the tree and create the* aurr, *the sacred clay, for the highest* blot *or offering and sacrifice. At times she seems to be the* völva, *the seeress, or maybe the* völva *is her. She carries the staff of the* völva, *the staff of becoming and evolving, to churn the white clay, to nurture and fertilize, to move with the* nornir, dísir, *and* valkyrjur *in the fateful matrix of* örlög. *And, yes, everybody talks about* Óðrærir, *the vessel*

that contains the drink of ecstasy, and the fury of Óðr, *aah yes, but don't you see what came before? Why do you think* Óðinn *is accused of* ergi, *of being unmanly, soft? One more thing about her which you need to remember if you want to be true to your ancestors: Many people say they don't understand the words* Vanir *for the spirits of old, such as* Freyja, *but some suspect it may have something to do with the star which rules her activities. Many of our kin have Venus on their belt or on their drum. Never do the work of* Freyja *with others when she does not show herself in the morning or the evening; this is the time to follow her into the great stone, the time to seek the power of the depths.*

Do not think about doing her work of seeing and healing before sacrificing your Self to the tree, before talking while sitting out, útiseta, *to your ancestors. Do not think you can pass by the guardian* Heimdallr *by just uttering the name of your ancestors. Yes, that you must do. But it is only the beginning. Until you have not been picked apart in the deep darkness of all the changes, all the history which the well of memory,* Urðarbrunnur *contains, until you have not shed the tears of memory, until you have not plunged into the shadow of all and everything our ancestors have wrought, until then: Work to remember the tree! Do not attempt to pass* Heimdallr, *because you are a lost soul, and lost you will be in the world you are trying to enter.*

You ask about sitting out, útiseta, *the calling for the ancestral spirits while out in the night, you ask about sacrifice,* blót, *the offerings to the different spirits at different times, you ask about* seiðr, *the seeing magic through drum-*

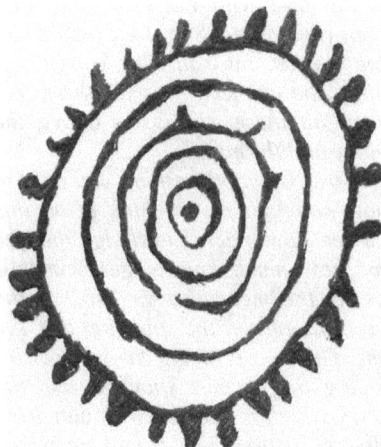
Art by Mariana Castro de Ali

ming and singing, the workings for protection and healing. And I tell you: None of this can be done without Freyja. *To reach her you have to travel up the tree and pass the test of wholeness which the guardian* Heimdallr *poses. He checks whether you are traveling alone, by force of your ego only, - or whether you have drunk from the well of memory,* Urðarbrunnur, *and are traveling with the ancestors, your other relations, and all else you need to have along. When you walk across that bridge you better know where you are going, you better remember the old stories which guide you to the places in the matrix, the places of origin, the trees, where you can do your work as* völva *or* vitki, *as seeress or seer, walk with your ancestors, walk with your* dísir, *your protective spirits, honor* Freyja *as you step forward, call upon the bird spirits, the* valkyrjur, *to show you the fateful lines in the white clay you need to see. And then do your work. Because then you will know whether it is meant to be done or not, then you see the fateful weave in the matrix. And then you will know what to do. All this is healing, and in all this is healing.*

This much I can tell you tonight, but you have to know: Much of this knowledge has been passed down with the help of our neighbors, and there have been many influences. One group of neighbors seems to have been particularly important in our past; they called them derogatively jötun, *giants, but some called them that to honor their mastery of the forces of* auður. *There are people who think the* Vanir *would be nothing without them, because they are the master magicians and they know how to nurture the mother of creation best. If you ever want to deepen this story, if you ever want to find missing pieces, go visit them. I honor the people who are now known as Sámi, and their relatives to the east. These are people we have traded with since the most ancient times we can track, back when we were neighbors on the river Don near the Black Sea.*

This story is the place of evocation, the place which I chant in ceremony. It is my place of origin. *Blót* (sacrifice), *útiseta* ("sitting out" to seek spiritual guidance), and *seiðr* (shamanic visioning ceremony for prophecy and other purposes) are the three ceremonies of which we have a historical record (traces of the original *blot* remain in practice in the far north). No need to reify what the literature contains, but there is a need to re-inspirit what we know and to understanding through ceremonial practice and dreaming. *Eiríks saga rauða,* the Saga of Eirik the Red, gives a beautiful description of a seeing ceremony and the chants sung for the seeress, the *völva*; I take this as a wonderful example of the old seeing practices (a late example, for sure), but not as dogma for the implementation of *seiðr.* The rich traces we have require our ceremonial responses to be inspirited and guide contemporary practices.

Into the Gap – Coming-To-Presence

As a way of summarizing my practice I have developed twenty-five statements for consideration, contemplation, meditation, inquiry, and practice; they were discussed and refined in communal discussions at one stage of their development.[15] These statements invoke a shamanic practice that centers shamanic healing on decolonization as initiation, a path of shamanism especially for people of dominant societies who have lost their connections with their ancestry, most importantly people of European ancestries; the practices are concerned with individual healing as much as with cultural healing. It is radical in its communal political stance and personally challenging as far as the individual practice is concerned. It is committed to an indigenous presence in place that is profoundly traditional it the sense of tradition ever unfolding through the deep visionary work of its practitioners, ever-renewing, ever-changing. Tradition is not a given, it cannot be found in museums, it is always alive when all its aspects are attended to; even when apparently dead the ancestors can still be listened to and spoken to.

The following statements are mere signposts to identify necessary ingredients of a practice recovering indigenous presence (while I would say they are comprehensive, I don't think they are complete). This is not the place to provide explanations beyond what I have already discussed above (see Kremer [2002] and Beyman et al. [2001] for some explanations). Instead, each statement can be used as occasion and inspiration for meditation and reflection. Each of the statements starts with the repeating refrain "Participating with awareness…." which should be read before each statement.

These meditative reflections guide my invocations and prayers when my shamanic practice connects the healing work of decolonization and personal healing. Working ceremonially in this framework has changed my interactions with indigenous Elders in conversation and ceremony and has resulted in dreams providing instructions for ceremonies and triggering echoes across time that may help healing across the generations. When I dance my ancestral body markings I dance them in this framework of participatory awareness, rather than an individualistic evocation of ancestry that can only result in supremacist presence. Haudenoshonee Elders told the U.N. that the spiritual is the political and these statements are intended to facilitate political and historical healing through spiritual healing.

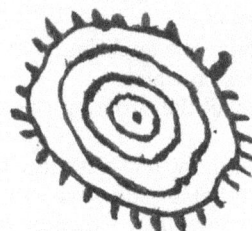

Art by Mariana Castro de Ali

Participating with awareness in the Great Cycle of Nurturing and Being Nurtured I give away as food the following practices in order to nurture myself and those around me, whether human, spirit, animal, plant, rock or other being.

Dedication
Participating with awareness In the Great Cycle of Nurturing and Being Nurtured I dedicate myself to the inner and outer work, the ceremonial and spiritual work that allow me to nurture what I am here to nurture through the gifts I have been given. I dedicate myself to the inner and outer work that allow me to receive nurturance in balance and gratitude.

Participating with awareness In the Great Cycle of Nurturing and Being Nurtured I dedicate myself to creating balance within myself and creating balance between myself and all my relations.

The Point of Beginning and the Point of Ending
Participating with awareness In the Great Cycle of Nurturing and Being Nurtured I see that the Great Love and the Great Peace require self-love and forgiveness.

Obligation and Grounding

Participating with awareness in the Great Cycle of Nurturing and Being Nurtured...

•...I observe the cycles of the stars, the planets, the seasons, human life.
•...I am aware that I am a link in the circle and cycle of nurturing and being nurtured.
•...I cultivate to come to awareness how my personal patterns, whether mental, emotional, somatic or spiritual, and I notice how they may cause suffering in myself and others.

Speaking and Inquiry

Participating with awareness in the Great Cycle of Nurturing and Being Nurtured ...

•...I am aware of the power of words and the realities they create. I dedicate myself to mindfulness in the use of all words.
•...I know that many of my relations do *not* speak using words.
•...I notice how words can create suffering or happiness.
•...I honor the spirit of all inquiry in service of balance and healing.
•...I notice the suffering brought about when we impose our views on others.
•...I see all the suffering created by fanaticism and intolerance.
•...I see how the historical dissociations and divisions have created the addictive virus of progress.
•...I see that great violence and injustice have been done to our environment and society.

Healing Personal Story

Participating with awareness in the Great Cycle of Nurturing and Being Nurtured ...

•...I see how lack of communication always creates separation and suffering.
•...I notice how my personal patterns may shield me from the surrender and vulnerability necessary for receiving the gifts of nurturing through my medicine.
•...I notice how anger may block communication and create suffering.
•...I see that much suffering is caused by war and conflict.
•...I see that sexual relations motivated by dissociative craving cannot dissipate the feeling of loneliness but will create more suffering, frustration, and isolation.
•...I see the suffering caused by exploitation, social injustice, institutionalized racism, stealing, and oppression.
•...I see how attachment and addiction to views and perceptions creates limitations and imbalance.
•...I look deeply at the nature of suffering so that I may develop compassion, love, and find ways out of suffering.
•...I see that true happiness is rooted in the peace, solidity, love, freedom, and compassion of nurturing conversations.
•...I see how lack of communication always creates separation and suffering.

•...I see that I am only in this life and body because of all my ancestors.
•...I honor all my different forms of awareness: wakefulness, dreaming, meditation, visionary journeying, others.

Goals or Intentions

Participating with awareness in the Great Cycle of Nurturing and Being Nurtured ...

•... I see that the essence and aim of any community dedicated to indigenous presence is the practice of the Nurturing Conversation.
•... I am aware that life is available only in the present moment and that it is possible to live happily in the here and now.

Participating with awareness
In the Great Cycle of
Nurturing and Being Nurtured

I see that
the Great Love and
the Great Peace
require
self-love and
forgiveness.

Within the matrix of awareness thus evoked dreams may help to occasion embodied visions in place that heal individuals and the painful burdens of history.

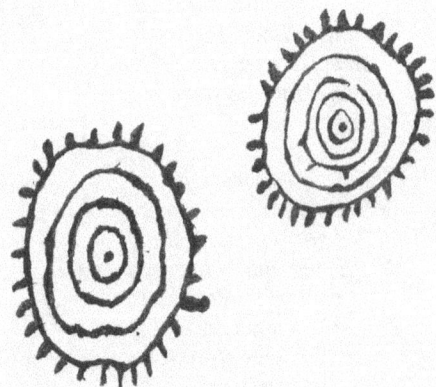

Art by Mariana Castro de Ali

NOTES

1. These are all my own dreams; for a variety of reasons it felt right to write them in the third person using one of my names, Muninn, referring to the raven of memory in Old Norse.

2. My thanks to Apela Colorado for the persistence and care with which she catalyzed the initial stage of my journey of the recovery of indigenous mind process.

3. Huginn and Muninn are the two ravens sitting on Óðinn's shoulders; however, this tradition goes way back before patriarchy, reaching beyond Óðinn to Óðr and past him the Eurasian village shamans. Kenin-Lopsang (1993) has pointed out that in Tuva the shaman, as a rule, has two ravens on the shoulders.

4. Thanks to Hanson Ashley for his explanations.

5. The gap, *Ginnungagap*, will be explored further below in the teaching story.

6. Auður, a term that appears several times below, is, from what I have gathered, a central term in Old Norse understanding of the world. It refers to life sustaining energies.

7. This story summarizes my shamanic understanding of the Old Norse traditions; it could not have been written without the collaborative work with Valgerður Bjarnadóttir. It is based on thorough research in the extant sources; see Bjarnadóttir & Kremer (2000), Beyman & Kremer (2003), and Kremer (2000, 2004 & 2006) for further details.

8. Plural of völva, seeress.

9. This quote is from *Völuspá*, presumably the oldest extant record of Old Norse cosmology.

10. Vanir are presumably the oldest identifiable layer of indigenous Norse spirits. The Æsir are spirits or gods and goddesses that arrived with the Indo-Europeanization of Northern Europe.

11. Freyja *and* Freyr simply meaning lady and lord.

12. Njörðr *and* Nerþuz – Nörd is the father of Frey and Freyja, according to Snorri Sturluson in charge of the movement of the winds, sea, and flames, a very prosperous Vanir fertility god; Nerthus is a fertility goddess, described in Tacitus; together they may represent sacred union.

13. Þór – the mightiest of the Æsir, giant-killer and thunderer.

14. The meaning and etymology of the names Hænir and Lóður remains somewhat mysterious.

15. Drafting these statements would not have been possible without the inspiration of Thich Nhat Hanh and the precepts of the Buddhist traditions, without the inspiration from PRATEC, the Andean *Proyecto Andino de Tecnologias Campesinas* and the statements of countless Elders, Teachers, and friends from a wide variety of Indigenous traditions. I want to acknowledge Rebecca Beyman, Linda Sartor, Jacqueline Whitmore, and Annie Wildwood with appreciation for their well considered suggestions.

REFERENCES

Beyman, R., & Kremer, J. W. (2003). The spirit of integration – Mythic androgyns and the significance of shamanic trance. *ReVision*, 26(1), 40-48.

Beyman, R., Kremer, J. W., Sartor, L., Whitmore, J., & Wildwood, A. (2001). Coming to presence. In: *Proceedings of the 18th International Conference on the Study of Shamanism and Alternate Modes of Healing* (pp. 233-241). Berkeley: Independent Scholars of Asia.

Bjarnadóttir, V. H., & Kremer, J. W. (2000). The cosmology of healing in vanir Norse mythology. In H. Kalweit & S. Krippner (Eds.), *Yearbook of Cross-Cultural Medicine and Psychotherapy 1997* (pp. 127-176). Mainz, Germany: Verlag für Wissenschaft und Bildung.

Borges, J. L. (1999). Islandia. In A. Coleman (Ed.), *Selected Poems I* (H. Rogers, Trans.) (pp. 400-401). New York: Viking.

Grimm, J. (1966). *Teutonic Mythology* (4 vols.). New York: Dover. Originally published 1883-1889.

Kafka, F. (1970). Wunsch, Indiander zu werden. In F. Kafka, *Sämtliche Erzählungen* (Complete Stories) (p. 18). Frankfurt, Germany: Fischer.

Kenin-Lopsang, M. B. (1993). Tuvinian shamans and the cult of birds. *ReVision*, 19(3), 33-36.

Kremer, J. W. (2000). Shamanic initiations and their loss -- decolonization as initiation and healing. *Ethnopsychologische Mitteilungen*, 9(1/2), 109-148.

Kremer, J. W. (2002). Radical presence. *ReVision*, 24(3), 11-20.

Kremer, J. W. (2004a). Remembering ancestral conversations. Afterword in B. Bastien, *Blackfoot Ways of Knowing - The worldview of the Siksikaitsitapi* (pp. 184-193). Calgary, Canada: University of Calgary Press.

Kremer, J. W. (2004b). Ethnoautobiography as Practice of Radical Presence - Storying the Self in Participatory Visions. *ReVision*, 26(2) (pp. 5-13).

Kremer, J. W. (2006). Freyja – The Great Shaman Spirit of the North. In *Proceedings of the 24th International Conference on the Study of Shamanism and Alternate Modes of Healing*. Berkeley: Independent Scholars of Asia.

Kremer, J. W. (2008). *Bear*ing Obligations. In K. Kailo, *Women and Bears: The Gifts of Nature, Culture and Gender Revisited* (pp. 219-272). Toronto, Canada: Inanna.

Vizenor, G. (2003). *Hiroshima Bugi: Atomu 57*. Lincoln: University of Nebraska Press.

AUTUMN AFTERNOON

Afternoon
And the late Autumn sunlight
And the broad canna leaves
Curling brown along their edges

Today we pause
Enjoy coffee on the deck
Amazed at this November heat
And forget
That Winter's shadow
Has already edged its way
Across the garden

-- Michael Sheffield

Art by Mariana Castro de Ali

Artist in Residence:

Mariana Castro de Ali

I am passionate about all kinds of art. I find manifestations of beauty and creativity in my daily life. I believe that art can be found in the streets, the homes, the closets, the personal journals, the kitchens, and in the backpacks of ordinary people. Art is an influential vehicle that entails sensitivity towards humanity. Through my art, I attempt to encourage people to take action in matters that concern our well being as individuals and also as members of society.

I came to the United States a few years after NAFTA and the so-called December's mistake which caused a huge economic recession in Mexico. I have been married for ten years with my Pakistani spouse. When we just got married, I could not communicate with him with words because of our lan-

fear that we have about other people, languages and races is a product of ignorance; we are more similar that different; what makes this world beautiful are those little differences among each other.

I work in various mediums including painting, printmaking, sculpture, audio and video. My art has been somewhat provocative, raw, edgy, and visceral. Through my work I intend to give voice to immigrants, to minorities, people suffering from different maladies such as AIDS, cancer and anorexia. I get inspired from daily mundane routines. I use common elements of every day life such as tickets, tea bags, coffee filters, tampons, threads and common conversations. I enjoy the juxtaposition of opposite elements such us the sacred and the profane, the in-

The flowers that I lost, 2007
Acrylic and tampons on canvas, 18 x 36

Domestication, 2007, Tampons and plaster, life size

guage differences, so we communicated with drawings. Every single day of my marriage is a learning experience by sharing my life with someone that comes from the other side of the world. We enrich each other's lives with our little differences. My personal experiences, my multicultural marriage, being an immigrant and having traveled has made me understand one thing: the

spiring and the debilitating, the kitsch and the chaste, the obvious and the ambiguous.

Domestication

Domestication was inspired by the women's invention: maize. Indians modified seeds gradually in what is known as "plant domestication" until

they developed the corn we know today. This piece was presented in my first solo show in 2007 in Ciudad Obregon, Sonora, Mexico the town where I was born. An agricultural town where Norman Bourloug did his experiments on genetic engineering that resulted in the Nobel Peace Prize of 1970 for his "Green Revolution." Many women in Sonora are dying from cancer caused by the agrochemicals used in the fields. This piece was dedicated to the women suffering from cancer and to the ones that already passed away, including some members of my own family. I delivered a message that made people question themselves in the use of agro-chemicals and the human losses that we are all suffering along with the erosion of the agricultural fields.

This piece was created to stimulate the audience imagination of a better world; I wanted the viewers to leave with a sense of appreciation for life, to celebrate their gender and to demand adequate ways to produce food without harming people. The piece was sold in 2008 in an art auction that benefited a Recycled AIDS Medicine program in San Francisco.

The Flowers that I lost

The Flowers that I lost was created in the summer of 2007. It was inspired by the amenorrhea that is experienced by women suffering from anorexia nervosa. I wanted to create public awareness through this work. The emphasis on being slim is making people suffer in their attempt to satisfy social standards of beauty and acceptance.

Reflection

This piece was inspired on my desire to inspire people to live life openly in a manner consistent with their sexual orientation. The colors on this painting depict the colors of the Rainbow flag.

A Matter of Survival, 2009, Print on sales receipts, 8 x 10 inches

It was part of a solo exhibition called True Colors at Lavender Library in Sacramento, CA.

A Matter of Survival

Immigration is a matter of survival.

Migratory birds travel thousands of miles for the same reasons as do Punjabis, Mexicans, Afghanis, Vietnamese and any other group of immigrants: to fight for life.

Mariana Castro de Ali uses bird migrations as a metaphor for the ordeal immigrants face daily. Corporations and governments constantly hunt people. We are being chased by mortgages, credit cards, unemployment, lack of social services and underfunded retirement plans.

Castro de Ali utilizes canvas, prints, sales receipts and price tags metaphorically and as artistic medium.

Reflection, 2008, Acrylic on canvas, 36 x 48 inches

Growth and Transformation among Women Healers

Gabrielle Pelicci

Cultural myths from around the world describe a time when only women knew the secrets of life and death, and therefore they alone could practice the magical art of healing. (Achterberg, 1991, p.1)

The presence and influence of women healers ranges from the celebrated to the controversial. Among scholars of Goddess Theology and Women's Spirituality, woman as healer is a tradition that spans several thousand years, stretching far back into prehistory when women were honored for their healing abilities (Achterberg, 1991; Gadon, 1989; Noble, 1991). Several universities including the California Institute of Integral Studies (CIIS) and the New College of California offer programs dedicated to the study of women's spirituality which incorporates female modes and powers of healing and embodied healing methods. Students of these and other informal groups celebrate the compassionate, nurturing and intuitive contribution that women make to health and medicine.

There is evidence of communities of priestesses and women's councils that existed for millennia in Old Europe and other places (Gimbutas, 2001). Almost all archeological sites in Italy, the Balkans and Central Europe, contain figurines etched with sacred symbols representing the sacred feminine. These objects can also be found in Asia Minor, the Near East and to a lesser extent in Western and Northern Europe (Achterberg, 1991; Eisler, 1987; Gimbutas, 2001; Noble, 1991; Stone, 1976).

Gabrielle Pelicci, Ph.D., is the Academic Director at Sober College, faculty in the Personal and Professional Development program at UCLA Extension, adjunct faculty in the Transformative Leadership Program at the California Institute of Integral Studies, instructor for UCLA Health System Ethics Center, and teacher trainer for several Kundalini Yoga Teacher Trainings. Gabrielle also presents at national educational and therapeutic conferences and assists individuals in creating personal and professional success through workshops and individualized coaching.

Women practiced midwifery and herbology during the eleventh, twelfth and thirteenth centuries. While the early part of the Middle Ages were times of excitement and diversity for women healers, the fourteenth through eighteenth centuries saw an orchestrated and thorough campaign to stamp out the woman healer (Brooke, 1997). During this time of calamity, crime, crop failures and illness, women and witchcraft were blamed for the disasters of the earth. The newly established medical professionals and the Church tried to establish a monopoly on the healing professions claiming that women healers were "idiots who gathered herbs and practiced religious nonsense" (Achterberg, 1990, p. 78). As a result of this unfortunate turn of events, women were forbidden to practice medicine. They were systematically tortured and burned by the hundreds and thousands for practicing healing arts. One medieval scholar estimates that more than one million women and healers were executed for the crime of helping other women (Robbins, 1998).

In the nineteenth century there were long and vicious battles to prevent women from entering medical school because medical education was considered unsuited to women (Brooke, 1997; Remen, Blau, & Hively, 1980). However, women were successful in reentering the health care system and eighty percent of the 12 million workers in health care today are women (Centers for Disease Control, 2001). Women have been working in free clinics, public health, geriatrics, preventive and complementary medicine and running their own hospitals (Brooke, 1997). In addition to practicing traditional medicine, women are working as botanical healers, midwives, chiropractors, homeopaths and an assortment of other lay healers (White House Commission on Complementary and Alternative Medicine Policy, 2002).

Although there is no research to support the theory that the public perceives women healers as respected practitioners today, the growing interest in Complementary and Alternative Medicine (CAM) suggests that the public perception of women healers is a positive one. More than $27 billion is spent annually on CAM (Eisenberg, et al., 1998) and, according to a 2004 nationwide government survey, 36 percent of U.S. adults aged 18 years and over use some form of CAM (Barnes, Powell-Griner, McFann, & Nahin, 2002).

The proportion of CAM providers who are female ranges from 30% to 85% depending on the type of practice. More women than men practiced massage therapy (85 percent) and acupuncture and naturopathy (almost 60 percent), but women represented only a minority of chiropractors (about 25 percent). In the United States, there are approximately 60,000 chiropractors, 100,000 massage therapists, 1300 naturopathic physicians, 3000 acupuncture physicians and an additional 11,000 non-physician acupuncturists. This population of 175,300 practitioners (62% female) represents a partial sample of the healing arts community (Eisenberg, et al., 2001).

Overview of the study

A combination of narrative analysis and life story was used to gather information about the experiences of growth and transformation among five women who maintained a successful practice in the healing arts for ten or more years. Ten years in practice was identified because it indicates a substantial amount of experience and a degree of maturity. A successful practice was important because the study called for the wisdom of accomplished, competent and effective healers. Life experience was a critical component for this research because it explores the common milestones that span a lifetime of practice.

I conducted five interviews between November and December of 2004. The five interviews were conducted face-to-face or over the telephone and were recorded for the purpose of creating transcripts. After the third interview, I began to notice several similarities in the stories. For example, four out of five women had experienced a life-threatening illness. The details of the stories, of course, were different. Two of the women suffered from breast cancer while the third had pelvic inflammatory disease. After the fifth interview, I felt confident that I had reached data saturation and I had collected enough information for the study.

Although it was a narrative research study, I did not use the structural or linguistic analysis often used in narrative analysis (Reissman, 1993). Instead, I used thematic analysis, a form of content analysis that involves searching for themes in the data. The first step in this process involved exploring the women's life stories for information that revealed the common experiences of growth and transformation. I began by reading and rereading the transcripts while listening to the audio recording. Each successive reading took me deeper into the life story of the women and allowed me to hear things that I didn't hear in the previous sittings. This also helped me to better understand the chronology of the life story since all the women told their stories in a nonlinear style.

After studying the text for several months, six themes were developed: Importance of a Support Network, Ongoing Learning and Self-transformation, Nature as a Teacher and Tool for Healing, Energy as a Universal Language, Integral Approach to Healing, and Purpose-driven Life. Once the themes were identified, I proceeded to weave the analysis of the life stories with the current literature and create a cultural, historical and social context for the themes identified in the life stories. This process of working with each theme to create a clear and coherent presentation lasted about 18 months and went through several transformations as the data became more integrated into my thinking.

Importance of a Support Network

Make sure you plan plenty of support, so you can totally fall apart, totally be in the mess and in the experience of pain. Because we have to go there in order to get through to the other side ... All good teachers say that you can only teach what you know. And you can only take people as far as you've gone. (Participant comment)

My analysis of the women's life stories demonstrated that throughout the process of growth and transformation, it was crucial to have a support system in place. As the women developed their practice, engaged in personal growth and worked with patients, it was their support system that helped them to clarity about their lives, manage their transformational development, and do self-healing. The support network also prevented them from feeling lonely, overwhelmed or disconnected.

The women healers in the study realize that they have to delve into their own self-healing to help others so they plan lots of support during the transformational process. Their support network allows them to heal and grow which allows them to help others do the same. The women can support their patients because they have a support network supporting them. Without a support network, they would not have been able to go through the necessary pain and growth to develop the skills needed to help others meet those same challenges.

The women described many challenges that required the use of their support system including running a business, developing their practice, surviving illness and disease. Gathering with other healers, spending time with mentors, and sharing experiences with friends are some of the ways that the women accessed their support network. The types of support that composed their support network included teachers, mentors, family friends and inner or spiritual guidance. The support network was crucial in providing the women with companionship, resources, inspiration, guidance, connection, and stability.

The current research on health care reports that social relationships serve important social, psychological, and behavioral functions across the lifespan (Berkowitz, 2002; Ornish, 2006; Uchino, Cacioppo & Kiecolt-Glaser, 1996). A review of 81 studies revealed that social support had beneficial effects on aspects of the cardiovascular, endocrine, and immune systems (Uchino, Cacioppo & Kiecolt-Glaser, 1996). Scientists as UCLA discovered that women respond to stress with a cascade of brain chemicals that cause them to make and maintain friendships with other women (Berkowitz, 2002). When the hormone oxytocin is released as part of the stress responses in a woman, it buffers the fight or flight

response and encourages her to gather with other women instead. This leads to a release of more oxytocin which further counters stress and produces a calming effect. Gathering with others also reduces the risk of disease, death, and physical impairments. Not having close friends or confidants is as detrimental to health as smoking or carrying extra weight (Berkowitz, 2002).

In addition to improving health, relationships between people also foster creative activity. Although creative individuals are often thought of as working in isolation, much of their intelligence and creativity results from interaction and collaboration with other individuals (Csikszentmihalyi, 1996). Since most healers work as independent contractors, they have to be creative in finding ways to meet other healthcare professionals. Some of the things I have done to stay involved with other healers include working part-time at wellness centers and doctor's offices, volunteering at health fairs, creating healing groups and practice groups, seeking out mentors in the field and connecting with pre-established networks of healers such as licensing boards or membership associations. I also encourage my students to plan a good support system. I recommend that they participate in learning communities and mentorship programs during the course of their studies so that they can experience the necessary support framework for their growth and development. In addition, I encourage them to build and maintain these systems when they graduate so they have the necessary resources for success when they start their healing practice.

Ongoing Learning and Self-Transformation

I'd say to my friends, "I feel I've completed a cycle, and I don't know what it is, but I've completed it." And then my life would take off in a whole new different direction ... like you have with certain seasons, you have a decay; so you've completed that, and then you have a rebirth ... that created more energy for me to be available to do new things. (Participant Comment)

The women described their ongoing learning and self-transformation as a tool that provided the necessary knowledge to do self-healing and healing with their clients. Some of the things they learned include learning to be still and listen deeply, learning to see the interconnectedness of everything, learning a common language based on energy, learning diverse approaches to healing from different cultures and disciplines, and learning to integrate all their experience to teach and empower others. They also came to interpret their experience of ongoing learning and self-transformation as a cyclical process of life-death-rebirth—a metaphor for the transformation of all things in nature.

For the women in the study, formal learning occurred in classrooms, universities, workshops and trainings. One woman spent 20 years meditating and studying alone in her home. Another woman has 5000 hours of training in bodywork and energy work modalities. A third woman has a formal education as a nurse and a forth is a licensed acupuncturist. Each woman followed a different path of education but they all experienced a similar type of learning and development. Mentors helped the women by giving them clarity about the concepts they were learning and frame it in a way that made sense. One woman said that her mentor gave her a few skeleton ideas that allowed her to "hang it together" and gave her "clarity about what's going on." Throughout the process of change, the women became more open and aware, learned to see the interconnectedness of everything, and empowered others to self-heal. They saw adversity as an opportunity rather than a curse and used it to develop awareness and skills that could be used to educate and heal others.

Patients presented an opportunity for learning because each treatment was unique and challenging in its own way and sometimes the women would run into situations that were unfamiliar. Encountering unfamiliar situations motivated the women to continue learning so that they could heal the patient. Personal illnesses and challenges presented a unique opportunity for ongoing learning and self-transformation because it enabled the women to learn about their own strength and authenticity. It also gave them a deeper understanding of the challenges that their patients face.

Becoming a healer requires the ability to grow beyond cultural conditioning and the conventional medicine

Photo: Mariana Castro de Ali

paradigm to embrace a new worldview. It requires openness to new ideas, ongoing learning and self-transformation, and the ability to integrate and communicate new insights and information to patients. In my own teaching, I address all aspects of healing (physiological, psychological, transpersonal, cultural, etc.) and all aspects of the person (physical, mental, emotional and spiritual). I explore the personal process of transformation in order to better prepare the student healer for the transformative learning experience. I also include discussions about the different worldviews and paradigms that accompany these varied approaches to healing in the curriculum. It is important to include curriculum about the historical and cultural dimensions of healing so that the healer understands the general context and personal context of her work. This awareness will enable her to be grounded in her profession and communicate about healing intelligently and effectively.

To receive a license or national certification in a healing modality, the practitioner may need as little as a high school diploma and 500 hours of training. While this serves as a good foundation for her work, the successful healer will want to acquire additional education which investigates the mind, body, pathology, spirituality, and all aspects of healing. In my practice, I have completed over 1000 hours of training in holistic modalities as well as a Bachelors degree in Psychology, a Masters degree in Education and a Doctorate on Women Healers. The

more a healer learns, the more tools she will have to use in the treatment room.

Nature as Teacher and a Tool for Healing

I have a lot of tools ... but you don't really need any. You just have to learn how to listen deeply. And you can never do that if you can't hear yourself and you don't have some kind of practice that allows you to be quiet and still ... You can't have activity without stillness because you won't really be there ... I think we can't really have an experience fully without being somehow connected to stillness. (Participant comment)

For more than 6,000 years, the concept that the body, mind and spirit are intertwined with nature has been present in the healing arts. The concept of elements can be found in many cultures including the Far East, ancient Greece and indigenous cultures around the world. Even the father of Western Medicine, Hippocrates described the human body in terms of the four elements: yellow bile (Fire), black bile (Earth), blood (Air), and phlegm (Water) (Hippocrene Books, 1931). In the study, nature represents people, plants, animals, the environment, the body and the natural elements that are present in everything. For the women in the study, their perception of nature was consistent with the role that nature plays in the Healing Arts. Nature was connected to the women's experience of body, listening, healing and teaching in a powerful way.

The women in the study had many extraordinary experiences and learned several significant lessons from nature. They connected to the energy of trees and animals, felt the awesome power of nature's creativity and beauty and learned to quiet their minds and listen deeply as a result of their interaction with nature. One of the women chose to work directly with animals and the environment as a means to teach people about the interrelationship between humans, animals and health. Another woman experienced deep healing after living alone on a mountain for an extended period of time. Each woman used their body and the skills they developed in nature as a teacher and tool for healing. The women in the study appreciate nature as the ultimate teacher and a framework for understanding the healing process.

Several researchers from diverse backgrounds including science, anthropology, philosophy and metaphysics have written about the sacred and intelligent power of nature (Abram, 1996; Chopra, 1989; Goodenough, 1998; Roads, 1990; Sahtouris, 2000; Tompkins and Bird, 1989). Chopra (1989) says each cell of the body harnesses the power and intelligence of nature. Abram (1996) says that the world is alive, awake and aware and each ecology has its own psyche. Within that ecology, each thing has its own unique mind or imagination and an active agency and power (Abram, 1996). Some authors have deeply explored the physical, emotional and spiritual relations between plants and people (Roads, 1990; Tompkins and Bird, 1989) and others say we are called to acknowledge our dependency on the web of life both for our subsistence and for our countless aesthetic experiences (Goodenough, 1998; Sahtouris, 2000).

Because nature serves as a foundation for many healing modalities as well as the practice of deep listening, I recommend that healers spend time meditating and reflecting in nature and practicing techniques to become more present and grounded in the body. We have many options for deepening our relationship with nature including yoga, martial arts, visiting sacred sites, and simple activities such as hiking or camping. I encourage my students to travel and work in different environments to increase their awareness of the ways in which diverse environments affect the healing process. Personally, I have traveled to multiple locations in North America, South America, Asia, Africa, and Europe to study different cultural approaches to healing. I also encourage my students to participate in experiential nature-based exercises and learn about nature's healing resources such as herbs, hydrotherapy (mineral springs, salt water), and so on.

Integral Approach to Healing

What I learned was that Taoism and CranioSacral are the same thing, because it's the same system that's utilized. The CranioSacral practitioners and the Shamanistic approach and the Tao are the same thing ... Nobody kind of sat down ... to make one language ... connecting the same systems. And luckily I studied the Western, the CranioSacral and acupuncture, so I really get that. (Participant comment)

The literature describes the ideal integral healer as someone who is transformed, deeply changed, healed and whole, expert in the world's healing traditions, expanded in consciousness, uses personal development and self-care and a holistic lens to view the world (Dasher, 1996; Khanna, 2004; Wilber 2004). The women in the study match the description in the literature because they use multiple healing traditions to treat patients, are expanded in consciousness, are committed to self-development, and use multiple ways of knowing and a holistic lens to view the world. In addition to the attributes of an integrally informed healthcare practitioner, their principles also match the principles of integrative medicine including a partnership relationship with patients, openness to new paradigms, and natural healing-oriented interventions.

Although they did not label themselves as integral healers, the women in the study talked extensively about their commitment to self-development that led to the characteristics of an integral approach to healing including openness, expansiveness, and wholeness. The women used many tools for self-development such as meditation, yoga, martial arts, workshops, fasting, retreats, spending time in nature, and so on. At the same time that they were working on themselves to become more healed and whole, the women in the study were also being trained in multiple healing modalities. One woman integrated many bodywork modalities together including Shiatsu and CranioSacral Therapy to treat the physical, mental and emotional aspects of her patients. Another woman studied everything from acupuncture to channeling to transcendental meditation to build her holistic approach to healing. Other modalities that were used by one or more of the women include Healing Touch, Quantum Touch, Breema, Shamanic Journeying, Hatun Karpey, and Energy Medicine.

The concept of interconnectedness between nature, people and healing is the foundation of healing arts and the holistic framework. The women in the study developed a holistic lens to view the world as they integrated learning from diverse cultures and healing modalities and participated in their own relationship with nature. This holistic framework is essential for an integral approach to healing because the integral perspective requires the practitioner to see how nature, people, lifestyle and transformation are inseparable. This perception allows them to bring their whole self into practice and use a whole-person approach to healing.

In my own teaching work, I aim to help students combine self-knowledge with knowledge about health and

> The women in the study developed a holistic lens to view the world as they integrated learning from diverse cultures and healing modalities and participated in their own relationship with nature.

medicine. I recommend that they develop their consciousness, intuition, and creativity and self-awareness. The curriculum that I have taught includes courses in anatomy, physiology, psychology, business practices, ethics, nutrition, fitness, yoga, meditation, martial arts, Traditional Chinese Medicine, Ayurvedic Medicine, CAM, shamanic healing, energy medicine, pathologies, contraindications, and so on. I attend conferences such as the North American Research Conference on Complementary and Integrative Medicine to stay current on research trends and meet like-minded professionals because it is important to build bridges between the conventional and alternative medical communities and create a future medical system that emphasize the both/and mentality rather than either/or thinking.

Energy as a Universal Language

Energy work is much more illusive than in physical health care, where we don't take blood tests or look at x-rays or things like that, that are very concrete measures how you can tell changes occurred. We're dealing with it in a different frame of reference. (Participant Comment)

The participants in this study describe energy as a force that is creative, moving, fluid, reproductive, generational and spiritual. They experience it as colors, tingling, vibration and connectedness. They exchange it with others through their words and their touch. They know it as a field around a person's body, invisible cords between people, pools and points on the body as well as a general feeling about the presence of a person. Doing healing work allows the participants to become more familiar with energy, learn the subtleties of energy, and distinguish the difference between their own energy and the energy of others. The more healing work they do, the more "open" and "free" they become. Doing healing work also raises their "vibration" and lets them "carry more light".

Energy is defined in the study as the life-force that is part of everything that exists and sustains living beings (Brennan, 1987, 1993; Hover-Kramer, 2002; Joy, 1979). Concepts of energy can be found in many cultures including India (prana) and China (chi). The women in the study each came to the same understanding about energy through different paths. Some came to the understanding through the science of the chakra system (India) or meridian system (China) and others developed their clairvoyant and clairaudient abilities. Several women combined multiple approaches.

The women came to their conclusion that energy is energy no matter how it is taught or where it is located by learning different energy modalities, spending time with healers from various cultures and making connections between different approaches to energy medicine. When one woman was working in South Africa, she was initiated as a traditional South African healer because they recognized her work as the same as their own. Another woman is in the process of compiling a book that outlines the similarities and compatibility of the diverse approaches to energy medicine. A third healer referred to quantum physics and the advances in technology imaging as evidence that energy is the underlying essence of the universe.

As they became more familiar with the dynamics of the life-force, the women learned that energy needs to be fluid and moving in order to maintain health. If the energy becomes blocked or stuck because of physical or mental obstructions, then the person will become sick. One woman said, "We are energetic bodies. And the energy either moves or doesn't. And if it doesn't move or moves a little bit but not sufficiently—we're out of balance." Whether they are doing Quantum Touch, Healing Touch or acupuncture, they are moving the life-force energy to restore health and balance to their patients.

Even though there are many cross-cultural frameworks for life-force energy, it has not been proven by western scientific methods and is not recognized by most conventional physicians in the United States. The success of western medicine over the last few centuries has been so impressive that we've come to equate western medicine with truth. In my practice, I have explored the diverse opinions and theories of energy and the ongoing research about energy medicine. I teach my students to approach discussions about energy and energy medicine intelligently citing the Eastern and Western philosophies as well as their personal experience. I inform them that energy medicine is not meant to replace common sense or professional or psychological help and it is not recommended for broken bones, acute pain, or any condition requiring immediate medical attention. Energy treatments are meant to be integrated with conventional western medicine and used appropriately.

Purpose-Driven Life

When a person is called, some ignore the call. They don't follow through with it and many times they become physically ill or mentally ill. And the only way they can get through it is if they answer the call to be a healer. (Participant Comment)

Several researchers describe elements of a life with purpose, destiny, meaning, and flow (Adrienne, 1998; Csikszentmihalyi, 1993; Hillman, 1996; Moore, 1992; Myss, 2001). According to the Acorn Theory, each person is born with a destiny written into the acorn—the seed of the self—which presents itself as a personal calling and a reason to be alive (Hillman, 1996). This theory is based on an ancient idea that the soul of each person is given a unique daimon (soul-companion or spirit guide) before they are born which stays with them throughout life and reminds them of their destiny (Hillman, 1996). In this perspective, a calling may be postponed or avoided but eventually it needs to be fulfilled.

In a similar vein, the Sacred Contract theory proposes that the soul of each person makes an agreement before birth to do certain things for divine purposes (Myss, 2001). Imbedded in the Sacred Contract is a mission or a quest that is unique to each individual. The Sacred Contract includes many individual agreements to meet and work with certain people, in certain places, at certain times and random events—whether positive or negative—are actually part of a life script that provides countless opportunities for spiritual transformation (Myss, 2001).

The meaning of a Purpose-driven Life, based on the Acorn Theory and the Sacred Contract theory, is to expand consciousness and fulfill a destiny with the help of spiritual guidance. Spiritual guidance manifests first as a calling to do something or be something and is followed by support in the form of intuition, dreams, hunches and coincidences to assist each person in fulfilling their life purpose (Hillman, 1996; Myss, 2001). All five women considered their practice to be a calling, not a profession. One woman said she was led to be a healer. Another said that she was called to help people. A third said that there was never any question that she was supposed to do anything other than healing. The women took their calling very seriously and worked hard to fulfill their destiny.

All of the women in the study were assisted by spiritual guidance once they stepped on the path of their life purpose. As they made important life decisions and encountered difficult obstacles, spiritual guidance was there to give them important information or point out the direction to travel. One woman met her spiritual guides on a shamanic journey (an ancient technique of journeying to the spirit worlds). Another woman had a premonition that she was going to work with the aborigines in Australia—which later came to pass. The spiritual voices also gave her advice about what career choices to make and which places to live.

In my teaching work, I encourage students to be intrinsically motivated and have a purpose-driven life. One of the most frequent failures in education is that students rarely say that they find studying to be intrinsically rewarding (Csikszentmihalyi & Larson, 1984). One of the most straightforward conclusions of research from the past two decades is that extrinsic motivation alone is likely to have precisely the opposite impact that we want it to have on student achievement (Lepper & Hodell, 1989). Intrinsically motivating activities are those in which people will engage for no reward other than the interest and enjoyment that accompanies them (Vockell, n.d.). I regularly encourage students to make choices that fulfill their calling and assist them in creating a life that is abundant with meaning, value and purpose.

Conclusion

If you consider conscious evolution, ongoing growth, and transformation to be the essential meaning of life, then you will engage yourself in the act of transformation ... ongoing transformation implies that you need to continuously dissolve the old

meaning of your life and create your life anew. (Kimura, 2002, p. 33)

The six significant themes that emerged in the study are *Importance of a Support Network, Ongoing Learning and Self-transformation, Nature as a Teacher and Tool for Healing, Integral Approach to Healing, Energy as Universal Language*, and *Purpose-driven Life*. Although these themes are listed as separate and independent, they are interconnected in the same way that the body is made of many parts that all work together to form the whole. The first theme, *Importance of a Support Network*, is the foundation that allows healers to engage in *Ongoing Learning and Self-transformation*. Without a support network, we would not be able to go through the necessary pain and growth to develop the skills needed to help others meet those same challenges. The process of ongoing learning and self-transformation is grounded in *Nature as a Teacher and Tool for Healing*. Nature provides a resource to learn about the self, the body and the healing process. It also teaches us how to be quiet, still and listen deeply which is also used as a tool in the treatment room. Energy gives healers a language we can use to describe the healing process and the spirit of nature. Additional tools come from studying many different approaches and methods of healing. Studying multiple methods and practices informs our *Integral Approach to Healing* and creates a holistic worldview with *Energy as the Universal Language* that we can use to communicate with practitioners of diverse modalities. Finally, the *Purpose-driven Life* is the way in which we use the other themes such as support, learning and self-transformation to create a meaningful experience and fulfill our destiny to serve others.

The future of healing arts requires leaders who can build bridges between people, integrate diverse ideas and practices, and create a united community. Practitioners are changing. Patients are changing. The healthcare system is changing. It is not possible to hold onto old paradigms and old models for long. Myss (2001) says that the essential characteristics of the healer include an inherent strength and the ability to assist people in transforming their pain into a healing process as well as having the necessary skill to gener-

ate physical and emotional changes. Honoring all forms of healers and healing will allow us to integrate the many different methods and practices to create the most complete medicine bag with all the diverse tools necessary to treat the uniqueness of each patient.

A future area of research includes delving more deeply into the theories about healing that female healers have developed over a lifetime of study and practice. Healing has been described by healers and patients alike, as everything from a mystery to a relationship to an expansion of consciousness. The women in the study described healing as reduction or elimination of pain, opening, clearing, peeling away layers, becoming freer and carrying more light. The Merriam-Webster Dictionary defines healing as: to make sound or whole; to restore to health; to cause (an undesirable condition) to be overcome; to mend; to patch up (a breach or division); to restore to original purity or integrity; and to return to a sound state (Merriam-Webster, 2006). One woman mentioned that she believed all healing systems from both the East and the West could be integrated into one 'theory of everything' not unlike Wilber's synthesis of ideas from science, spirituality, economics, and medicine (Wilber, 2001). Another woman had a plethora of transpersonal experiences that rival those of Carlos Castaneda (1993) or Lynn Andrews (1983). Unfortunately, many women healers do not write or publish about their experiences and so much is lost as a result. The more research we can do about women healers to give them a voice in the dialogue on healing the better.

REFERENCES

Abram, D. (1996). *Spell of the sensuous*. New York: Vintage Books.

Achterberg, J. (1991). *Woman as healer*. Boston: Shambala.

Adrienne, C. (1998). *The purpose of your life*. New York: Eagle Brook.

Andrews, L. (1983). *Medicine woman*. San Francisco: Harper San Francisco.

Barnes, P. M., Powell-Griner, E., McFann, K., & Nahin, R.L. (2002). Complementary and alternative medicine use among adults: United States, 2002. *Advance Data, 27*, 1-19.

Berkowitz, G. (2002). *UCLA study on friendship among women*. Retrieved August 17, 2006 from http://www.anapsid.org/cnd/gender/tendfend.html.

Brennan, B. (1987). *Hands of light*. New York: Bantam.

Brennan, B. (1993). *Light emerging*. New York: Bantam.

Brooke, E. (1997). *Medicine women: a pictorial history of women healers*. London: Theosophical Publishing House.

Castaneda, C. (1993). *The Art of Dreaming*. New York: Harper Perennial.

Centers for Disease Control – National Institute for Occupational Safety and Health. (2001). *Health Care Workers*. Retrieved August 10, 2006 from http://www.cdc.gov/niosh/topics/healthcare/.

Chopra, D. (1989). *Quantum Healing*. London: Bantam.

Csikszentmihalyi, M. (1996). *Creativity: Flow and the psychology of discovery and invention*. New York: HarperCollins Publishers.

Csikszentmihalyi, M & Larson, R. (1984). *Being adolescent*. New York: Basic Books.

Dacher, E. (1996). Towards a post-modern integral medicine. *The Journal of Alternative and Complementary Medicine, 2(4)*, 531-537.

Eisenberg, D.M., et al. (1998). Trends in alternative medicine use in the United States, 1990-1997: results of a follow-up national survey. *Journal of the American Medical Association, 280(18)*, 1569-75.

Eisenberg, D.M., et al. (2001). Perceptions about use and non-disclosure of complementary relative to conventional therapies among adults who use both. *Annals of Internal Medicine, 135*, 344-351.

Eisler, R. (1987). *The chalice and the blade*. San Francisco: Harper

Gadon, E. (1989). *The once and future goddess*. San Francisco: Harper San Francisco.

Gimbutas, M. (2001). *The living goddesses*. Berkeley: University of California Press.

Goodenough, U. (1998). *Sacred Depths of Nature*. New York: Oxford University Press.

Hillman, J. (1996). *The soul's code*. New York: Random House.

Hippocrene Books. (1931). Hippocrates, Volume IV: Nature of Man. Cambridge, MA: Harvard University Press.

Hover-Kramer, D. (2002). *Healing touch: A guidebook for practitioners* (2nd ed.). New York: Delmar Publishers.

Joy, W.B. (1979). *Joy's way: a map for the transformational journey*. Los Angeles: Jeremy P. Tarcher.

Khanna, S. (2004). *Challenges of integral medicine*. Retrieved August 17, 2006 from http://shiftinaction.com /node/102.

Kimura, Y. (2002). A philosopher of change. *What is Enlightenment? 22*, 22-35.

Lepper, M. R., & Hodell, M. (1989). *Intrinsic motivation in the classroom*. In C. Ames & R. Ames (Eds.), Research on motivation in education (Vol. 3) (pp. 73-105). San Diego, CA: Academic Press.

Maizes, V., Koffler, K., Fleishman, S. (2002). Revisiting the health history: an integrative approach. *International Journal of Integrative Medicine, 4(3)*, 7-13.

Merriam-Webster. (2006). *Healing*. Retrieved on October 10, 2006 from http://merriam-webster.com/.

Moore, T. (1992). *Care of the soul*. New York: Harper Collins Publishers.

Myss, C. (2001). *Sacred Contracts*. New York: Harmony Books.

Noble, V. (1991). *Shakti woman: Feeling our fire, healing our world*. San Francisco: Harper.

Ornish, D. (2006). *Love is real medicine*. Retrieved August 30, 2006 from http://www.msnbc.msn.com/ id/9466931/site/newsweek/.

Reissman, C. (1993). *Narrative Analysis*. Newberry Park, CA: Sage.

Remen, R. N. (1996). In the Service of Life. *Noetic Sciences Review, 37*, 24-25.

Remen, R., Blau, A., & Hively, R. (1980). The masculine principle, the feminine principle and humanistic medicine. In P. A. R. Flynn (Ed.). *The Healing Continuum: Journeys in the philosophy of holistic health*. Bowie, MD: R.J. Brady Co.

Roads, M. J. (1990). *Journey into nature*. Tiburon, CA: HJ Kramer Inc.

Robbins, J. (1998). *Reclaiming our health*. Tiburon, CA: HJ Kramer.

Sahtouris, E. (2000). *Earthdance*. iUniversity Press. Retrieved August 18, 2006 from http://www.ratical.org /LifeWeb/.

Stone, M. (1976). *When God was a woman*. New York: Harcourt Brace & Co.

Tompkins, P. & Bird, C. (1989). *The secret life of plants*. New York: Harper Perennial.

Uchino, B.N., Cacioppo, J.T. and Kiecolt-Glaser, J.K. (1996). The relationship between social support and physiological processes. *PsychoLogical Bulletin, 119(3)*, 488-531

Vockell, E. (no date). *Educational psychology: A practical approach*. Retrieved September 3, 2006 from http://education.calumet.purdue.edu/vockell/EdPsyBook/

White House Commission on Complementary and Alternative Medicine Policy. (2002). *WHCCAMP – Final report*. Retrieved July 25, 2006 from http://www.whccamp.hhs.gov/finalreport.html.

Wilber, K. (2001). *A brief history of everything*. Boston: Shambhala.

Wilber, K. (2005). Foreword. In M. Schlitz & T. Hyman, (Eds.). *Consciousness and healing*. St. Louis, MO: Elsevier Churchill Livingstone.

Beyond Monogamy and Polyamory:
A New Vision of Intimate Relationships for the Twenty-First Century

Jorge N. Ferrer

In Buddhism, sympathetic joy (*mudita*) is regarded as one of the "four immeasurable states" (*brahmaviharas*) or qualities of an enlightened person—the other three being loving kindness (*metta*), compassion (*karuna*), and equanimity (*upeksha*). Sympathetic joy refers to the human capability to participate in the joy of others, to feel happy when others feel happy. Although with different emphases, such understanding can also be found in the contemplative teachings of many other religious traditions such as the Kabbalah, Christianity, or Sufism, which in their respective languages talk about empathic joy, for example, in terms of opening the "eye of the heart." According to these and other traditions, the cultivation of sympathetic joy can break through the ultimately false duality between self and others, being therefore a potent aid on the path toward overcoming self-centeredness and achieving liberation.

Though the ultimate aim of many religious practices is to develop sympathetic joy for all sentient beings, intimate relationships offer human beings—whether they are spiritual practitioners or not—a precious opportunity to taste its experiential flavor. Most psychologically balanced individuals naturally share to some degree in the happiness of their mates. Bliss and delight can effortlessly emerge within us as we feel the joy of our partner's

Jorge N. Ferrer, Ph.D., is Chair of the Department of East-West Psychology at the California Institute of Integral Studies (CIIS), San Francisco. He is the author of *Revisioning Transpersonal Theory: A Participatory Vision of Human Spirituality* (SUNY Press, 2002) and co-editor of *The Participatory Turn: Spirituality, Mysticism, Religious Studies* (SUNY Press, 2008). He is the editor of the *ReVision* monograph "New Horizons in Contemporary Spirituality." He has explored integral approaches to education and transformation at CIIS, the Institute of Transpersonal Psychology, the Esalen Institute, and, more recently, Auroville, India. He can be contacted at jferrer@ciis.edu.

ecstatic dance, enjoyment of an art performance, relishing of a favorite dish, or serene contemplation of a splendid sunset. And this innate capacity for sympathetic joy in intimate relationships often reaches its peak in deeply emotional shared experiences, sensual exchange, and lovemaking. When we are in love, the embodied joy of our beloved becomes extremely contagious.

Jealousy in Monogamous Relationships

But what if our partner's sensuous or emotional joy were to arise in relation not to us but to someone else? For the vast majority of people, the immediate reaction would likely be not one of expansive openness and love, but rather of contracting fear, anger, and perhaps even violent rage. The change of a single variable has rapidly turned the selfless contentment of sympathetic joy into the "green-eyed monster" of jealousy, as Shakespeare called this compulsive emotion.

Perhaps due to its prevalence, jealousy is widely accepted as "normal" in most cultures, and many of its violent consequences have often been regarded as understandable, morally justified, and even legally permissible. (It is worth remembering that as late as the 1970s the law of states such as Texas, Utah, and New Mexico considered "reasonable" the homicide of one's adulterous partner if it happened at the scene of discovery!). Though there are circumstances in which the mindful expression of rightful anger (not violence) may be a temporary appropriate response—for example, in the case of the adulterous breaking of monogamous vows—jealousy frequently makes its appearance in interpersonal situations where no betrayal has taken place or when we rationally know that no real threat actually exists (for example, watching our partner's sensuous dance with an attractive person at a party). In general, the awakening of sympathetic joy in observing the hap-

piness of one's mate in relationship with perceived "rivals" is an extremely rare pearl to find. In the context of romantic relationships, jealousy functions as a hindrance to sympathetic joy.

What are the roots of this widespread difficulty in experiencing sympathetic joy in the arenas of sexuality and sensuous experience? What is ultimately lurking behind such an apparently defiled behavior as jealousy? Can jealousy be transformed through a fuller embodiment of sympathetic joy in our intimate relationships? What emotional response can take the place of jealousy? And what are the implications of transforming jealousy for our spiritually informed relationship choices? To begin exploring these questions, we need to turn to the discoveries of modern evolutionary psychology.

Evolutionary Map of Jealousy

The evolutionary origins and function of jealousy have been clearly mapped by contemporary evolutionary psychologists, anthropologists, and zoologists. Despite its tragic impact in the modern world—the overwhelming majority of mate battering and spousal murders worldwide is caused by jealous violence—jealousy very likely emerged around 3.5 million years ago in our hominid ancestors as an adaptive response of vital evolutionary value for both genders. Whereas the reproductive payoff of jealousy for males was to secure certainty of paternity and to avoid spending resources in support of another male's genetic offspring, for females it evolved as a mechanism for guaranteeing protection and resources for biological children by having a steady partner. In short, jealousy emerged in our ancestral past to protect males from being cuckolded and to protect women from being abandoned. This is why even today men tend to experience more intense feelings of jealousy than women do when they suspect sexual infidelity, while women are more likely than men to feel threatened when their mates become emotionally attached to another female and spend time and money with her. Modern research shows that this "evolutionary logic" in relation to gender-specific jealousy patterns operates widely across disparate cultures and countries, from Sweden to China and from North America and the Netherlands to Japan and Korea.

The problem, of course, is that many instinctive reactions that had evolutionary significance in ancestral times do not make much sense in our modern world. There are today many single mothers, for example, who do not need or want financial—or even emotional—support from their children's fathers, yet still feel jealous when their ex-partners pay attention to other women. And most contemporary men and women suffer from jealousy independent of whether they want children or plan to have them with their partners. As evolutionary psychologist

sensitive defense mechanism against the genetically disastrous possibility of having one's partner stray from monogamy. In the ancestral savannah, it was as imperative for females to secure a stable partner who would provide food and protect their children from predators as it was for males to make sure they were not investing their time and energy in someone else's progeny. Put simply, from an evolutionary standpoint the main purpose of both monogamy and jealousy is to provide for the dissemination of one's DNA.

In a context of spiritual aspiration aimed at the gradual uncovering and transformation of increasingly subtle forms of self-centeredness, we can perhaps recognize that jealousy ultimately serves a biologically engrained form of egotism which we may call "genetic selfishness"—not to be confused with Richard Dawkins' "selfish gene" theory, which reduces human beings to the status of survival ma-

humanely understandable and morally justifiable to favor the survival of one's own progeny over that of others? But, we may want to ponder, was the officer's decision the most enlightened action to take? What if by saving our only child we were condemning to death three or four children from another person? Should numbers be of any significance in these decisions? What course of action is most aligned with universal compassion in these admittedly extreme situations? Any effort to reach a generalized answer to these questions is likely misguided; each concrete situation requires careful examination within its context and from a variety of perspectives and ways of knowing. My aim in raising these questions is not to offer solutions, but merely to convey how tacitly genetic selfishness is embedded as "second nature" in the human condition.

Transforming Jealousy into Sympathetic Joy

The discussion of the twin evolutionary origins of jealousy and monogamy raises further questions: Can jealousy be truly transformed? What emotional response can take the place of jealousy in human experience? And how can the transformation of jealousy affect our relationship choices?

To my knowledge, in contrast to most other emotional states, jealousy has no antonym in any human language. This is probably why the Kerista community—a polygamous group located in San Francisco that was disbanded in the early 1990s—coined the term "compersion" to refer to the emotional response opposite to jealousy. The Keristas defined compersion as "the feeling of taking joy in the joy that others you love share among themselves." Since the term emerged in the context of the practice of "polyfidelity" (faithfulness to many), sensuous and sexual joy were included, but compersion was only cultivated when a person had loving bonds with all parties involved. However, the feeling of compersion can also be extended to any situation in which our mate feels emotional/sensuous joy with others in wholesome and constructive ways. In these situations, we can rejoice in our partner's joy even if we do not know the third parties. Experientially, compersion can be felt as a tangible presence in the heart whose awakening

> The cultivation of sympathetic joy can break through the ultimately false duality between self and others, being therefore a potent aid on the path toward overcoming self-centeredness and achieving liberation.

David Buss puts it in his acclaimed *The Evolution of Desire*, most human mating mechanisms and responses are actually "living fossils" shaped by the genetic pressures of our evolutionary history.

Our Genetic Instincts

Interestingly, the genetic roots of jealousy are precisely the same as those behind the desire for sexual exclusivity (or possessiveness) that we have come to call "monogamy." In contrast to conventional use, however, the term "monogamy" simply means "one spouse" and does not necessarily entail sexual fidelity. In any event, whereas jealousy is not exclusive to monogamous bonds (swingers and polyamorous people also feel jealous), the origins of jealousy and monogamy are intimately connected in our primeval past. Indeed, evolutionary psychology tells us, jealousy emerged as a hyper-

chines at the service of gene replication. Genetic selfishness is so archaic, pandemic, and deeply seated in human nature that it invariably goes unnoticed in contemporary culture and spiritual circles. An example may help to reveal the elusive nature of genetic selfishness. In the movie *Cinderella Man*, an officer from the electric company is about to cut off the power of the residence of three children who will very likely die without heat—it is winter in New York at the time of the Great Depression. When the children's mother appeals to the compassion of the officer, begging him not to cut off the power, he responds that his own children will suffer the same fate if he does not do his job. As I looked around the theater, I noted a large number of people in the audience nodding their heads in poignant understanding. We can all empathize with the officer's stance. After all, who would not do the same in similar circumstances? Is it not both may be accompanied by waves of warmth, pleasure, and appreciation at the idea of our partner loving others and being loved by them in nonharmful and mutually beneficial ways. In this light, I suggest that compersion can be seen as a novel extension of sympathetic joy to the realm of intimate relationships and, in particular, to interpersonal situations that conventionally evoke feelings of jealousy.

The reader acquainted with Vajrayana Buddhism may wonder whether such extension is novel at all. Has not the transformation of jealousy into sympathetic joy been described in the tantric literature? Well, yes and no. In Vajrayana Buddhism, jealousy is considered an imperfection (klesha) associated with attachment and self-centeredness that is transmuted into sympathetic joy, equanimity, and wisdom by the power of the Lord of Karma, Amoghasiddhi, one of the Five Dhyani Buddhas (Buddhas we visualize in meditation). From the green body of Amoghasiddhi emanates his consort, the goddess Green Tara, who is said to also have the power of turning jealousy into the ability to dwell in the happiness of others.

At first sight, it may look as if the green gods and goddesses of the Buddhist pantheon have defeated the green-eyed monster of jealousy. Upon closer inspection, however, it becomes apparent that this perception needs correction. The problem is that the Buddhist terms translated as "jealousy"—such as issa (Pali), phrag dog (Tibetan), or irshya (Sanskrit)—are more accurately read as "envy." In the various Buddhist descriptions of "jealousy" we generally find illustrations of bitterness and resentment at the happiness, talents, or good fortune of others, but very rarely, if ever, of contracting fear and anger in response to a mate's sexual or emotional connection to others. In the Abhidhamma, for example, jealousy (issa) is considered an immoral mental state characterized by feelings of ill will at the success and prosperity of others. The description of the "jealous gods" realm (asura-loka) also supports this assertion. Though commonly called "jealous," the asuras are said to be envious of the gods of the heaven realm (devas) and possessed by feelings of ambition, hatred, and paranoia.

Discussing the samsaric mandala, Chögyam Trungpa writes in Orderly Chaos, "It is not exactly jealousy; we do not seem to have the proper term in the English language. It is a paranoid attitude of comparison rather than purely jealousy . . . a sense of competition." As should be obvious, all these descriptions refer to "envy," which the Oxford English Dictionary defines as "To feel displeasure and ill-will at the superiority of (another person) in happiness, success, reputation, or the possession of anything desirable," and not to jealousy, which is a response to the real or imagined threat of losing one's partner or valued relationship to a third party. Since Buddhist teachings about jealousy were originally aimed at monks who were not supposed to develop emotional attachments (even those who engaged in tantric sexual acts), the lack of systematic reflection in Buddhism upon romantic jealousy should not come as a surprise.

Let us explore now the implications of transforming jealousy for our intimate relationships. I suggest that the transformation of jealousy through the cultivation of sympathetic joy bolsters the awakening of the enlightened heart. As jealousy dissolves, universal compassion and unconditional love become more easily available to the individual. Human compassion is universal in its embrace of all sentient beings without qualifications. Human love is also all-inclusive and unconditional—a love that is both free from the tendency to possess and that does not expect anything in return. Although to love without conditions is generally easier in the case of brotherly and spiritual love, I suggest that as we heal the historical split between spiritual love (agape) and sensuous love (eros), the extension of sympathetic joy to more embodied forms of love becomes a natural development. And when embodied love is emancipated from possessiveness, a richer range of spiritually legitimate relationship options organically emerges. As people become more whole and are freed from certain basic fears (e.g., of abandonment, of unworthiness, of engulfment), new possibilities for the expression of embodied love open up which may feel natural, safe, and wholesome rather than undesirable, threatening, or even morally questionable. For example, once jealousy turns into sympathetic joy and sensuous and spiritual love are integrated, a couple may feel drawn to extend their love to other individuals beyond the structure of the pair bond. In short, once jealousy loosens its grip on the contemporary self, human love can attain a wider dimension of embodiment in our lives that may naturally lead to the mindful cultivation of more inclusive intimate connections.

Social Monogamy as a Mask for Biological Polyamory

Even if mindful and open, the inclusion of other loving connections in the context of a partnership can elicit the two classic objections to nonmonogamy (or polyamory): First, it does not work in practice, and second, it leads to the destruction of relationships. (I am leaving aside here the deeply engrained moral opposition to the very idea of polyamory associated with the legacy of Christianity in the West.) As for the first objection, though polygyny ("many wives") is still culturally prevalent on the globe—out of 853 known human cultures, 84 percent permit polygyny—it seems undeniable that with a few exceptions modern attempts at more gender-egalitarian open relationships have not been very successful. Nevertheless, the same could be said about monogamy. After all, the history of monogamy is the history of adultery. As H. H. Munro wrote, monogamy is "the Western custom of one wife and hardly any mistresses." Summing up the available evidence, David Buss estimates that "approximately 20 to 40 percent of American women and 30 to 50 percent of American men have at least one affair over the course of the marriage," and recent surveys suggest that the chance of either member of a modern couple committing infidelity at some point in their marriage may be as high as 76 percent—with these numbers increasing every year. Though most people in our culture consider themselves—and are believed to be—monogamous, anonymous surveys reveal that many are so socially but not biologically.

In other words, social monogamy frequently masks biological polyamory in an increasingly significant number of couples. In her Anatomy of Love, prominent anthropologist Helen Fisher suggests that the human desire for clandestine extramarital sex is genetically grounded in the evolutionary advantages that having other mates provided for both genders in ancestral times: extra opportunities to spread

DNA for males, and extra protection and resources plus the acquisition of potentially better sperm for females. It may also be important to note that the prevalent relationship paradigm in the modern West is no longer lifelong monogamy ("till death do us part") but serial monogamy (many partners sequentially), often punctuated with adultery. Serial monogamy plus clandestine adultery is in many respects not too different from polyamory, except perhaps in that the latter is more honest, ethical, and arguably less harmful. In this context, the mindful exploration of polyamory (i.e., practiced with the full knowledge and approval of all concerned) may help alleviating the suffering caused by the staggering number of clandestine affairs in our modern culture.

Furthermore, to disregard a potentially emancipatory cultural development because its early manifestations did not succeed may be unwise. Looking back at the history of emancipatory movements in the West—from feminism to the abolition of slavery to the gaining of civil rights by African-Americans—we can see that the first waves of the Promethean impulse were frequently burdened with problems and distortions which only later could be recognized and resolved. This is not the place to review this historical evidence, but to dismiss polyamory because of its previous failures may be equivalent to having written off feminism on the grounds that its first waves failed to reclaim genuine feminine values or free women from patriarchy (e.g., turning women into masculinized "super-women" capable of succeeding in a patriarchal world).

Polyamory as a Path toward Emotional and Spiritual Depth

But wait a moment. Dyadic relationships are already challenging enough. Why complicate them further by adding extra parties to the equation? Response: From a spiritual standpoint, an intimate relationship can be viewed as a structure through which human beings can learn to express and receive love in many forms. Although I would hesitate to declare polyamory more spiritual or evolved than monogamy, it is clear that if a person has not mastered the lessons and challenges of the dyadic structure he or she may not be ready to take on the challenges of more

complex forms of relationships. Therefore, the objection of impracticability may be valid in many cases.

The second common objection to polyamory is that it results in the dissolution of pair bonds. The rationale is that the intimate contact with others will increase the chances that one member of the couple will abandon the other and run off with a more appealing mate. This concern is understandable, but the fact is that people are having affairs, falling in love, and leaving their partners all the time in the context of monogamous vows. As we have seen, adultery goes hand in hand with monogamy, and lifelong monogamy has been mostly replaced with serial monogamy (or sequential polyamory) in our culture. Parenthetically, vows of lifelong monogamy create often-unrealistic expectations that add suffering to the pain involved in the termination of any relationship—and one could also raise questions about the wholesomeness of the psychological needs for certainty and security that such vows normally meet. In any event, although it may sound counterintuitive at first, the threat of abandonment may be actually reduced in polyamory, since the loving bond that our partner may develop with another person does not necessarily mean that he or she must choose between them or us (or lie to us).

More positively, the new qualities and passions that novel intimate connections can awaken within a person can also bring a renewed sense of creative dynamism to the sexual/emotional life of the couple, whose frequent stagnation after three or four years (seven in some cases) is the chief cause of clandestine affairs and separation. As recent surveys show, the number of couples who successfully navigate the so-called four- and seven-year itches is decreasing every year. Mindful polyamory may also offer an alternative to the usually unfulfilling nature of currently prevalent serial monogamy in which people change partners every few years, never benefiting from the emotional and spiritual depth that only an enduring connection with another human being provides. In a context of psychospiritual growth, such exploration can create unique opportunities for the development of emotional maturity, the transmutation of jealousy into sympathetic joy, the emancipation of embodied love from exclusivity and pos-

sessiveness, and the integration of sensuous and spiritual love. As Christian mystic Richard of St. Victor maintained, mature love between lover and beloved naturally reaches beyond itself toward a third reality, and this opening, I suggest, might in some cases be crucial both to overcome codependent tendencies and to foster the health, creative vitality, and perhaps even longevity of intimate relationships.

I should stress that my intent is not to argue for the superiority of any relationship style over others—a discussion I find both pointless and misleading. Human beings are endowed with widely diverse biological, psychological, and spiritual dispositions that predispose them toward different relationship styles: celibacy, monogamy, serial monogamy, or polyamory. In other words, many equally valid psychospiritual trajectories may call individuals to engage in one or another relationship style either for life or at specific junctures in their paths. Whereas the psychospiritual foundation for this diversity of mating responses cannot be empirically established, recent discoveries in neuroscience support the idea of a genetic base. When scientists inserted a piece of DNA from a monogamous species of mice (prairie voles) into males from a different—and highly promiscuous—mice species, the latter turned fervently monogamous. What is more striking is that some people carry an extra bit of DNA in a gene responsible for the distribution of vasopressin receptors in the brain (a hormone associated with attachment bonds), while others do not, and that piece of DNA is very similar to the one found in the monogamous prairie voles. Although the implications of this finding for our understanding of human mating await further clarification, it strongly suggests that a diversity of relationship styles—both monogamous and polyamorous—may be genetically imprinted in humans.

Religious Decree on Sexual Behavior

I address the objections to polyamory because lifelong or serial monogamy (together with celibacy) are still widely considered the only or most "spiritually correct" relationship styles in the modern West. In addition to the traditional Christian prescription of lifelong monogamy, many influential contemporary Buddhist teachers in the

West make similar recommendations. Consider, for example, Thich Nhat Hanh's reading of the Buddhist precept of "refraining from sexual misconduct." Originally, this precept meant, for the monks, to avoid engaging in any sexual act whatsoever and, for lay people, to not engage in a list of "inappropriate" sexual behaviors having to do with specific body parts, times, and places. In *For a Future to Be Possible*, Thich Nhat Hanh explains that the monks of his order follow the traditional celibate vow in order to use sexual energy as a catalyst for spiritual breakthrough. For lay practitioners, however, Thich Nhat Hanh reads the precept to mean avoiding all sexual contact unless it takes place in the context of a "long-term commitment between two people," because there is an incompatibility between love and casual sex (monogamous marriage is a common practice for lay people in his order). In this reading, Thich Nhat Hanh reinterprets the Buddhist precept as a prescription for long-term monogamy, excluding the possibility of not only wholesome polyamorous relations, but also spiritually edifying intimate encounters. (It is important to note, however, that "long-term commitment" is not equivalent to "monogamy," since it is perfectly feasible to hold a long-term commitment with more than one intimate partner.) In *The Art of Happiness*, the Dalai Lama also assumes a monogamous structure as the container for appropriate sex in intimate relationships. Since reproduction is the biological purpose of sexual relations, he tells us, long-term commitment and sexual exclusivity are desirable for the wholesomeness of love relationships.

Despite the great respect I feel for these and other Buddhist teachers who speak in similar fashion, I must confess my perplexity. These assessments of appropriate sexual expression, which have become influential guidelines for many contemporary Western Buddhists, are often offered by celibate individuals whose sexual experience is likely to be limited, if not nonexistent. If there is anything we have learned from developmental psychology, it is that an individual needs to perform a number of "developmental tasks" to gain competence (and wisdom) in various arenas: cognitive, emotional, sexual, and so forth. Even when offered with the best of intentions, advice of-

fered about aspects of life in which one has not achieved developmental competence through direct experience may be both questionable and misleading. When this advice is given by figures culturally venerated as spiritual authorities, the situation can become even more problematic. What is more, in the context of spiritual praxis, these assertions can arguably be seen as incongruent with the emphasis on direct knowledge characteristic of Buddhism.

It may be worth remembering that the Buddha himself encouraged polyamory over monogamy in certain situations. In the *Jataka 200* (stories of Buddha's former births), a Brahmin asks the Buddha for advice regarding four suitors who are courting his four daughters. The Brahmin says, "One was fine and handsome, one was old and well advanced in years, the third a man of family [noble birth], and the fourth was good." "Even though there be beauty and the like qualities," the Buddha answered, "a man is to be despised if he fails in virtue. Therefore the former is not the measure of a man; those that I like are the virtuous." After hearing this, the Brahmin gave all his daughters to the virtuous suitor.

As the Buddha's advice illustrates, several forms of relationship may be spiritually wholesome (in the Buddhist sense of leading to liberation) according to various human dispositions and contextual situations. Historically, Buddhism hardly ever considered one relationship style intrinsically more wholesome than others for lay people and tended to support different relationship styles depending on cultural and karmic factors. From the Buddhist perspective of skillful means (*upaya*) and of the soteriological nature of Buddhist ethics, it also follows that the key factor in evaluating the appropriateness of any intimate connection may not be its form but rather its power to eradicate the suffering of self and others. There is much to learn today, I believe, from the nondogmatic and pragmatic approach of historical Buddhism to intimate relationships—an approach that was not attached to any specific relationship structure but was essentially guided by a radical emphasis on liberation.

As is well known, Judaism permitted and even encouraged polygyny ("many wives") for centuries until Rabbeinu Gershom (c. 960-1028) enacted an edict against marrying more

than one wife, unless allowed on special grounds by at least 100 rabbis from three different countries. Interestingly, Rav Yaakov Emden explains, the reason for the ban was not moral or spiritual, but social. The edict was a reaction to the danger that having more than one wife could bring to the Jews in a Europe increasingly dominated by Christianity, which had been trying to abolish polygamy from about 600CE to 900CE. In short, the purpose of the edict was to protect the Jewish people from being attacked or even killed by resentful Christian fundamentalists. Furthermore, according to most authorities, the ban was supposed to have validity only until the end of the fifth millennium of the Jewish calendar, so it never actually had the force of an edict (*cherem*) after the year 1240CE, though it continued as a custom in many places. (Originally, the prohibition was also limited geographically to certain European countries and regions.) If the Torah and the Biblical law permitted polyamory, if the rationale for the prohibition was contextual, and if the validity of the edict was supposed to last only until the year 1240CE, then the current observance of the Cherem Rabbeinu Gershom seems unjustified. Of course, in light of the modern reconstruction of Judaism carried out by Rabbi Michael Lerner and others (see Lerner's *The Jewish Renewal*), contemporary Jews may regard the traditional endorsement of polygyny and prohibition of polyandry ("many husbands") as a "sexist" trend of ancient Judaism and, consequently, may want to creatively explore more egalitarian forms of polyamory.

For a variety of evolutionary and historical reasons, polyamory has "bad press" in Western culture and spiritual circles—being automatically linked, for example, with promiscuity, irresponsibility, inability to commit, and even narcissistic hedonism. Given the current crisis of monogamy in our culture, however, it may be valuable to explore seriously the social potential of responsible forms of nonmonogamy. And given the spiritual potential of such exploration, it may also be important to expand the range of spiritually legitimate relationship choices that we as individuals can make at the various karmic crossroads of our lives.

Beyond Monogamy and Polyamory

It is my hope that this essay opens avenues for dialogue and inquiry in spiritual circles about the transformation of intimate relationships. It is also my hope that it contributes to the extension of spiritual virtues, such as sympathetic joy, to all areas of life and in particular to those which, due to historical, cultural, and perhaps evolutionary reasons, have been traditionally excluded or overlooked—areas such as sexuality and romantic love.

The culturally prevalent belief—supported by many contemporary spiritual teachers—that the only spiritually correct sexual options are either celibacy or monogamy is a myth that may be causing unnecessary suffering and that needs, therefore, to be laid to rest. It may be perfectly plausible to hold simultaneously more than one loving or sexual bond in a context of mindfulness, ethical integrity, and spiritual growth, for example, while working toward the transformation of jealousy into sympathetic joy and the integration of sensuous and spiritual love. I should add right away that, ultimately, I believe that the greatest expression of spiritual freedom in intimate relationships does not lie in strictly sticking to any particular relationship style—whether monogamous or polyamorous—but rather in a radical openness to the dynamic unfolding of life that eludes any fixed or predetermined structure of relationships. It should be obvious, for example, that one can follow a specific relationship style for the "right" (e.g., life-enhancing) or "wrong" (e.g., fear-based) reasons; that all relationship styles can become equally limiting spiritual ideologies; and that different internal and external conditions may rightfully call us to engage in different relationship styles at various junctures of our lives. It is in this open space catalyzed by the movement beyond monogamy and polyamory, I believe, that an existential stance deeply attuned to the standpoint of Spirit can truly emerge.

Nevertheless, gaining awareness about the ancestral—and mostly obsolete—nature of the evolutionary impulses that direct our sexual/emotional responses and relationship choices may empower us to consciously co-create a future in which expanded forms of spiritual freedom may have a greater chance to bloom. Who knows, perhaps as we extend spiritual practice to intimate relationships, new petals of liberation will blossom that may not only emancipate our minds, hearts, and consciousness, but also our bodies and instinctive world. Can we envision an "integral *bodhisattva* vow" in which the conscious mind renounces full liberation until the body and the primary world can be free as well?

REFERENCES

Barush, D. P., & Lipton, J. E. (2001). *The Myth of Monogamy: Fidelity and Infidelity in Animals and People.* New York: Henry Holt and Company.

Buss, D. (1994). *The Evolution of Desire: Strategies of Human Mating.* New York: Basic Books.

Buss, D. (2000). *The Dangerous Passion: Why Jealousy Is as Necessary as Love or Sex.* New York: Free Press.

Fisher, H. (1994). *Anatomy of Love: A Natural History of Mating, Marriage, and Why We Stray.* New York: Ballantine.

Fisher, H. (2004). *Why We Love: The Nature and Chemistry of Romantic Love.* New York: Henry Holt & Co.

HAIKU

silently
on the pond
migrating geese

morning fog--
framed by the window
a world of nothing-at-all

Autumn morning
the daylily offers
one last blossom

through the flutter
of yellow leaves
falling walnuts

cracked milkweed pod-
above the drifting fluff
a raven calls

-- Michael Sheffield

Art by Mariana Castro de Ali

Children with Knives: When Theory Becomes Ideology

Karen Ann Watson-Gegeo

all photographs by Karen Ann Watson-Gegeo

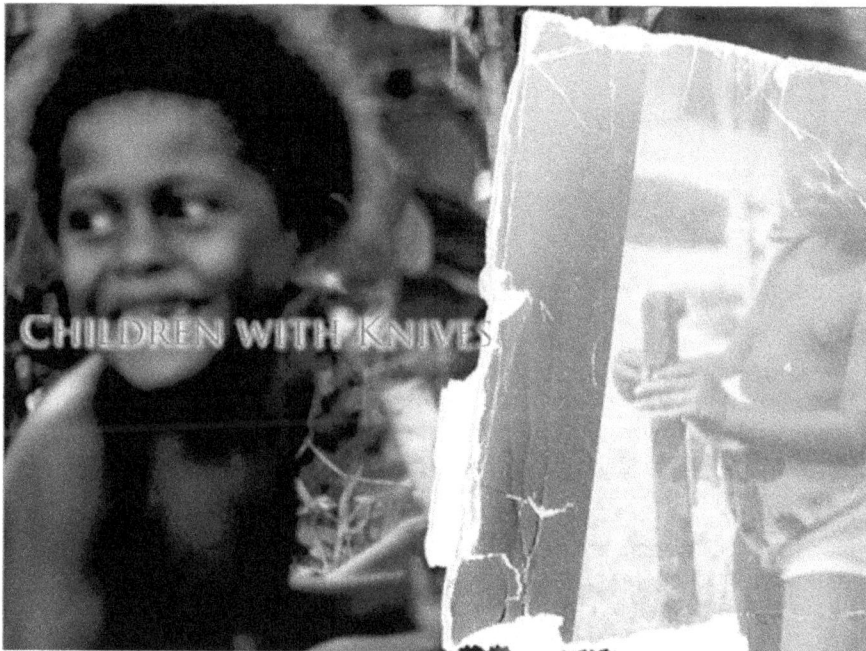

In a special double issue of ReVision titled "Revisioning Higher Education" (Bronson, 2005, 2006), the authors questioned conventional assumptions about teaching, learning, and interpersonal relationships in colleges and universities. They argued for the importance of incorporating the whole human being, including spirituality, into higher education, drawing on their own teaching and curricular experiences (e.g., Grand, 2005; Wexler, 2005). The rich and varied discussion was a follow-on to previous ReVision issues concerned with the nature of wisdom and knowledge. In the double issue on higher education, my contribution was to examine the 'dark side of

Karen Ann Watson-Gegeo is an anthropologist, poet, and professor of language, literacy and culture, School of Education, University of California, Davis. She taught for several years at Harvard University and the University of Hawai'i. Her research on language learning, indigenous epistemology, and community development has been in rural and urban areas of Hawai'i and Solomon Islands.

being professional,' critiquing the way that 'professionalism' can be used (for instance) to mystify epistemic processes, and cover hostilities with surface politeness. In this article[1], I extend the discussion in another direction: the

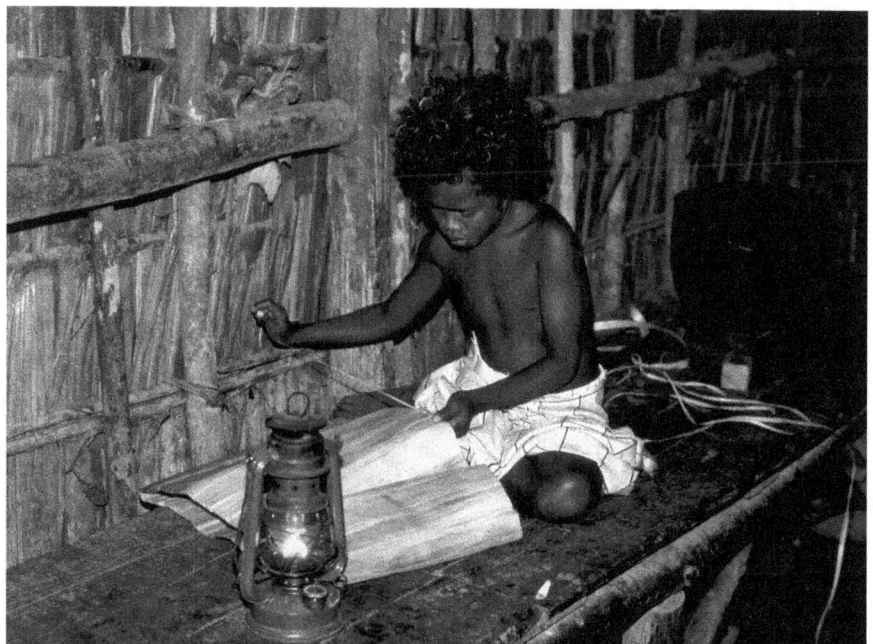

way in which knowledge construction can be sabotaged when theory becomes ideology. My particular focus is the jockeying for position, fame, and influence in academic politics. The presumed neutrality of Western theory-construction and research methodologies is compromised by academic politics far more often than scholars admit. Such compromising threatens the integrity of academe as a center for knowledge construction.

We first need to acknowledge that epistemological arguments can readily become ideological arguments, because despite the methodological claims of value neutrality by positivistic Western science, no knowledge construction is politically or ideologically neutral. This point has been repeatedly and convincingly made by philosophers of science (Habermas, 1971; Kaplan, 1964) at least as far back as the 1960s, and more recently by feminist standpoint theorists (Alcoff & Potter, 1993; Harding, 1993; Yeatman, 1994) and indigenous scholars (e.g., Gegeo, 1994; Gegeo & Watson-Gegeo, 2001, 2002; Meyer, 1998; Sinha, 1997; Smith, 1999) writ-

ing about indigenous epistemologies. Nevertheless, academic researchers – who live by 'publish or perish' in the so-called 'tier one' universities – have been hesitant to fully embrace the idea that their research strategies are not politically and ideologically neutral, and that their assumptions often spring from deeply held epistemological assumptions that are tied to social class, race, ethnicity, culture, and gender. Equally problematic, interpersonal politics and power concerns are always operating in what is going on in theory construction and validation in an academic discipline. The step from justified disagreement to ideological enforcement may be a small one where there is a power differential between different 'sides' of a debate or discussion.

In this article, then, I examine three occasions in my career, beginning in graduate school, when 'theory as ideology' became especially salient for me as a participant in epistemological encounters that were potentially damaging to my career. I reflect on what I have come to understand about them over time.

On choosing unwisely

As a working-class child speaking a non-standard variety of English, my early life experiences radicalized me. When I entered a Ph.D. program in anthropology, I was committed to research and activism for social justice and the transformation of conscious-

ness. My entering statement of purpose was to study myth and symbolism, and I was assured by the department chair that they had a program on myth waiting for me. So imagine my surprise when I arrived on campus to discover that the fellowship I'd been given tied me to a 4-year training program in psychological anthropology, with an emphasis on conventional child development. The faculty were highly conservative and seriously into academic politics. For me as for many others, graduate school was my first exposure to theory as ideology.

Threatened by the faculty that they would terminate my fellowship, I nevertheless resisted what I felt to be indoctrination into mainstream human

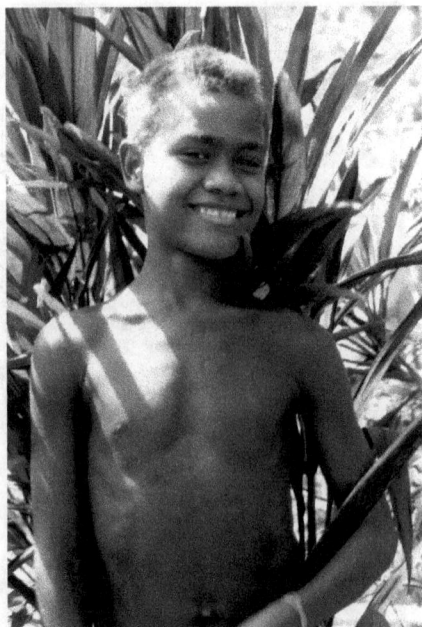

development theory. The great scholar Gregory Bateson, who I so admired, took me on as his graduate student. Although I fully enjoyed my academic work, I was also eager to do something of use in the local community while going to school. The opportunity came when a visiting professor from the Mainland invited me to volunteer as a classroom aide at an elementary school attended by Native Hawaiian homestead children in rural 'Oahu, where he was doing research. But once in the classrooms, I was horrified by the gap between how the teachers judged the abilities of Native Hawaiian children, and what I saw of their abilities outside teacher awareness. In my third year of graduate school, I told Gregory that I had already begun doing ethnographic research in the classroom where I was an aide. Deeply committed to these children, I said that I was going to write my dissertation on their talk story oral discourse, with the intent of showing the high-level linguistic and reasoning skills these children had developed in their first language, Hawai'i Creole English (typically referred to as "Pidgin" in Hawai'i). At the time, as Gregory and I both knew, Native Hawaiian creole-speaking children were represented in educational research and by the state department of education as cognitively and culturally deficient. I hoped my study would contribute to improving education for these children, because so many were failing school.

To my shock, Gregory said to me disdainfully, "That's a waste of your time! There's nothing meaningful there for theory!" He went on to say that if I came to my senses and changed my topic, he might still chair or be a member of my dissertation committee. That was the end of my relationship with Gregory. My dissertation did turn out to be significant for the education of Hawaiian children (Au & Jordan, 1981; Boggs, 1985) and for theory in oral narration and child discourse (Watson, 1973, 1975; Watson-Gegeo & Boggs, 1977). My study was one of several on discourse abilities of ethnic minority children at that time, countering the 'culture of deficit' interpretation of sociolinguistic differences between middle-class and poor children. On the basis of my dissertation, I was offered a 'revolving door' (seven years and out) faculty position at Harvard Graduate School of Education, which I took

in the fall of 1977. Interestingly, though, several anthropologists were dismayed that I had taken my first faculty job in an applied field, warning me that when I began looking for a tenure-track position, it had better not be in education. "Don't take a job in an applied field again, it is the kiss of death to your anthropological career," was a common sentiment.

Reflecting on what happened, I realized that as a multi-disciplinary graduate student who found it easy to integrate theories from multiple sources, I had not yet realized the strong bias against that sort of 'mixing.' In fact, members of academic disciplines patrol the boundaries and make judgments as to whether a given person is properly thinking 'inside' versus 'outside' the boundaries, and then they intervene with corrective action as needed. I began to see that not only is theory construction and loyalty to a body of theory ideological, but so are disciplines themselves. Even today when much more cross-disciplinary sharing of shrinking resources brings academic departments into alliances, those boundaries are often being patrolled. New faculty who are hired in joint positions crossing two departments may find this to be true when it comes time for them to go up for tenure. Finally, for academic anthropology of the time, my dissertation study represented 'wrong' choices in several ways. First, I was working with children, not adults – children are not the powerful in a

society, the study of children is typically a 'female' focus, and women as well as children are relatively less powerful than men. Second, narrative theory was important in the humanities, but not yet in the social sciences at that time. Gregory expected me to focus on communication theory, systems theory, cybernetics, or another of the 'in' theories of his interest. Third, schools, perhaps because they are associated with women and children, are the least respected among social institutions when it comes to theory and research. Fourth, applied work has historically been second-class work in the social sciences because it involves 'practice' rather than (or more than) 'theory.'

On being a romantic

Once I found narrative theory and discourse analysis, I never expected to return to child development theory. Three years out of graduate school, however, I met David Welchman Gegeo from Kwara'ae (Solomon Islands), and we married. Shortly after, on the basis of my Hawaiian research, as mentioned above, I accepted a junior faculty position at Harvard Graduate School of Education, and David and I began research in Kwara'ae. From the late 1970s through the 1990s, my energy was directed toward holding on to and building a career while holding out for a more realistic, honest, and 'true' representation of children and adults

against prevailing academic ideologies in human and community development.

When we began research on Kwara'ae children's language socialization (LS), the work of Soviet psychologist Lev Vygotsky (1978, 1981) was just starting to be embraced in human development and education. Neo-Vygotskyian theory was welcome to David and me because so many of Vygotsky's postulates are similar to Kwara'ae beliefs about learning. Vygotsky argued, for instance, that children's cognitive skills develop through social interaction with adults and children who are more competent than they, and especially through talk. Kwara'ae adults believe the same thing, and interact almost continuously with infants and young children through a well-defined set of discourse routines in various degrees of difficulty intended to meet and accelerate the child's linguistic and cultural skills. When David and I moved back to Hawai'i in 1986, I was already a member of a multidisciplinary, feminist Vygotsky research group at the university, where I was now teaching. A prominent senior scholar in child development from the Mainland, who I will call Vivian, was advising us before our third major conference presentation, at the American Educational Research Association in 1989.

Our panel on extending Neo-Vygotskian theory attracted a very large audience, among whom were psychologists, educators, anthropologists, and several leading Vygotskian theorists. We offered a critique of Neo-Vygotskian theory as too narrow in its conception of children's learning, including the notions of 'cognitive apprenticeship' and 'scaffolding,' neither of which are concepts in Vygotsky's own writings. We argued that 'cognitive apprenticeship' as it was being conceptualized was becoming stage-oriented and rigid, losing the fluidity and flexibility of Vygotsky's original ideas, and increasingly resembling mainstream child development theory, which is stage-based.

Part of my presentation critiqued Leont'ev's (1981) 'leading activities' assumptions. Leont'ev claimed that children learn through a chronologically invariant sequence of three leading activities – first, play; then school; and finally work, in late teenage or early adulthood. In contrast, Kwara'ae children are pushed to be adult as soon as possible. At age 3 years, children are given bush knives (machetes), have many work responsibilities including subsistence gardening and caregiving younger siblings, are taught through both informal and formal discourse registers of the language, and begin to command features of high-level argumentation and logical reasoning. To help themselves accomplish all this, children take on *adult mode* style of embodiment (Watson-Gegeo, 2001) – interactional routines and positioning through which they anticipatorily assume and perform the role and behavior of adults. I concluded that Leont'ev's developmental sequence for leading activities is not universal. For Kwara'ae children and others in subsistence life-worlds, play and work are first and simultaneous, and school comes after. Some years later, Leont'ev withdrew his fixed sequence, and there have been much deeper critiques of Neo-Vygotskian theory since then.

That afternoon the reception to our panel and my presentation was mixed, and Vivian said nothing to me. That night at my hotel room, I received a telephone call from a respected psycholinguist and good friend of Vivian. She said that Vivian had criticized my work to her and other important scholars around her at the session. Vivian's lines that I will never forget were, "Karen is a romantic. Three-year-olds can't do the tasks she says they can. It is beyond their developmental level.

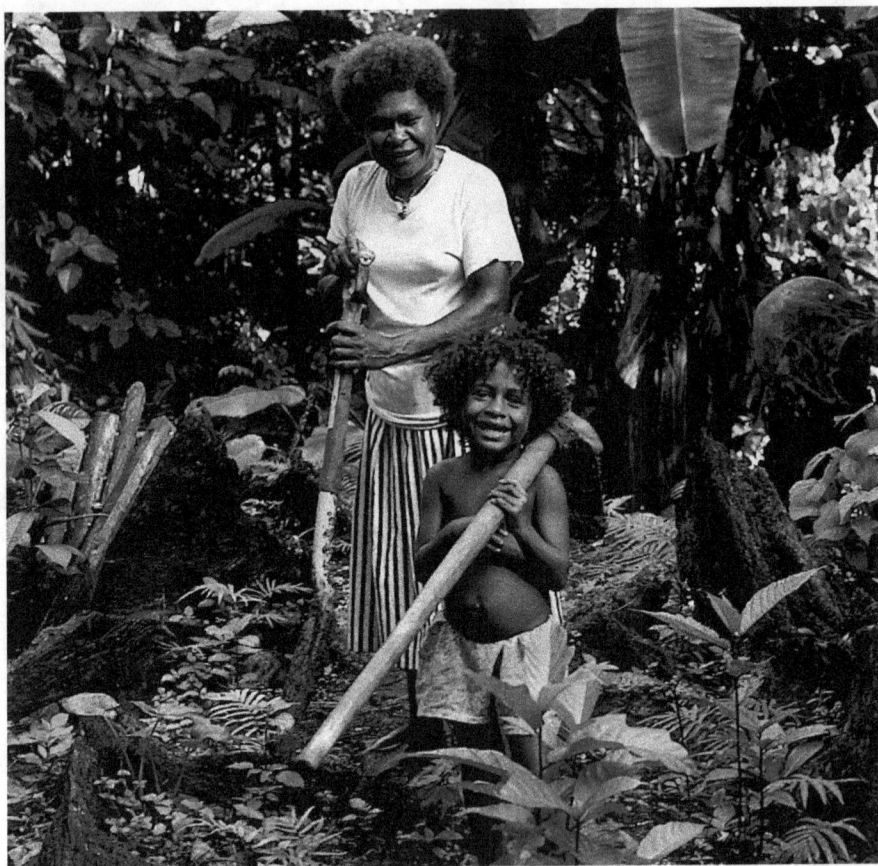

She just wants to believe that. She is naïve."

This was not the first time I was charged with romanticizing Solomon Islanders, although it is difficult to see how small children working sometimes to exhaustion in gardens is romantic. However, Vivian's words were effective. A week later one of our Vygotsky group and I did a panel on research methods at a respected child language conference. A group of leading and rising scholars of our generation who knew Vivian sat down front in the audience, smirking, whispering, and ridiculing points as we made them. After these two sessions, I found that invitations to me to participate in child language panels and publications dropped dramatically.

The challenges our AERA panel made to child development theory were not answered in either of these situations. Instead, the strategy was to discredit me as observer and analyst. One take-away message to all who were trying to build a career was that certain aspects of developmental theory are ideological and not open to question. These aspects involve deeply rooted Western values and assumptions about children, development, and language.

Anyone who has spent time in working-class or poor communities whether in the US or 'Third World' knows that children in those communities work early and develop skills accordingly. When I have told this story to researchers who are not child development experts but who have worked in the 'Third World,' they have been surprised because all of them casually noticed 3-year-old children working in the fields, taking care of infants, and such as laundry or cooking.

Reflecting on what happened, I suspect the problem here is not just the difference between the limitations of experimental research (on which most child development theory is based) versus the clarity of observing children in their naturally-occurring everyday life. I suspect that the issue is much more personal. For ironically, privileged people, including professors who do child development research, want to see their own children as precocious and unusually talented if they perform above research-established developmental levels, especially in socially preferred academic or artistic skills. Poor children of color failing school and experimental testing is lamentable, but to be expected. Poor children ex-

celling in ways that counter expected developmental levels threatens the unique ability status of children of privilege.

Some 15 years after the foregoing incidents, mainstream human development research has finally produced studies showing that the developmental abilities of 3-year-olds had previously been underestimated. Today there is a critical literature in human development and family studies, the sociology of childhood, cultural and cross-cultural psychology, and related disciplines that continues to expand our understandings of children's lives, and hopefully is moving human development away from the narrow models that create what Jeffrey Lewis and I call 'fictions of childhood' (Burman, 1994; Canella, 1997; Davies, 1984; Lewis & Watson-Gegeo, 2004; Mayall, 2002; Morss, 1990; Stephens, 1995). This includes a new generation of indigenous scholars doing research in their own societies, using indigenous or indigenized theoretical models (Gegeo 1994; Gegeo & Watson-Gegeo 2001, 2002; Meyer, 1998; Sinha, 1997;

Smith, 1999). Also important have been carefully reconstructed histories of how 'the child' and 'childhood' have been conceptualized across time in Western societies (Cunningham, 2005; Heywood, 2001).

On going native

Having grown up with a working-class worldview, and then learning middle-class culture in college, part of my criticalist[2] agenda in graduate school was to understand ways of being and thinking beyond the narrow ones I knew. Once in anthropology, I became increasingly uncomfortable with the term 'worldview.' It seemed to me that whereas we in the so-called 'First World' have what philosophers of science call *ontology*, everybody else just has 'worldview.' The vague, unspecified characterization of 'worldview' makes it a dismissive way of treating the thinking and being of others. In long late-night conversations, David and I talked through this and other problematic ways that Westerners position the thought of Pacific Islands villagers.

For his Ph.D. dissertation in political science, David examined the failure of rural development in Kwara'ae, from both a postmodern and an indigenous positioning. In the process of trying to explain to his politically divided committee how he could reach the level of how people think, he chose the term 'indigenous epistemology.' It isn't only 'Other' people's *ontology* that is dismissed as mere worldview, it is also their *epistemology* – their ways of knowing, and creating and validating knowledge. Epistemology is essential to what I now call 'deep culture,' the set of propositions and images that shape perception, information processing, and the assignment of values in a culture (Watson-Gegeo & Gegeo, 2004, p. 21).

All of this evolution in our thinking was taking place despite the growing pressure I felt from anthropological colleagues to distance myself from Kwara'ae people and perspectives. The point of distinguishing between 'emic' and 'etic' descriptive language and positioning in anthropology is to balance the outside researcher's perspective (*etic*) with that of the members of a culture or group (*emic*). Etic is from the outside, but more importantly, it has been assumed to be *neutral* in

judgment, values, and meanings. Hopefully by now the feminists have taught us that there is no neutral research, and that the default for 'etic' is usually Western ontology, and middle-class male at that. And what about feelings, emotional connection, spirituality, and experience?

'Going native' implies that one has lost oneself in the fantasy of being the 'Other.' It implies that the work that a person does is now suspect because he or she has lost objectivity. The conundrum I faced with colleagues thinking that I had 'gone native' was complex. On the one hand, the hallmark of good research as conventionally defined is keeping one's emotional distance. On the other hand, having married into David's family, I had entered a permanent *liminality* in which neutrality could never even be a fiction again. I was in the community and of the community in a way that no outside researcher ever is, with real responsibilities and cultural expectations for performance, and participation in situations never shared with outsiders.

So it was that I began to experience encounters between villagers and researchers through two sets of eyes, those of the outsiders, and those of the villagers. I saw that even anthropologists who had some level of understanding of local cultural expectations constantly violated those expectations in multiple ways. Though, unfortunately, I have witnessed multiple examples, I can only briefly allude to one here.

When Solomon Islands erupted in ethnic conflict on Guadalcanal in 1998, anthropologists on the e-mail list-serve for Pacific anthropologists immediately began theorizing about the causes, and within days tried to organize a session on the topic at an upcoming national meeting. A well-known Solomon Islander in graduate school in New Zealand, who I'll call Sale, e-mailed back that it was far too early to organize such a session. He argued that as he himself and other Solomon Islanders living abroad did not know what was going on in the Solomons, even though they were in constant telephone contact with the islands, how could outside researchers thousands of miles away be already creating theories? He argued that everyone should wait until more was known. His posting was immediately answered by a well-known anthropologist I'll call Frank. Using all

caps for many of his sentences (which of course is 'shouting' on e-mail), Frank retorted that what was proposed was only an informal session, not a formal session. The posting was structured in a highly insulting manner, as if Sale failed to understand the difference between informal and formal. Moreover, Frank said that he and his colleagues had expertise to help solve the problems in the Solomons. With other Solomon Islander members, David and I then responded on Sale's part, posting a message explaining in indigenous epistemological terms why he was upset. We added that too often anthropologists and other outsiders want to intervene before they understand what is happening. The correct route is to wait to be asked for assistance, should that happen. In the meantime, if anthropologists really wanted to help, they could donate or raise money for all the Solomons families who were made homeless by the conflict. Our message set off an angry tirade of messages against us.

The interesting thing is that weeks later, most of the white anthropologists had 'made up' with Sale and with David (who was first author on all our posts), but had stopped communicating with me. The participants needed to be sure not to offend Solomon Islanders, of course, since that could stand in the way of their gaining entry visas to return to the Solomons to do research. However, I was already positioned as having 'gone native,' which my participation in this debate had reaffirmed for them, and therefore I was now out-

side the boundary of 'good anthropology.'

In conclusion

When I contemplate the charge of romanticizing Kwara'ae children, one of the ironies is that all along I had the evidence I needed to answer my critics. A few months ago I began putting together a coffee-table book of some of the best of the 3,000 photographs I took in Solomon Islands. One day my co-author Daniel Ryman and I were at the computer, and I pulled up a file of photographs of Kwara'ae children at work and play. Daniel stared at the screen, and then said jokingly, "We could do a whole book on 'children with knives'!" I looked at the several dozen photographs on screen, and realized with surprise that a very large percentage of them depicted children of 2 to 10 years old carrying and using bush knives, or carving wood with butcher knives. I had taken the photographs so as to never forget the children and people I love, and to make a slideshow for my graduate classes. I had not thought of them as primary data.

In the best cases, theory is built from carefully collected data in multiple situations over time, and represents our most accurate depiction of human behavior, given what we have to work with so far. But even theorists operate out of unexamined, implicit 'theories' about reality, people, and what is natural or normal. All of this becomes entangled with the jockeying for power and position in the careers of research-

ers. I am not saying anything that hasn't been said before, of course, and no doubt some of my readers have experienced the truth of it themselves. It is important, however, to continually examine in our personal lives our own stories of precisely how it happens, if we are to keep theory honest.

NOTES

1. An earlier version of this paper was originally presented at the panel on Critical Re-visitations: Disciplinary Ideologies and Knowledge-making Practices, Annual Meeting of the American Association of Applied Linguistics, 21-24 April 2007, Costa Mesa, California.

2. I use 'criticalist' as a descriptive term to group together all critical approaches from the political, social, and philosophical left, including critical ethnography, critical theory, critical linguistics, radical feminism, queer theory, postmodernism, post colonialism, etc.

REFERENCES

Alcoff, L., & Potter, E. (Eds.). (1993). *Feminist epistemologies*. New York: Routledge.

Au, K. H., & Jordan, C. (1981). Teaching reading to Hawaiian children: Finding a culturally appropriate solution. In E. T. Trueba, G. P. Guthrie, & K. H. Au (Eds.), *Culture and the bilingual classroom: Studies in classroom ethnography* (pp. 139-152). Rowley, MA: Newbury House.

Boggs, S.T. (1985). *Speaking, relating and learning: A study of Hawaiian children at home and at school*. Norwood, NJ: Ablex.

Bronson, M. C. (Ed.). (2005). Revisioning higher education for the twenty-first century, Part I [Special issue]. *ReVision, a Journal of Consciousness and Transformation, 28*(2).

Bronson, M. C. (Ed.). (2006). Revisioning higher education for the twenty-first century, Part II [Special issue]. *ReVision, a Journal of Consciousness and Transformation, 29*(1).

Burman, E. (1994). *Deconstructing developmental psychology*. London: Routledge.

Canella, G. S. (1997). *Deconstructing early childhood education: Social justice and revolution*. New York: Peter Lang.

Cunningham, H. (2005). *Children and childhood in Western society since 1500*. London: Longman.

Davies, B. (1984). Children through their own eyes. *Oxford Review of Education, 10*(3), 275-292.

Gegeo, D. W. (1994). Kastom *and* Bisnis: *Toward integrating cultural knowledge into rural development in the Solomon*

Islands. Unpublished doctoral dissertation, University of Hawai'i, Honolulu.

Gegeo, D. W., & Watson-Gegeo, K. A. (2001). "How we know": Kwara'ae rural villagers doing indigenous epistemology. *The Contemporary Pacific*, 13, 55-88.

Gegeo, D. W., & Watson-Gegeo, K. A. (2002). Whose knowledge? Epistemological collisions in Solomon Islands community development. *The Contemporary Pacific*, 14, 377-409.

Grand, I. J. (2005). The practice of embodied emergence: Integral education in a counseling psychology program. *ReVision*, 28(2), 35-42.

Habermas, J. (1971). *Knowledge and human interests.* Boston: Beacon Press.

Harding, S. (1993). Rethinking standpoint epistemology. In L. Alcoff & E. Potter (Eds.), (1993). *Feminist epistemologies* (pp. 49-82). New York: Routledge.

Heywood, C. M. (2001). *A history of childhood: Children and childhood in the West from medieval to modern times.* Malden, MA: Blackwell.

Kaplan, A. (1964). *The conduct of inquiry.* Scranton, PA: Chandler.

Leont'ev, A. N. (1981). *Problems of the development of the mind.* (M. Kopylova, Trans.). Moscow: Progress.

Lewis, J. L., & Watson-Gegeo, K. A. (2004). Fictions of childhood: Toward a sociohistorical approach to human development. *Ethos*, 32(1), 3-33.

Mayall, B. (2002). *Towards a sociology for childhood: Thinking from children's lives.* Philadelphia: Open University Press.

Meyer, M. A. (1998). *Native Hawaiian epistemology: Contemporary narratives.* Unpublished doctoral dissertation, University of Hawai'i, Honolulu.

Morss, J. R. (1990). *The biologising of childhood: Developmental psychology and the Darwinian myth.* Hillsdale, NJ: Lawrence Erlbaum Associates.

Sinha, D. (1997). Indigenizing psychology. In J. W. Berry, Y. H. Poortinga, & J. Pandey (Eds.), *Handbook of cross-cultural psychology* (pp. 129-169). Needham Heights, MA: Allyn & Bacon.

Smith, L. T. (1999). *Decolonizing methodologies: Research and Indigenous peoples.* New York: Zed Books.

Stephens, S. (1995). Children and the politics of culture in "late capitalism." In S. Stephens (Ed.), *Children and the Politics of Culture* (pp. 3-48). Princeton, NJ: Princeton University Press.

Vygotsky, L. S. (1978). *Mind in society: The development of higher psychological processes.* Cambridge, MA: Harvard University Press.

Vygotsky, L. S. (1981). The genesis of higher mental functions. In J. W. Wertsch (Ed.), *The Concept of Activity in Soviet Psychology* (pp. 144-188). Armonk, NY: M. E. Sharpe.

Watson, K. A. (1973). A rhetorical and sociolinguistic model for the analysis of narrative. *American Anthropologist*, 75, 243-264.

Watson, K. A. (1975). Transferable communicative routines: Strategies and group identity in two speech acts. *Language in Society*, 4, 53-70.

Watson-Gegeo, K. A. (2001). Fantasy and reality: The dialectic of work and play in Kwara'ae children's lives. *Ethos*, 29, 1-26.

Watson-Gegeo, K. A. (2004). Mind, language, and epistemology: Toward a Language Socialization paradigm for SLA. *Modern Language Journal*, 88, 331-350.

Watson-Gegeo, K. A., & Boggs, S. T. (1977). From verbal play to talk story: The role of routines in speech events among Hawaiian children. In S. Ervin-Tripp & C. Mitchell-Kernan (Eds.), *Child Discourse* (pp. 67-90). New York: Academic Press.

Watson-Gegeo, K. A., & Gegeo, D. W. (2004). Deep culture: The epistemological boundaries of multicultural education. In G. Goodman & K. Carey (Eds.), *Critical multicultural instructions: A guide to strategies that enhance the performance of all students* (pp. 235-256). Cresskill, NJ: Hampton.

Wexler, J. (2005). Toward a model of integral education. *ReVision*, 28(2), 29-34.

Yeatman, A. (1994). *Postmodern revisionings of the political.* New York: Routledge.

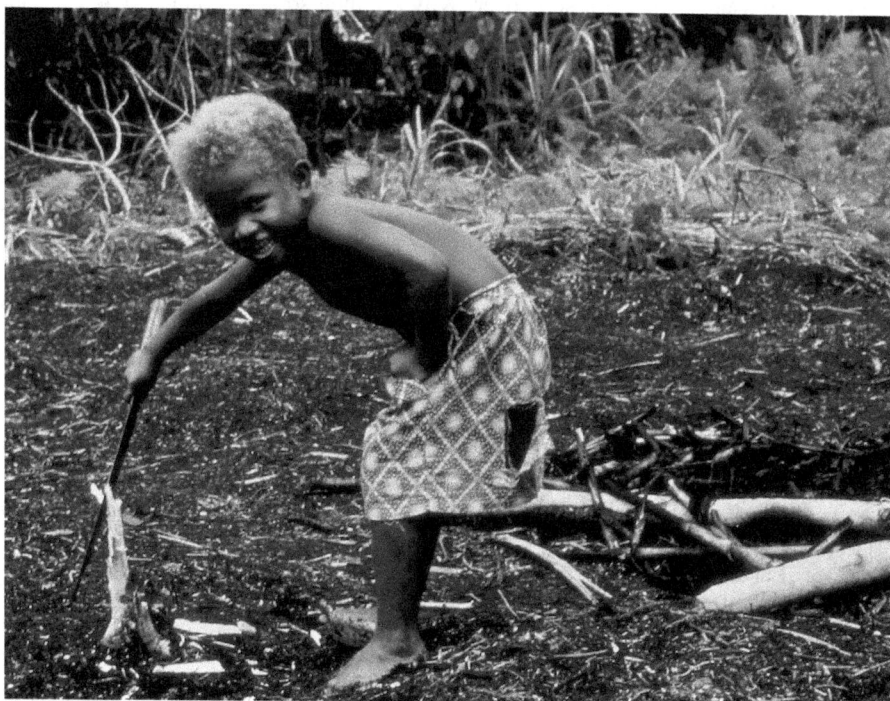

Are Boys Being Trained for Obsolescence?

Philip Slater

One day in early 2007 I was listening to Bulgarian and Rumanian students being interviewed on the BBC about having just joined the European Union. Most of the women were excited about the new opportunities this would open up for them, while the men were gloomy and pessimistic. And it struck me how familiar this seemed to me: how often women appear confident and eager about the future, men doubtful and resistant. From American high school students to women in developing countries, women seem more hopeful, men more confused.

Thinking about this I was reminded of a new trend in the way men are portrayed in film and TV comedies today: they're getting *Dumb and Dumber*. Comedies have always celebrated stupidity, but until recently there were certain rules about who could or could not look like an idiot. By and large you had to be unattractive, middle-aged or older, member of a minority, working class, or all of the above. The only exception was that an attractive leading lady could be ditzy—in the tradition of Carole Lombard, Lucile Ball, and Marilyn Monroe. But leading men could never be stupid. Lou Costello, the Three Stooges, Ralph Kramden and Morton could be stupid, but not Cary Grant.

Of course no red-blooded macho hero was ever a Mensa candidate. In old Hollywood action movies, men with exceptional mental ability were either mad scientists trying to rule the world or well intentioned but doddering and ineffectual eggheads—often the heroine's father or grandfather. And the heroes of action flicks, like film noir private eyes, always *did* stupid

Philip Slater has an A.B. and Ph. D. from Harvard, taught sociology at Harvard, Brandeis, and University of California, Santa Cruz, and is currently teaching at California Institute for Integral Studies. He is the author of *The Pursuit of Loneliness* and nine other nonfiction books. His most recent is *The Chysalis Effect: The Metamorphosis of Global Culture*.

things—so they could be captured, beaten up, and nearly killed to advance the plot—but they never *looked* dumb.

All this began to change toward the end of the 20th century. The dimwitted, loud, beer-swilling oaf—the hick villain or comic foil of earlier films—began to be treated positively. Films like *Dumb and Dumber*, *Dude, Where's My Car*, *Saving Silverman*, *American Pie*, and so on, are increasingly common and well-received. Beer ads show men grunting like apes, repeating the same word moronically, and generally reveling in a kind of good-natured idiocy. While women are more and more often portrayed as smart, competent, motivated, and busy, today's everyday-life male protagonist is often pictured as a brainless, lazy, unrealistic, insensitive, unreliable, and unmotivated slob.

This unflattering portrait fits the negative stereotype voiced by many women today. But most of these roles aren't created by women. They're written, directed, acted, and enjoyed, by men. And obviously men who drink beer like being portrayed as idiots, since it sells beer. Why are men so accepting of this unappealing image? It's as if they were saying: "Yes, we're dumb, and proud of it! That's what it means to be a real man!"

Painting Themselves into a Corner

Men today seem to be struggling to define themselves. Which creates a severe dilemma: to define masculinity is to limit it, for it has always meant distinguishing it from femininity. But defining 'man' as 'not woman' has the unfortunate consequence of eliminating a great deal of what it means to be human. 'Masculinity' must include only what 'femininity' leaves out; so to be macho, men had to content themselves with leftover scraps from the women's behavioral dinner table.

When women burst the bonds of gender constraint and decided to define themselves as complete human beings, many men found themselves clinging desperately to ever-shrinking definitions of masculinity. As women have

expanded into 'male' arenas, for example, there has been an increase in bodybuilding and steroid use by men—part of what Harrison Pope calls the "Adonis Complex"—a growing male preoccupation with body image. He suggests that men are retreating to gyms as a way of asserting their manhood:

> The courts can decree that girls must be admitted to the Citadel, but they cannot decree that a woman can bench press 300 pounds. The male body is becoming the last refuge for men who are trying to hang on to certain masculine distinctions (Pope, 2000).

The reason for all this male confusion is that today's world is one for which women happen to be better prepared and better suited than men.

The Feminine Renaissance

In the United States a few decades ago twice as many men as women went to college, but today women account for 58% of the bachelor's degrees and 60% of the master's degrees. In 1963 female medical school applicants numbered only 8%. By 1983 the number was 34%. In 2003 it was 49.7 % and in 2004 women applicants outnumbered males. In 1970 only 10% of first-year law students were women. By 2001 they were a majority. And since legal training is often a prerequisite to a political career, we're also more likely in the future to see women in positions of power as this cohort moves up.

Women are outdistancing men in quality as well as quantity. Men get worse grades and women are winning a disproportionate share of the honors degrees—in some public universities three-fourths of them. "Male and female students alike agreed that the slackers in their midst were mostly male, and that the fireballs were mostly female" (Lewin, 2006).

Half of the world's countries now have no gender gap in education and in eighteen countries, mostly Latin American, girls outnumber boys in secondary schools. Several Islamic countries and a few Sub-Saharan African nations are among those who have made the greatest strides. In Iran, for example, women are a majority of university students. This is important in the developing world, since educating women is associated with both economic development and population control. And educated mothers—far more than educated fathers—tend to produce educated children.

Change in the business world is slower, but no less striking. Between 1999 and 2002 the percentage of female corporate officers in Fortune 500 companies almost doubled, despite the economic downturn, and the increase is still steady, despite the glass ceiling. In the U.S. between 1997 and 2006, women-owned businesses grew 43.3% (compared with 23.3% for all businesses). They generated almost two trillion dollars in sales and employed almost 13 million people.

The Employment Policy Foundation predicted in 2002 that by 2030 women will outnumber men in professional occupations. "The prediction seems absurdly conservative today. If the male was the prototypical industrial worker, the information worker is typically a woman....Of the people whose job title falls under the category of 'professional'...the majority are women" (Naisbitt and Aburdene, 2000). Why has this change come about? And why is it happening so swiftly?

Women are Better Prepared

Women have a head start in today's world—a shrinking world with a global economy in which communication is everything. Because the ability of men to communicate on an emotional level has been limited by the straitjacket of macho competitiveness, it has for centuries fallen to women to take care of those human needs irrelevant to combat. Women have had to become skilled at negotiation and compromise, at recognizing and anticipating the needs of others, at mediating ("Your father-son-brother really loves you, dear, he just doesn't know how to say it").

This gives women an advantage in a shrunken world in which communication and cooperation are vital to our survival as a species. As a group women are better attuned to the demands of a modern democratic society

than men are. Men talk constantly about 'being firm', 'standing tall', and 'standing up to' people, as if working collectively on a problem were a matter of maintaining an erection. But rigidity is not a virtue in a democracy, and solving collective problems is not a form of hand-to-hand combat.

Men tend to have more developed 'left brains', women more developed 'right brains'. In the past this difference was seen as an indication of female inferiority—the right hemisphere was intuitive and artistic but not really IQ-smart. But today linear, left hemisphere intelligence is less important. After all, it's easily automated. What it can do a computer can do 100 times better and 1,000,000 times faster. So now the scorned, right-hemisphere intelligence of women has become the key to the future. "We've progressed from a society of farmers to a society of factory workers to a society of knowledge workers. And now we're progressing yet again—to a society of creators and empathizers, of pattern recognizers and meaning makers" (Pink, 2005, 50).

Collaborating

Since young girls aren't trained to be compulsively competitive the way men are, it's a lot easier for women to join forces to achieve common goals. Women in all fields of activity are getting together to pool resources and improve skills. They have writing groups, artists' groups, executive support groups, entrepreneurial support groups, professional support groups, academic support groups—whatever women set out to do, they tend to do in a cooperative setting. In sports, in an era in which male athletes have become notoriously egocentric, women excel at teamwork.

Deborah Tannen finds that women often make better managers than men because they tend to involve employees in decision-making, leading to more enthusiastic implementation (Tannen, 1990, 181). Women in business, says Carol Frenier, have less need than men to have their egos stroked and their ideas copyrighted. And while there are always a few women managers who try to 'out-male' men, most women managers want primarily to be acknowledged for "carrying their weight" (Frenier, 1997, 86 ff).

Leadership maven Tom Peters believes women will lead most compa-

nies within 20 years, partly because: "Women have traditionally been stronger than men at such things as forming relationships, using intuition and not being threatened by strong people . . . all qualities that leaders need" (Murphy, 2000).

Research studies find that women try to maintain equality in relationships while men tend to compete for status—a difference well-entrenched by the 2nd or 3rd grade; women focus on community, men on competition; men boast regularly, women do not; women tend to seek out the wishes of others, men do not; men tend to take suggestions as being ordered around, women do not. In short, a man tends to see himself as a competitor in a pecking order, while a woman sees herself "as an individual in a network of connections" (Tannen, 1990, Gilligan, 1982).

While men have tried to dominate their environment and make it predictable, women have always had to live with confusion and chaos. In traditional households they had to adapt daily to the unexpected, between body changes, active small children, and the whims of demanding husbands. Women are also used to being involved in several activities at the same time, of being in the midst of chaos. It's this difficulty in adapting to a changing world that has left so many men confused and angry today. "Women have spent a lot of time preparing for a world that's different. Men have not done that . . . .We don't know what we want to be" (Zernike, 1998).

Making Men

What is it in the conditioning of men that makes adaptation to our new world difficult? For it's hard to escape the conclusion that this masculine failing is the direct result of male gender training—that what we consider right and proper behavior for young boys, which, while quite serviceable in preparing men to serve in a medieval army, makes them utterly unfit for constructive roles in the modern world.

The problem, I would suggest, is that men are still being raised as if they were to spend their lives engaged in hand-to-hand combat—a useful training when most men could expected to be forced to utilize these skills from time to time, but one of little value today, when war is becoming so counter-productive that none of the world's wealthiest nations engage in it. Furthermore, war today is mostly a matter of dropping bombs, or firing missiles. Even gun are usually fired at some distance from their targets. Hand-to-hand combat is rarely involved.

For nine thousand years, whether a society was actually at war or enjoying a peaceful spell, war has dominated male consciousness: "The male psyche is, first and foremost, the Warrior psyche….All men are marked by the warfare system and the military virtues" (Keen, 1991, 37-38).

When Shakespeare described the seven ages of man and wanted to define young adulthood—between his adolescent lover and his middle-aged judge—he chose: "A soldier, full of strange oaths…jealous in honour, sudden and quick in quarrel, seeking the bubble reputation even in the cannon's mouth."

And Henry V, encouraging his soldiers before Agincourt, ties masculinity to war in the same competitive way: "And gentlemen in England now a-bed shall think themselves accursed they were not here, And hold their manhoods cheap whiles any speaks that fought with us…" Being a soldier was the masculine ideal, and men whose young adult years occurred between wars often felt cheated and emasculated.

To distinguish themselves from women, the creators, men were trained to be killers and destroyers. This is why men who were artists, writers, musicians, etc., have traditionally been considered effeminate. To be manly was to be ready to destroy, not to create.

So what qualities would you want to instill in men who were going to devote their lives to war? Especially war as it existed when military training began—that is, hand-to-hand combat?

First of all, you'd want them not to be easily intimidated—you'd want them to be insensitive to the boasts and threats of their antagonists. You'd also want them to be pitiless—to show no mercy in battle. Finally, you'd want them to be unquestioningly obedient to their leaders.

Part of military training even today consists of what Lt. Col. Dave Grossman—a former paratrooper and military trainer—calls "seemingly sadistic abuse and hardship"—browbeating, frequent and degrading punishment, humiliation, pointless tasks, and so on

(Grossman, 1995, 82). It's often claimed that such practices will 'make a man' out of someone who could not otherwise lay claim to the title. "Boot camp was awful," some men say, "but it made a man of me." And while it certainly won't make a man for all seasons, it definitely makes a soldier-man.

Learning to accept abuse and not react produces the numbness needed for physical combat. It helps the soldier deaden himself to feeling, and hardens him to suffering—both his own and (since he witnesses the abuse of his fellow soldiers) that of others. This is important in warfare since the soldier is primarily engaged in inflicting suffering and shouldn't go around feeling bad about it. What we want in a soldier is an unfeeling, obedient man who can kill designated opponents on cue and without remorse.

But this last requirement poses a problem. Normal humans have an instinctual, genetic reluctance to kill members of their own species. This reluctance has to be trained out of soldiers. In World War II only about one-sixth of the soldiers ever fired their guns in combat. And according to Grossman, most soldiers in most wars have fired over the heads of their opponents.

More soldiers suffer psychiatric disorders than die in battle. And Grossman shows that it's not fear but the stress of killing. Those who don't have to kill at close range, or who don't have to kill at all, are less prone to psychiatric disorders *even when exposed to greater danger*.

Most primitive tribes also show extreme reluctance to kill face-to-face. This is also why, Grossman says, gangland executions are carried out by a shot to the back of the head, and why men are blindfolded when shot by a firing squad. Hostages and kidnap victims are far more likely to be killed if blindfolded. (There are, of course, exceptions to this reluctance. In any armed force, Grossman says, about 2% are sociopathic—men incapable of empathy, who enjoy killing.)

We still seem confused today about whether we want men in modern society to approximate this military ideal. We generally want more complexity, a wider range of values. Yet we still—judging from movies and TV—admire the man who kills, and all men are infected to some degree with macho values. Particularly when other men are

around to enforce conformity through ridicule and shame.

We've been indoctrinated to associate manliness with domination. The media refer to significant events in human history as 'conquests': the 'conquest' of the sea, the 'conquest' of polio, the 'conquest' of Everest, the 'conquest' of space. Many men never feel they're winning in life unless someone or something is losing.

Out of Work

Even though they still run the world, many men today express feelings of powerlessness. They're angry that women are invading previously all-male domains, and upset that women aren't as dependent on them as they used to be—especially since most men still feel dependent on women: sexually, emotionally, domestically.

This sense of loss—of uselessness, of vanishing function—echoes the feelings of skilled 19th-century craftsmen displaced by machines. Like those craftsmen, modern men have been trained in macho skills over many years and at severe cost, only to discover that those skills are no longer of any use to anyone. Strutting, boasting, fighting, destroying, and killing just don't seem as important to the world as they used to.

Yet some men feel that our world today offers advantages—freeing us from the role behavior that abuses us—the competitiveness that isolates and stresses us, the status-hunger that separates us from loved ones and keeps us from enjoying what we have, the belligerence that turns the world hostile, the stoicism that prevents relief.

In a 1993 survey three-fourths of the men polled said more time with their children was the most desired change in their lives. Seventy percent were willing to slow their careers to bring this about. Warren Farrell found that out of 10,000 men asked, 80% would prefer to take six months to a year off work to be with a new baby full time, while only 3% would prefer to keep working full time (Farrell, 1993, 20).

There are three million children in the United States today living only with their fathers. And in one out of five intact families the husband is the primary parent (Kimbrell, 1995).

Such men are pursuing an uncharted course with little support from others. Women who gather with their children in parks are often as unwelcoming of 'Mr. Moms' as firemen are of women firefighters. And I've seen women intrude with astonishing arrogance and officiousness into the parenting of men who have been a child's primary caretaker since it was born. Women, too, have trouble giving up old patterns.

Making Yesterday's Men Today

It's always easier to prepare our children for the future than it is to change our own ingrained habits. Immigrants have been doing it for centuries. Carole Gallagher, who studies successful women executives, commented in an interview that male CEOs who have been blind to discrimination against women quickly regain their sight when their daughters encounter it. It's easier to support change for the next generation than for your own.

But few parents are as forward-looking when it comes to their sons. Many men have a horror of their son being seen as a sissy—despite the fact that so many of the 'great men' of history were called sissies or mama's boys when they were young. There are five times as many boys as girls classified as "Gender Identity Disorders" (Burke, 1996, 201)

Women, too, seem nervous about this, and often—against their own instincts—encourage their sons to be exactly the insensitive, selfish, inconsiderate, and boorish men they're always complaining about.

It isn't just in boot camp that men are trained in military values. "Be a good soldier", a male child is often told when asked to deal with an unpleasant, painful, or tiresome situation. Traditionally, young boys are not supposed to cry, show fear, or be quiet and studious, or emotional, or nurturant, or play with girls. They're expected to be tough, stoical, competitive, noisy, boisterous, not too bright, and enjoy destroying things. This is what will earn them the proud honor: "he's all boy." It's what William Pollack calls the 'Boy Code', and it's still prominent today (Pollack, 1998). Boys, in our interdependent, shrinking world, are still being trained—by parents, schools, other adults, and older children—as if they were destined to spend their lives engaging in hand-to-hand combat. Much of the world's constant slaughter can be attributed to the fact that men simply aren't trained to share power.

Children who are abused tend to become abusers. So it's no surprise to find that boys, who commit the majority of violent acts, are treated more harshly as children than girls are. They're half again more likely to receive corporal punishment at home, and six times more likely in school.

Some people believe these traits are in the genes, although they're entirely absent from many cultures. And if they were 'natural' you'd think boys would be happy and comfortable in their assigned roles. Yet eighty-five percent of teen suicides are boys (Kindlon, 1999).

And in fact nothing about the "Boy Code" is natural or genetic. David Gilmore, who looked at cross-cultural studies hoping to find some universals in male behavior, was compelled to admit defeat, and research efforts to find a biological foundation for male aggression have failed repeatedly, despite the immense popularity of the idea (Gilmore, 1991).

Biologically men are no more prone to aggression than to nurturing or generosity or any other trait in the vast repertory of human impulses. Male babies are actually more emotionally expressive than girl babies, and until the age of four or five—by which time they've been thoroughly indoctrinated with the Boy Code—boys are just as interested in infants as girls are. In some cultures nurturance is considered as much a masculine trait as a feminine one. Infant males in our own culture, moreover, are just as empathic as females.

But by four or five years old, in most cultures, emotional intelligence, tenderness, and empathy have been largely squelched by the Boy Code. Boys are being systematically deprived of many of the right-brain qualities Daniel Pink says will be most needed in the future.

The toughness and stoicism that are supposed to be genetic in men turn out to be easily discarded when permission is backed up by strong enough group support. When Robin Ely, a Harvard Business School professor, studied workers on an oil rig in the Gulf of Mexico, she was shocked to discover that these men, who rode Harleys, went hunting, made crude jokes, and did all the other things 'real men' are supposed to do, were completely open in expressing emotional and physical vulnerability. They told the others when they didn't feel safe, or wanted help

and support staying focused because of an emotional problem at home. This openness was the result of a safety campaign initiated by the company, and was successful partly because of the very real dangers on the rigs, and the fact that the men worked and lived so closely together. Older workers told Ely that before the program was instituted the rig had just the kind of competitive atmosphere she had expected to find, with workers continually trying to out-macho each other (Henig, 2007).

Efforts to demonstrate biological gender differences are often based on studies of children several years old, when gender training is firmly entrenched. Deborah Blum, for example, cites the fact that boys five years old are rougher and tolerate much louder noises than girls of the same age as evidence that boys are genetically from Mars (Blum, 1997, 68). But if you tell people an infant is a boy they'll treat it more roughly and talk louder to it, which renders Blum's observation meaningless.

Louann Brizendine has written perhaps the most comprehensive survey of innate gender differences, but even she fails to take into account the powerful impact of gender training. She also places great emphasis on the fact that the communication center is bigger in the female brain, and that it "develops a greater ability to read cues" (2006, 13). But if people talk louder to infants they believe are boys, and treat them more roughly, obviously their ability to read cues is going to be less highly developed.

There are, of course, hard-wired gender difference, but at present it is impossible to tell how much the differences we see are created or exaggerated by gender training. Brain growth is not a simple genetic unfolding, but is part of an open loop. The brain develops in interaction with others.

Those most insistent on a biological origin for gender behavior are the very ones who get most upset when it isn't manifested. But if gender behavior is based on biology, we should all be able to sit back and let nature take its course. Instead we see hordes of otherwise intelligent people forcefully imposing traits on children who are supposed to already possess them.

Gender indoctrination begins at birth. The very first question people ask about a newborn is whether it's a boy or a girl. They want to know how to behave toward it—how to train it. People will get upset if you dress a child in the wrong color or give it a gender-ambiguous name.

Adults watching an infant crying will interpret it as anger if told it's a boy, and fear if told it's a girl. If they think an infant is a boy they'll talk about its firm grasp; if they think it's a girl they'll comment on its softness and fragility. Parents of newborn boys will describe their offspring as stronger, larger, better coordinated and more alert than will the parents of newborn girls, even when no differences exist. Infant boys and girls will be given different clothing and toys and their rooms will be decorated differently (Matlin, 1987; D. Archer, personal communication, 1997).

Sociologist Dane Archer found that merely dressing the same infant in pink or blue would elicit different responses. Dressed in pink, the infant was always said to be beautiful, in blue, almost never. In blue, many career choices were prophesied, in pink, only one—Miss America.

Of what value is traditional masculine gender training in the modern world? Will it help a boy become a corporate manager, programmer, teacher, or film director? Encouraging insensitivity, belligerence, and selfishness might have been excellent training for a boy growing up in war-torn 9th-century Scotland but it isn't clear that it's useful in our woven world, where communication skills are in more demand.

Parents who instill macho values, habits, and attitudes in a young boy today may be sentencing him to a life of failure, frustration, and irrelevance—to be one of the drudges, the grunts, the expendable bodies in a world that demands flexibility and receptivity. Such parents are burdened by "outmoded ideas about masculinity and what it takes for a boy to become a man. These models...simply have no relevance to today's world" (Pollack, 1998, xxii).

Yet few parents—even those antagonistic to the macho worldview—see this as anything remotely approaching an emergency. This despite the fact that traditional male gender training takes place everywhere—in the media, in schools, with older children, in toy stores, etc. While it would be absurd, and probably harmful, for a parent to attempt to shield a boy from this barrage of conditioning, parents who want their boys to have a meaningful place in today's world could at least avoid adding to the din. They can create an attitude of acceptance—a space that will permit a young boy to widen his range of responses, to reject the crippling aspects of the Boy Code when it becomes oppressive, to decide for himself what kind of behavior is appropriate for a man.

REFERENCES

Blum, D. (1997). *Sex on the brain.* New York: Viking.

Brizendine, L. (2006). *The female brain.* New York: Morgan Road.

Burke, P. (1996). *Gender shock.* New York: Anchor Books.

Farrell, W. (1993). *The myth of male power.* New York: Simon & Schuster.

Frenier, C.R. (1997). *Business and the feminine principle.* Boston, Mass.: Butterworth-Heinemann.

Gilligan, C. (1982). *In a different voice.* Cambridge, Mass.: Harvard University Press.

Gilmore, D. G. (1991). *Manhood in the making.* New Haven, Conn.: Yale University Press.

Grossman, Lt. Col. D. (1995). *On killing.* Boston, Mass.: Little, Brown.

Henig, S. (2007, September/October) Manhood reconsidered. *Harvard Magazine, 110* (1), 16-18.

Keen, S. (1991). *Fire in the belly.* New York: Bantam.

Kimbrell, A (1995). *The masculine mystique.* New York: Ballantine Books.

Kindlon, D.J., and Thompson, M. (1999). *Raising Cain: protecting the emotional life of boys.* New York: Ballantine Books.

Lewin, T. (2006, July 8). At colleges, women are leaving men in the dust. *The New York Times.*

Matlin, M. W. (1987). *The psychology of women.* New York: Holt, Rinehart and Winston.

Murphy, D. (2000, September 17). What bosses don't know. *The San Francisco Examiner,* pp. J1-2.

Naisbitt, J. and Aburdene, P. (1990). *Megatrends 2000.* New York: William Morrow.

Pink, D.H. (2005). *A whole new mind.* New York: Riverhead.

Pollack, W. (1998). *Real boys.* New York: Random House.

Pope, H. G., Jr., Phillips, K. A., & Olivardia, R. (2000). *The Adonis complex.* New York: Free Press.

Tannen, D. (1990). *You Just Don't Understand.* New York: William Morrow.

Zernike, K. (1998, May 17) Men on the verge post-feminism, the other gender is stirring, reasserting its strength. *The Boston Globe.*

Art by Mariana Castro de Ali

A Radical Approach to Delinquency Reform

Marty Mendenhall

Several million juveniles commit delinquent acts each year. Violent and property crimes committed by juveniles are one of the foremost social and public health problems in America. In 2002, law enforcement agencies in the United States made an estimated 2.3 million arrests of persons under age 18. Although juvenile crime rates have gradually decreased since peaking in 1994, according to the Federal Bureau of Investigation, juveniles still accounted for 17% of all arrests and 15% of all violent crime arrests in 2002 (Office of Juvenile Justice and Delinquency Prevention, 2004, p. 1).

On any give day in the United States 108,700 juveniles are held in detention or correctional facilities. On average, a year of incarceration costs taxpayers $43,000 per juvenile (The National Center on Addiction and Substance Abuse, 2004). In addition to the monetary costs of juvenile delinquency there are other costs including: lost property and wages, medical and psychological expenses, decreased productivity, pain and suffering, and decreased quality of life.

The importance of the need for effective interventions for serious juvenile offenders cannot be overstated as

Marty Mendenhall, Ph.D., is a Licensed Professional Counselor. He completed his doctoral program at Saybrook Graduate School and Research Center in San Francisco specializing in spirituality and consciousness. He also completed a two-year post-graduate certificate program in Socially Engaged Spirituality at Saybrook. He has been employed by the Utah State Department of Juvenile Justice Services for twenty-two years working to incorporate and nourish the spiritual roots of restorative justice in the programs that he directs. Marty is also an adjunct faculty member at the University of Phoenix and provides mental health services for children who have been removed from home due to abuse and neglect. He owns and operates Mendenhall Martial Arts and Holistic Health Center in Pleasant View, Utah, where he advocates the harmonious development of mind, body, and spirit.

this group poses a significant challenge to criminal justice agencies both in terms of frequency and seriousness of their offending and their later behavior as adults. Juvenile court judges continue to commit chronic juvenile offenders to large secure care facilities although these facilities have never proved effective in rehabilitating youthful offenders. Recidivism from large training schools is uniformly high. In virtually every study examining recidivism among youth sentenced to juvenile training schools in the past three decades has found that at least 50 to 70 percent of offenders are arrested within one or two years after release (Mendel, 1999, pp. 50-51). This pattern

of behavior imposes enormous costs on society and on the local, state and federal governments, not to mention the tremendous loss of human potential.

New evidence in juvenile justice literature calls for radical change, because it demonstrates clearly that today's widespread practices are often ineffective and at times counterproductive. It is precisely due to the ineffectiveness of conventional juvenile justice practices that led me to develop a radical approach to delinquency reform based on a synthesis of my experience as a martial artist, a student of Buddhism, and meditation practitioner. I borrowed the term *Chuan Fa*—an ancient form of Buddhist martial arts to identify this practice.

During the spring of 2006 I conducted research that investigated the lived experience of incarcerated juvenile delinquents who practiced a form of Buddhist martial arts daily for twelve weeks. The particular focus was on the subjective experience of participants who practiced meditation and martial arts to help resolve emotional problems, curb aggressive tendencies, develop self-awareness, and cultivate a strong moral foundation.

A group of 12 selected residents at Mill Creek Youth Center (Utah's largest Division of Juvenile Justice Services secure care facility) ranging in age from 16 to 21 participated in the twelve-week Buddhist martial arts training program. Training consisted, in part, of observance of *panca-sila* (the five moral precepts), and practice of

> New evidence in juvenile justice literature calls for radical change, because it demonstrates clearly that today's widespread practices are often ineffective and at times counterproductive.

the Four Noble Truths, the Eightfold Noble Path, and the six *parami* (generosity, discipline, patience, endeavor, meditative concentration, and wisdom). Participants also engaged in rigorous martial arts training, dharma teachings, and *vipassana* meditation.

My purpose for conducting this study was is in part a reaction to the primarily secular response to the rehabilitation of troubled young people. The intention *Chuan Fa* is to help young people understand the truth of who they are, and how to allow that truth to begin to guide their lives. The underlying philosophy of the program is that the truth in each of us is our best teacher.

Many of the Buddha's thoughts were conveyed during the study due to the fact that he was a profound philosopher and psychologist whose instructions

Photo: Marty Mendenhall

can empower human beings to improve their lives. The sharing of Buddhist teachings and philosophy however, should not be construed as an attempt to convert participants to Buddhism. His teachings were presented along with other philosophers, sages, prophets, poets, and avatars because they contain clear techniques to effectively deal with situations in daily life. The Buddha discussed the workings of one's mind, and realistic and practical ways to deal with daily problems. Describing one's difficulties and their causes, the Buddha also explained the way to eliminate them. He talked of humanity's great potential and how to develop it. Participants of the study had opportunities to learn that it is up to each human being to ascertain through logic and personal experience the truth of what he taught.

Of the copious psychological characteristics studied over the past several years, the attribute of external locus of control is the most recurrently identified indicator of juvenile delinquency. For example, Kumchy and Sayer (1980), in a study of the attitudinal responsibility of juvenile delinquents, report that juvenile delinquents are more likely to demonstrate an external locus of control than non-delinquents of the same age. Locus of control is the tendency of individuals to either perceive life's circumstances as a product of forces outside their control (external locus of control), or, as a result of their own behavior or personal attributes (internal locus of control).

IMPACT OF MEDITATION ON JUVENILE DELINQUENTS

Meditation can remedy the characteristics of external locus of control. It leads to a variety of beneficial effects in the areas of physiology and behavior studies. There is empirical evidence supporting the use of meditation techniques to enhance internal locus of control, lower anxiety, and improve the ability to monitor both internal and external stimuli (Murphy, 1988).

Meditation is the core practice of *Chuan Fa*. It may be thought of as the directing, stilling, quieting, or focusing of one's attention in a systematic manner. Meditation is a method of training a disorderly, disorganized mind to become proficient and creative. When asked about his experience of meditation during the twelve-week study, one participant commented:

Meditation practice has helped me open up and stay focused. Not only that, it has expanded my awareness and helped me understand other people's perspectives on life, and that there is not only one way to handle the issues that I have. Ever since I started this practice I feel more at peace with my mind, I'm not trying to fight with myself anymore, I'm learning to help myself.

The Buddha taught the importance of internal locus of control. He said: "Your own self is your master; who else could be? With yourself well controlled, you gain a master very hard to find" (Easwaran, 1985, p. 121). The Buddha emphasized that by examining one's own nature one examines the phenomenon of a human being. Laying all preconceptions aside, he explored reality within and realized that the only way to free oneself from suffering is through self-awareness. The Buddha developed a system for developing self-knowledge as a means of self-transformation. He taught that by attaining an experiential understanding of reality of one's own nature, one could eliminate the misapprehensions that cause one to act wrongly and to make oneself unhappy. One thus learns to act in accordance with reality and therefore to lead productive, useful, happy lives (Hart, 1987, p. 146).

Chuan Fa teaches participants that their bodies, in collaboration with their minds and spirit, are marvelously blessed with self-healing abilities. The body is the vehicle of one's life. Mind and spirit are the dwellers within the vehicle. Mind and spirit sustain the vehicle. Mind's intelligence and spirit's inspiration vitalize and animate the body. The three together cooperate to produce the most profound medicine ever known right within oneself. When practicing meditation one practices the harmonious balance of mind, body, and spirit in perfect oneness.

One participant reported that her experience with meditation was so helpful that she learned to develop meditative practices beyond her practice of sitting. She indicated:

When I'm weight training or running, and even in daily activities when I'm down in cottage I am learning to practice centering myself by focusing on my breath. Being in the moment helps me not to stress so much. That has really helped because sometimes my mind is all over the place. Initially I seemed to be able to practice mindful awareness more easily when my body was in motion during martial arts or when I was running. However, now I have learned to recall the state of mind while practicing *kata* (a succession of martial arts movements committed to memory) or other forms of moving meditation and that helps me stop, calm, and focus my mind during silent sitting.

When one practices looking deeply during meditation one begins to see clearly the conditions that have caused one to be the way one is. One begins to see that suffering has not been imposed by some external force but that one's thoughts are the root cause of one's suffering and misbehavior.

Incarcerated juvenile delinquents are in need of eradication of suffering brought about by a transformation of consciousness or a "turning of the heart." Eradication of suffering is freedom from greed, ignorance, and aversion. This differs from usual methods of delinquency reform, which typically only addresses the delinquent's problems superficially. In Buddhist practice one is taught that one must get to the root of one's problems if one is to achieve lasting happiness. This can only be done through an in depth examination of the workings of the mind. Through the diligent practice of meditation one may transform the callous heart of one lost in delusion into the heart of the enlightened mind. This type of transformation has been the endeavor of meditation practitioners for thousands of years. It consists of learning how to stop all one's "doing" and shift to a "being" mode, learning how to make time for oneself, and how to slow down, and nurture calmness and self-acceptance, learning to observe what one's own mind is up to from moment to moment, how to watch one's thoughts and how to let go of them without getting so caught up and driven by them, how to make room for new ways of seeing old problems and for perceiving the interconnectedness of things.

One participant talked about her early experience with meditation noting that the benefits of her training did not come suddenly or without effort:

Sometimes when I first started this practice, I wouldn't want to get up at 5:30 a.m. it was so early and I would be tired. I would get frustrated but the inside part of me, my inner core would say 'come on, get up, you can do it' so I would get up and that gave me a feeling of strength. Every time I get up early and practice now, I feel real strong. I feel mentally and physically strong and that gives me a lot of confidence. It makes me know that I can handle tough times, that I can keep going, because there are times when I want to quit, but again, my inner core allows me to keep going.

Sometimes during moving or sitting practice I will be off focus but still a part of me is quiet and still. This has helped me learn that there is a part of me that cannot be affected by outside things...do you know what I mean? I don't know, it's like when I'm practicing a part of me knows I am getting stronger, that I don't have to use drugs...you know what I mean? I don't know I just feel like a warrior. Like I'm getting ready, I'm getting prepared for when I go out there (back into society), I'm going to have to fight a lot of temptations and I know that if I can make it through this training I'll be able to just keep going.

Juvenile delinquents are often impulsive and frequently ignore inner promptings to correct behaviors. They have forgotten how to think with their heart. In Buddhist practice, thinking with the heart is encouraged through the practice of meditation. Through deep contemplation and dedicated practice one can transforms one's delu-

the present moment. As one calms one's mind and develops moment-to-moment awareness of one's breath, sensations, emotions, and thoughts, one gains insight into one's life and the world. Insight and knowledge is not the same thing. Insight is entirely different than knowledge. It is one's own inner wisdom. Insight is what one already knows inside one's heart. When one has an insight one feels familiarity, as if one had known it all along. Or one recognizes its truth intuitively, rather than intellectually. One understands oneself better, or learns a truth of the world. One participant commented on his experience of understanding himself better through the practice of meditation:

Meditation has strengthened my mind it has helped me to know when I'm getting mad so I can handle the situation a lot better. It has helped me to get to know myself better, which allows me to speak

> Recent research shows that martial arts practice is a discipline with promise to help remedy mental health problems by curbing aggressive tendencies, developing compassion and respect, and cultivating a strong moral foundation

sion, greed, self-centeredness, and negativity. Through meditation practice one has the possibility of healing the afflictions of anger, hatred, loneliness, sorrow, and unhealthy attachments. In this way of practice, one develops a noble heart filled with the abundance of wisdom, compassion, and love. In time, these sublime qualities of love become natural and spontaneous—a constant life affirming attitude radiating from one's heart bringing benefit and happiness to all. The Buddha taught that if the heart is full of love and compassion, which is the inner state, the outer manifestation is care and connectedness (Salzberg, 1995, p. 172).

There is no better way to have a practical, personal understanding of the principals of truth than to embark upon a meditation practice. In *vipassana* meditation one's mind stays connected and aware of whatever is happening in

a lot more freely to other people. I've also learned more how to control emotions in general. I discovered that certain feelings in the body always show up with powerful emotions and learning to recognize those feelings and be able to identify them keeps me from having an emotional outburst. It has helped me be more aware of my feelings. I feel I have a better understanding of who I am because ever since I started meditation I have been able to see myself more clearly.

Mindfulness methods can be taught as therapeutic procedures that are of real value. For example one who gets overwhelmed by emotion may find, if one stops to examine it, that there are a number of stages contributing to their feelings. Each of these stages is accompanied by physiological changes, such as rising or falling temperature in different parts of the body, tightness in the chest, muscular tension, as well as more psychological signs such as particular imagery, memories or thoughts. All these can be observed. A person who learns to observe them gains greatly in self-control as evidenced by this participant's comments:

This practice has helped me do better and doing good has made me more aware and sensitive to bad behavior. The other day I was having a bad day in cottage, so I went in my room and I was so angry I was just crying, but I noticed this feeling of negativity all over me, like it was just 'on me.' When I told my mom on the phone later that day about it, I told her that I never want to feel that way again. I know that I will probably have times where I will feel like that again but what makes me feel good is that I know my 'practice' can pull me out of it. Before I started practicing I would get stuck in these real negative places and didn't have the skills or maybe even the motivation to get out of them. I have learned that it is all up to me. I can create a world of misery or I can create a world of happiness. My brother is getting out of prison soon and it's going to be hard, like really hard, but I'm hoping that he can follow what I'm doing now. Even though I'm younger than him, I'm hoping that I can set a good example for him. I think my mom and everyone is working hard to change to help us change. I'm hoping that my whole family can start practicing this way so that we can all be happy.

It seems quite possible that the meditative aspects of *Chuan Fa* offer a unique approach to the long-standing problem of juvenile delinquency. Through the process of moving and seated meditation, the practitioner gradually develops *sila* (moral and ethical development), *samdhi* (the ability to concentrate without being distracted), and *panna* (wisdom). By so doing, the practitioner expands the resources of self via the increased sense of continuity and authenticity that develops from intense concentration and turning one's attention inward with an accepting and non-judgmental awareness of all the body and mind offers. Through the practice of *Chuan Fa,* one cultivates attention firmly rooted in the body, which strengthen one's connection to that aspect of the self that has been the experiential witness of the private physiological, emotional and cognitive events of one's ongoing process. This enhanced connection with what William James (1997) has referred to as the "self as

knower" or the existential "I" can also facilitate an adolescent's sense of authenticity or realness. Developing a greater connection to a sense of authenticity or realness can also be a vital resource for adolescents as they face the demands of their social world to define who they are.

Through the practice of *Chuan Fa,* the adolescent may gain more access to his or her inner sense of self and what is real or meaningful about it. With this understanding, the adolescent may be more likely to withstand the temptations of peers that threaten to push him or her off course. An inner sense of self allows one to make choices that are informed by a greater sense of awareness while being mindful of one's personal opinions and convictions. Meditation may remedy the characteristics of external locus of control and allow one to be "true" to one's self. They may lead to a variety of beneficial effects in the areas of physiology and behavior (Goleman, 2003). There is empirical evidence supporting the use of meditation techniques to enhance internal locus of control, lower anxiety, and improve the ability to monitor both internal and external stimuli (Goleman, 2003).

THE IMPACT OF MARTIAL ARTS ON JUVENILE DELINQUENTS

Practice of martial arts was another vital component of the study. Recent research shows that martial arts practice is a discipline with promise to help remedy mental health problems by curbing aggressive tendencies, developing compassion and respect, and cultivating a strong moral foundation. Over the past decade or so, studies have shown that certain types of martial arts practice are connected with lowered rates of aggression. The practice of focusing on breath and awareness of the sensations of the body when anger arises in consciousness has also been found to disrupt the cycle of anger. This process is a catalyst for the relaxation response, which is the antidote for the fight-or-flight stress response. As a result, the mind is restored to balance more rapidly and destructive behavior is avoided (Trulson, 1986; Zivin, et al., 2001).

Because the history of martial arts is rooted in training programs for psychological and spiritual growth, it is understandable that one finds increasing

Western interest in the martial arts' ability to promote physical and mental health (Weiser, Kutz, Kutz, & Weiser, 1995). This interest is manifested partly in psychology and martial arts literature. These literatures include both theory and applied research that has explored concepts ranging from Eastern, Zen-like concepts (Back & Kim, 1979) to Western ideas and constructs.

One of the most abstract benefits of the martial arts is "self-actualization and enlightenment" (Back & Kim, 1979; Becker, 1982; Thirer & Grabiner, 1980). This formless and sometimes esoteric concept has been defined in a variety of ways. Becker (1982) provided an explanation, which emphasizes harmony with nature. According to this theory, since karate movements correspond to various aspects of nature (Russell, 1976), when the marital artist practices these movements he or she becomes more harmonious with nature. A second definition of enlightenment suggests that it is related to a state of awareness or being. For example, Back and Kim (1979) discuss the martial arts students' learning to interact with their environments in a spontaneous manner in which thought is precluded. Thirer and Grabiner (1980) discuss a similar concept, which they refer to as "peak experience." Peak experience is defined as an internal state involving a sense of total immersion, oneness, and the feeling of effortless movement. Other interpretations of enlightenment are more psychological in nature. Russell (1976) discusses self-acceptance. Specifically, Russell believes that through the deep experience of his or her emotions, the martial artist develops a deeper sense of self-knowledge and acceptance.

Recent research is demonstrating that martial arts practice that incorporates physical techniques and exercises with meditation and brief lectures reduces aggressive behaviors, disrupts the anger cycle, solicits the relaxation response, reduces anxiety, and balances the mind. Research also shows that this type of martial arts practice leads to more warm-hearted easy-going individuals and increases self-confidence, self-esteem and self-control (Brown, et al., 1995; Leith & Taylor, 1990).

In practical usage, *Chuan Fa* incorporates "hard" and "soft" elements in self-defense strategies and techniques. Common to "hard" and "soft" elements is the practice of calmness, focus on respiration and body sensations, emptying the mind of all thoughts, and the awareness of *Chi* flowing throughout the body. Through this practice, over time the practitioner may begin to realize pure consciousness, consciousness free from desire, aversion, and ignorance.

At the center of *Chuan Fa* as a spiritual path is *chi*, the cosmos-forming energy that also lies at the core of each human being, waiting to be realized. While the concept of *chi* originates with the seminal thinkers of ancient China—Lao-tzu, Chuang-tzu, Huainan-tzu, as well as Kuan-tzu, Ch'engtzu, Confucius and Mencius—it is not limited to them; it underwent changes in evolution of history. The connotation of *chi* takes on multihued colorings and nuances in the different cultural spheres and time periods of East Asian civilizations. In Japan after this concept

with the eyes of the spirit means viewing it from the viewpoint its real essence. When one looks in this way one sees that all of creation, the whole world, all humanity, are of the same womb with trees, grass, everything even the clouds and the mists. *Chuan Fa* practitioners use this way of seeing and this description of the basic essence of the universe to obtain an understanding of the spirit of loving and protecting all things and the injunction against fighting (Tohei, 1978).

Suzuki (1959) taught that when human beings are aware of *chi* they "will know how to behave on every occasion… as long as they are one with *chi* they will never err in proper behavior however variable the situation may be" (p.174).

According to the Chinese philosopher Chuang-tzu, by relinquishing psychic turbulence through "mind-fasting" human beings can hear and see with

to love, reverence, and protect all sentient beings.

During *Chuan Fa* practice participants are taught that their lives are part of the universal *chi* enclosed in the flesh of their bodies. Even though *chi* is encased in flesh, it is in conflux with and active as part of the universal life force. When human beings breathe they breathe the *chi* of the universal in with their entire bodies (Tohei, 1978). When the conflux of a human beings *chi* and that of the universal is unimpaired that human being is considered to be in good health and can be characterized as lively, loving, and unselfish. When the flow is dull, human beings become listless, and selfish, and when it stops, the body dies.

SUMMARY OF THE FINDINGS

It seems that mindfulness or full mental absorption in a task is at the root of the therapeutic aspects of *Chuan Fa*. Absorption in a task frees up psychic energy that would otherwise be constrained by the perpetual habits of the ego. This freeing of psychic energy brings a sense of enjoyment and a more vital relationship to the world. Whether the experience is felt as a moment of simple clarity or an insight that has a profound effect on the core of one's being, whether it occurs while in meditation, martial arts practice, attending to a loved one, running, weight-training, or washing the dishes, the principle seems to be that absorption is happiness. When one is absorbed in a task the thoughts that typically one finds troublesome are neutralized through the process of absorption or mindfulness; this brings about a relaxed state of body and mind. When one recalls a distressing thought, while at the same time is in a state of deep relaxation, the disturbing thought will lose its hold and thoughts about it will be converted into objective and relatively non-emotional concerns. If one deliberately allows distressing thoughts to arise while relaxed in a detached state of meditation this can bring about a critical change in a person's reaction to those thoughts and this change may be more or less permanent in its effect.

The mindful absorption that was cultivated in sitting and moving meditation seemed to have a healing effect on participants. It may have brought about an awareness of wholeness. From this place of wholeness, partici-

> When troubled young people begin to connect to their domain of wholeness they start to realize that there is a way of being, a way of living, a way of paying attention that is like starting anew, that is liberating.

was introduced it interacted with the native ethos to form a distinctive world-view, encompassing attitudes to nature, life, and death (Ueshiba, 1984).

Chi can be simply defined as vital energy or the fundamental creative principle. Like the Sanskrit *prana*, it is conceived to be a subtle breath, spirit, or energy that pervades the universe (Murphy, 1992). *Chuan Fa* philosophy holds that *chi*, is the essential substance of the universe. It has no beginning and no end; its absolute value neither increases or decreases. Human beings were born of *chi*, to which they must someday return.

To understand *chi* one must learn a special way of seeing. One must learn to see with the eyes of spirit. To see with the eyes of the body, our lives seem to disappear at death, but from the viewpoint of the spirit, nothing disappears at all. Life existed before birth of the human body and will exist in the hereafter. Looking at something

chi to apprehend "the emptiness (*kyo, hsu*) in which infinite possibilities are harbored" (Murphy, 1992, p. 451).

One objective in the practice of *Chuan Fa* is the unification of the fundamental creative principle, *chi*, permeating the universe, and the individual *chi*, inseparable from the breath, of every person. Through the diligent training of mind and body, the individual *chi* harmonizes with the universal *chi*, and this harmony appears in a vibrant, flowing movement of *chi*-power that is free and fluid, indestructible and invincible.

The practice of *chi* development can be presented to incarcerated juvenile delinquents as a practice of awakening an astounding healing power that lies within them waiting to be accessed in order to liberate them from their suffering. This cosmic-power has the capacity to transforms hearts, minds, and worlds. With the cultivation of positive *chi* comes a spontaneous commitment pants appeared to develop the ability to come to terms with their problems and suffering in a more skilful way. As a result of their practice there seemed to come about a different way of seeing that created a different context within which they were able to see and work with their problems. It seemed to be a perceptual shift away from fragmentation and isolation toward wholeness and connectedness. With this shift of perspective there seemed to come about a feeling of being more in control and an acknowledgement of what is possible, a sense of acceptance and inner peace. There also seemed to be a definite attitudinal and emotional transformation.

As a result of their practice participants seemed to have been able to cultivate a sense of connectedness. This is significant because when one feels connected to something, that connection immediately gives one a reason for living. Affiliation, meaning and a sense of coherence are attributes of wellbeing. When one feels well one typically has healthier relationships and makes better decisions in one's life.

Meaning and relationships are strands of connectedness. They weave one's life as an individual into the larger community of the human family, which one might say, actually gives one's life its individuality, which is a fundamental task of adolescence.

It may be that the cultivation of connectedness was one of the most powerful aspects of the practice of *Chuan Fa* in terms of its relationship to participants' emotional health. The studies of social involvements and health certainly suggest that this is so (Kabat-Zinn, 1990). It might be said that the degree to which a person's mind and body are connected and in harmony reflects the degree of awareness that a person brings to present moment experience. If one is not in touch with oneself, it is very unlikely that one's connections with others will be satisfactory. The more centered one is the easier it will be for one to be centered in relationships, to appreciate connectedness with others.

When troubled young people begin to connect to their domain of wholeness they start to realize that there is a way of being, a way of living, a way of paying attention that is like starting anew, that is liberating. It doesn't matter how much turmoil or suffering one has experienced, one learns to be with things just as they are but one now sees in a different way.

Chuan Fa practice provided the troubled young people of this study an opportunity to walk the path of their own lives with their eyes open and minds alert, responding consciously in the world instead of reacting automatically, mindlessly. The end result of this practice seemed to be subtly different from the other way of living in that participants seemed to know that they were walking a path, that they were following a way, that they were awake and aware. No one was dictating to them what the path was. No one was telling them to follow "my way." It was suggested to participants that perhaps there is only one way, but that way manifests in as many different ways as there are people. Each person individually is responsible to walk the path in a way that they find meaningful.

REFERENCES

Back, A., & Kim, D. (1979). Towards a Western philosophy of the Eastern martial arts. *Journal of the Philosophy of Sport, VI,* 19-28.

Becker, C. B. (1982). Philosophical perspectives on the martial arts in America. *Journal of the Philosophy of Sport, 9,* 19-29.

Brown, D. R., Wang, Y., Ward, A., Ebbeling, C. B., Fortlage, L., Puleo, et al. (1995). Chronic psychological effects of exercise and exercise plus cognitive strategies. *Medicine and Science in Sports and Exercise, 27,* 765-775.

Easwaran, E. (1985). *The dhammapada.* Berkeley, CA: Blue Mountain.

Goleman, D. (2003). *Destructive emotions: How can we overcome them.* New York: Bantam Books.

Hart, W. (1987). *The art of living: Vipassana meditation.* San Francisco, CA: Harper Collins.

Ingram, J. C., Marchoni, P., Hill, C., Caraveo-Ramus, E., & McNeil, B. (1985). Recidivism, perceived problem abilities, MMPI characteristics, and violence: A study of black and white incarcerated male offenders. *Journal of Clinical Psychology, 41,* 425-432.

James, W. (1997). *The varieties of religious experience.* New York: Simon and Schuster.

Kabat-Zinn, J. (1990). *Full catastrophe living.* New York: Doubleday Publishing.

Kumchy, C., & Sayer, L. (1980). Locus of control in a delinquent population. *Psychological Reports, 46,* 1307-1310.

Leith, L. M., & Taylor, A. H. (1990). Psychological aspects of exercise: A decade literature review. *Journal of Sport Behavior, 13,* 219-239.

Mendel, R. A. (2000). *Less hype, more help: Reducing juvenile crime, what works—what doesn't.* Washington, DC: American Youth Policy Forum.

Murphy, M. (1992). *The future of the body: Exploration into the further evolution of human nature.* New York: Penguin.

Office of Juvenile Justice and Delinquency Prevention. (2004, September). *Bulletin.* Retrieved November 13, 2008, from www.ojp.usdoj.gov/ojjdp.

Russell, W. S. (1976). *Karate: The energy connection.* San Francisco: Delacorte Press.

Salzburg, S. (1995). *Loving-kindness: The revolutionary art of happiness.* Boston: Shambhala.

Suzuki, D. T. (1959). *Zen and Japanese culture.* New York: Princeton University Press.

The National Center on Addiction and Substance Abuse at Columbia University (2004). *Criminal neglect: Substance abuse, Juvenile Justice, and the children left behind.* Retrieved November 13, 2008 from http://www.casacolumbia.org.

Thirer, J., & Grabiner, M. D. (1980). Self-actualization through Zen and the martial arts. *Review of Sport and Leisure, 5,* 79-92.

Tohei, K. (1978). *Ki in daily life.* Tokyo: Ki No Kenkyukai.

Trulson, M. E. (1986). Martial arts: A novel "cure" for juvenile delinquency. *Human Relations, 39,* 1131-1140.

Ueshiba, K. (1984). *The spirit of aikido.* Tokyo: Kodansha International.

Weiser, M., Kutz, I., Kutz, S. J., & Weiser, D. (1995). Psychotherapeutic aspects of the martial arts. *American Journal of Psychotherapy, 49,* 118-127.

Zivin, G., Hassan, N. R., Depaula, G. F., Monti, D. A., Harlan, C., Hossain, K. D., et al. (2001). An effective approach to violence prevention: Traditional martial arts in middle school. *Adolescence, 36,* 443-460.

Art by Mariana Castro de Ali

Therapeutic Horseback Riding With Children Placed In The Foster Care System

Amy Kesner & Steven R. Pritzker

Many of the estimated 500,000 children (National Foster Parent Association, 2000) placed in Therapeutic Foster Care (TFC) have experienced physical, emotional, or sexual abuse, as well as abandonment so they struggle with trusting others and forming quality relationships. Interaction with family and friends is often guarded because they have difficulty dealing with emotional intimacy.

TFC is reserved for children with severe emotional disturbances. While they do not meet the criteria for inpatient hospitalization care, placement in TFC is considered an inpatient service. Issues for these children may include poor self-esteem and self-concept, poor boundaries, lack of empathy, attachment issues, and difficulty feeling loved (Bodmer & Grob, 1996; Foster

Amy Kesner, Ph.D., is a Licensed Professional Counselor in the state of Oklahoma where she has worked as a therapist for 13 years. She currently works for Human Skills and Resources as a therapist to children who have been abused and are placed in state custody. She also works as a substance abuse counselor for adults and families and assists in foster parent training. Current projects include advocating for funding to implement animal-assisted therapy for emotionally disturbed children in state custody.

Steven R. Pritzker, Ph.D., is an Executive Faculty member at Saybrook Graduate School and Research Center where he is Director of the Consciousness and Spirituality Concentration, the M.A. in Psychology with an Emphasis on Creativity Studies. He is Co-Editor-in-Chief of *The Encyclopedia of Creativity* (2nd ed. in 2011). Dr. Pritzker edited a special edition of *Psychology and Marketing* (May 2009) related to creativity research and film. Recent book chapters include "Characteristics of Eminent Screenwriters" in *Psychology and Writing* (Cambridge, 2009) and "Audience Flow: Creativity in Television Watching With Applications to Teletherapy" in *Everyday Creativity and New Views of Human Nature* (American Psychological Association, 2007).

Family-Based Treatment Association, 2001). Mental health problems include an inability to form emotional attachments, depression, explosive tantrums, excessive aggressiveness, refusal to follow rules or respect authority, conduct disorder (lying, stealing, destruction of property, hurting others), drug use, and other self-destructive behaviors.

Children in TFC often demonstrate a lack of response to more traditional therapy approaches including talk therapy. Corson, et al. (1977) found that Animal Assisted Therapy was effective with clients who were unresponsive to other forms of treatment. The field of animal-assisted therapy (AAT) is based on evidence that indicates relationships with animals can be therapeutic and beneficial to psychological well-being (Arkow, 1984; Melson, 2001; Polsbuck, 1997). Human-animal interaction may facilitate a healing relationship. In some situations, children may feel more comfortable forming attachments to animals. Animals can assist children in the development of healthy self-esteem, ability to set boundaries, and build trust.

Studies concerning animal-assisted therapies and therapeutic horseback riding have shown positive results with specific populations, including individuals with physical disabilities, developmental disorders, the elderly and at-risk youth. However, we could not find any studies that looked at the effect of therapeutic horseback riding on children in TFC. Obviously anything that could help these children develop trust and relationship might have the power to improve their lives so a research study was launched in 2007 asking: What are the effects of therapeutic horseback riding on abused children placed in the therapeutic foster care system?

In this article, we will present a background on the historical aspects and psychological perspectives regarding human-animal relationships that frames the rationale for this study. Then we will discuss the results of the study with emphasis on the children's own reports of the experience.

Historical and Spiritual Aspects of Human-Animal Relationships

The healing power of a relationship with animals is not a new concept. Scully (2002) stated, "Whether of natural or supernatural origin, the moment

Note: Children were not participants in the study.   Photo: Mariana Castro de Ali

that humanity acquired reason and language we were set apart forever from the natural world, and nothing was ever the same" (p. 1). This is illustrated by the fact that, "The earliest indication of the spiritual significance of the human-animal relationship can be found in the 20,000-year-old cave wall paintings of Cro-Magnon people" (Randour, 2000, p. 3). In many cultures, animals were "linked with supernatural forces, acting as guardians and shamans, worshiped along with gods and goddesses, and appeared in images of an afterlife" (Randour, 2000, p. 3). Literature and religious teachings from Eastern and Western traditions suggest that treating animals with responsibility, respect, and reverence contributes to an individual's spiritual growth.

The Hebrew word *nephesh*, which translates as, "that which animates living beings with personality, desires, feelings, and volition, what we know as soul, refers to both animals and humans throughout the Hebrew bible" (Randour, 2000, p. 108). According to Randour, the New Testament uses *psuche*[1], the Greek version of *nephesh*, meaning "breath of life," to refer to animal souls (Revelations: 8:9, 16:3, King James Version and The Companion Bible). This demonstrates that historically, people believed that animals experienced feelings and desires, had interests, and consciousness. Hyland (2000) identified scriptures that described God as having relationships with humans and animals.

Hinduism and Buddhism, as well as other Eastern religions, base their beliefs on the doctrine of interdependence of all species. "Eastern religions do not separate human and non-human animals the same way as Judeo-Christian traditions often do. They often assign spiritual attributes to animals, and give them moral consideration (Randour, 2000, p. 105).

Islamic tradition supports the concept that kindness to animals is respect for Allah (Scully, 2002). Masri (1989), in his book *Animals in Islam*, taught that all elements of nature, including all the animal kingdoms, function in harmony with God's laws, and that only humans disobey and bring suffering on themselves. This affliction can appear as disease, illness, or emotional hardships. This theme is repeated throughout the *Qur'an* to emphasize that humans should work toward harmony with nature, according to the laws of God, as does all of creation.

Ayurveda, the ancient Hindu medical science, is based on principles that pertain to the life of humans, plants, and animals, and is considered by some scholars to be the oldest healing system (Lad, 2002). Hinduism also advocates *ahimsa*, the practice of not causing harm to all living things (Randour, 2000). Hindu texts state that humans must interact with the universe to be balanced since the human being represents the universe: "Ayurveda defines life as the conjunction of body, mind, and spirit found in Cosmic Consciousness and embracing all of Creation" (Lad, 2002, p. 1). If this balance or harmony is disrupted, a person may become ill. Therefore, treatment of disease in Ayurveda is to restore this balance, including functioning of the body's systems, emotions, creativity, psychological systems, and integrating relationships with nature, including animals, family, self, and God (Lad, 2002). When these relationships are weakened, an imbalance is created and the individual may suffer from various maladies. One way to reconnect with nature and recapture a sense of true balance may be accomplished by having relationships with animals.

Many indigenous cultures address the important role of animals in their daily lives. Extensive symbolic use of animals can be found within Native American culture (Randour, 2000). Native Americans do not classify animals as separate from humans. McGaa (1992) explained that the lifestyle of Native Americans demonstrates an interdependent relationship with nature. McElroy (1996) stated, "Indigenous people look upon wild animals as living incarnations of special powers, traits, or virtues that humans might learn from if they watched closely and with reverence" (p. 98). Sun Bear and Wabun Wind (1992) explained that Native Americans believe in the equality and interdependence of all creatures, including minerals, plants, animals, and that survival and harmony is maintained through a blending with nature.

Animal medicine is the energy of the animal that helps a person reconnect to the universe. Sams and Carson (1988) argued that medicine is anything that improves one's connection to all life forms, for healing the body, mind, and spirit. They explained that Native American medicine promotes harmony with creation and that an illness is viewed as disharmony in one's soul.

Animals exhibit patterns and habits that convey messages of healing. According to Sams and Carson (1988), these patterns offer lessons based on one concept, and each animal has been designated to teach a lesson. Storm (1972) explained that Indian elders teach that all things, except humans, know of their harmony with nature. He stated that all things of the universe have a spirit, and that people can be made whole by learning to have harmony with all things in the universe. Many shamans speak about the importance of the relationship between humans and animals as it relates to health and healing using spirit animals and totems.

The biophilia hypothesis, advanced by Wilson (1984), proposes that humans have an innate urge to "affiliate with other life forms" (p. 85). Wilson explained that the brain has evolved over millions of years, from a time when people lived in hunter-gather communities, having intimate contact with the natural world around them. He proposed that the brain has stored this information through time, as exemplified by our current behavior. Wilson is not describing "instinct" but information that has been stored genetically as learned from very early experiences (p. 108).

This innate urge to connect with nature influences human development on an emotional and cognitive level. Children are assumed to have "a connection with other living things" during initial stages of life and that the "emotions and personalities of animals are immediate to children in the same way that the emotions and personality of

> This innate urge to connect with nature influences human development on an emotional and cognitive level.

people are" (Melson, 2001, p. 19). As a society, we seem to understand that children have a natural affinity for animals as "we fill children's lives with animal presences through books, art, and videos" (Randour, 2000, p. 15). This is evident in television shows, movies, and learning programs designed for children. Animals and symbols such as stuffed animals help children learn and provide comfort and communication.

Shepard (1978) explained:

Human intelligence is bound to the presence of animals. They are the means by which cognition takes its first shape and they are the instruments for imagining abstract ideas and qualities, they are the code images by which language retrieves ideas and traits. Animals are used in the growth and development of the human person, in those most priceless qualities we lump together as 'mind'. Animals are basic to the development of speech and thought. (p. 249)

Wilson stated:

We are literally kin to other organisms. The phylogenetic continuity of life with humanity seems an adequate reason by itself to tolerate the continued existence of apes and other organisms. This does not diminish humanity; it raises the status of non-human creatures. (p. 130)

The theory of biophilia purports that "humans are predisposed to respond to friendly animals as sentinels of safety and as partners in dialogue" (Melson, 2001, p. 131). Wilson (1984) asked, "How could our relation to nature, on which survival depended minute by minute for millions of years, not in some way be reflected in the rules of cognitive development that generate the human mind?" (p. 9).

Psychological Perspectives

Freud (1994) was interested in how frequently animals appeared in children's dreams. He proposed that animal figures were projections of threatening adults, possibly parents. In contrast, Jung stressed that animal symbols express aspects of the interpretative self.

Jung believed that animal figures appeared in our dreams as part of the evolution of our psyche that represents the "legacy of our ancestral life" (Ryan, 2002, p. 24). Ryan argued that these animal images represent human psychic integration. Jung considered

this integration a "wholeness that is both God and animal, the totality of being rooted in animal nature and reaching out to the divine" (p. 74). Ryan explained that archetypal symbols, such as animal figures, function as images of instinct as "the symbols enlist and employ the deep instinctive wisdom of nature which healed body and mind for millennia before consciousness and the ego seized the reigns" (p. 147). One participant's description reflected this process:

I believe that all animals are equal and if you are disrespectful toward a horse it is as bad as being disrespectful to another person. I have thought a lot about this and I can sense that my horse knows I feel this way. He comes to me in my dreams and lets me know that I am going to be alright, even if I am different.

Erikson (1968) proposed that the developmental stages of initiative and industry[2] involves exploration and investigation of the natural environment, which is often met by children playing outside and interacting with animals, as well as other people. These experiences lead to an understanding of one's relationship with nature and help develop identity.

Piaget's (1970) theory of cognition implies that children, aged 7 and younger, may view animals as peers. Piaget's view opens the possibility that teaching children to be empathetic with an animal may be easier than with adults. Cognitive research indicates that teaching children to be kind and respectful to animals may eventually result in similar behavior to people (Nebbe, 2000).

Melson (1989) alluded to the psychological relationship between humans and animals by reporting that animals are "finely tuned barometers of human feelings, readily reflecting and reacting to the emotional climate as shown in clinical accounts of pets mirroring anorexia, depression, and other disorders in their human owners" (p. 42). As noted by one participant:

I am less angry and depressed. I think my horse makes me happy. Jim [The Riding Instructor] told me that he had to change horses with me because I was so angry it made my horses angry. That isn't fair. I shouldn't take my anger everywhere.

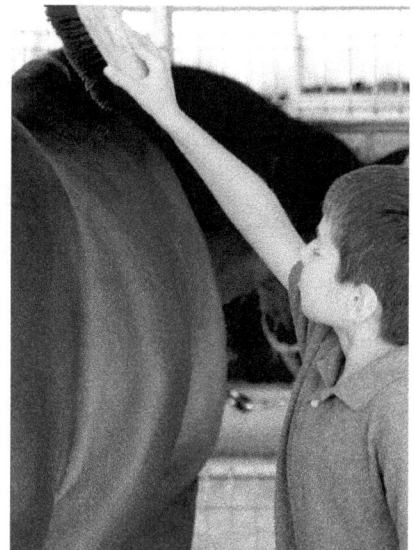
Photo: Mariana Castro de Ali
Note: Child is not a participant in the study.

Animal Assisted Therapy

Boris Levinson is often credited with being a pioneer in the field of animal-assisted therapy (AAT). During one of his sessions he noticed that the presence of his dog Jingles prompted positive responses from a withdrawn child. Levinson tested techniques of using the dog's presence to make visits to therapy less threatening for other children. Levinson's initial observations led to his 1969 book *Pet-Oriented Child Psychotherapy.* He theorized that for children who require hospitalization, animals might humanize the setting and help distract a child from inner conflicts (Levinson, 1997).

Mental health professionals realize that animals can be very powerful in helping children at risk because they can encourage learning, cooperation, and expression. Animals can stimulate exercise, reduce anxiety, provide comfort and an external focus of attention, and may decrease loneliness and depression (All, et al., 1999). A supportive relationship is beneficial to individuals who experienced stressful circumstances (Arkow, 1984; Jennings, 1997).

In a series of studies, including the 1996 study by Beck and Katcher, it was found that children's blood pressure decreased in the company of a friendly dog (Altschuler, 1999; Katcher, et al., 1983), and children who demonstrated empathy toward animals, were empathetic to other humans (Ascione, 1992; Ascione & Weber, 1996; Melson, 2001).

Children with varying disabilities who participate in AAT may improve communication and social skills as well as demonstrate academic improvements (Polsbuck, 1997). There are also indications that some children may be more responsive to an animal than to another person (Kaufmann, 1997). Gonski (1985) did a study with children in traditional, long-term foster care and found that when dogs were part of the treatment, children seemed to develop empathy and demonstrate improved behavioral response as compared to children in treatment without dogs.

Therapeutic horseback riding

Therapeutic horseback riding is a specialized form of AAT. Horses offer aspects to treatment that may not be available with smaller animals (Granger & Kogan, 2000). Therapeutic riding is a process in which a rider and their horse can interact to address physical, mental, and emotional needs (North America Riding for the Handicapped Association, 2000; Equine Assisted Growth and Learning Association [EAGALA], 2003).

Horseback riding gives people with various disabilities the opportunity to participate and succeed at something that others may not try. Children are given the opportunity to socialize with peers who have similar problems and interests, including riding. Individuals are encouraged to give the horse the necessary commands, such as go or walk, and to move in different directions, which teach riders the benefits of using meaningful speech. When they speak to the horse they get results, which encourages additional interaction, articulation, and verbalization.

The therapeutic value of riding stems from the relationship developed between a rider and their horse. Becker (2002) noted, "the horse is just being the horse, walking fast or slow around the ring," depending on the rider's instructions "people bring their issues to the horse, no matter what they are, and see them reflected back in stark relief" (p. 132). Horses offer passive therapy just through clients sitting on their backs as their perspective of the world may change and provide a sense of power. Riding offers active therapy through the learning of behaviors,

which result in a positive response from the horse, and may offer benefits for psychological or social problems (Granger & Kogan, 2000). Jorgenson (1997) asserted that riding encourages risk-taking and the development of patience, emotional control, and self-discipline. Learning to maneuver a large animal can be empowering and promote confidence and self-esteem. Becker (2002) said that exercising power and control are key issues to those who suffer from "depression, anxiety, eating disorder, and whom have a history of abuse" (p. 132). He stated that working with horses offers the opportunity to "engage the root of fear, allows a person to see a problem more clearly, and that the encounter brings up the struggle to integrate mind and body; to have our actions and our stance reflect our true intentions" (p. 133).

Children in TFC have usually participated in various therapeutic interventions and have been placed in a variety of therapeutic settings, including group homes and hospitals. However, positive results from these interventions were minimal as evidenced by continued behavioral and emotional problems. "As more traditional therapy methods are not producing outcomes people want, the use of horses is gaining more recognition as a powerful and effective approach to emotional healing" (EAGALA, 2003, p. 7).

Becker (2002) explained, "In traditional therapy, the patient and therapist sit in chairs and discuss events that took place outside the room. In equine-

Photo: Mariana Castro de Ali
Note: Child is not a participant in the study.

assisted therapy the event takes place in the stall with the horse" (p. 132). He noted that this experience could help with roadblocks that have interfered with therapeutic progress. Kersten (2003) stated:

The benefits to adolescent clients include respect and responsibility as a by-product of basic equine care and upkeep. As sessions with the animals progress and intensify, appropriate communication, confidence, and self-esteem are learned through trial and error and accomplishment with equine counterparts. (p. 17)

Results

Fourteen children aged 5-17 (8 boys, 6 girls) were selected based on face-to-face interviews with foster parents, where they were invited to allow their foster children to participate in the study. The participants in this study were placed in TFC yet there were no set criteria pertaining to placement established for specific behavior or emotional issues or DSM-IV-TR diagnosis. Selection Criteria for participants included the following:

1. Stabilization of any presenting dangerous behaviors preceding the study, including incidents of self-harm or threats to harm others.
2. No expressed fear of animals.
3. Cognitive ability to process feelings and thoughts

Each child and their TFC parents were interviewed. Additional data included observations of children in the riding session, interviews with the riding instructor and parents' journals. Children completed both the Tennessee Self-Concept Scale (TSCS) and the Piers-Harris 2 Children's Self-Concept. TFC parents completed the Conduct Disorder Scale (CDS) prior to the riding session and afterwards.

Children participated in 10 therapeutic horseback riding sessions. Sessions were scheduled in 1-hour increments for each riding group. Riding sessions focused on learning the basics of horse care, riding etiquette, and mastery of riding skills including maneuvering the horse. Horses are "large and powerful, and are naturally intimidating to many people," and riding a horse can offer an "opportunity to overcome fear and develop confidence" (EAGALA, 2003, p. 8). Becker (2002) explained that the

Table 1 N=14 *Participant demographics for therapeutic horseback riding program.*					
Participant	**Age**	**Race**	**Gender**	**Diagnosis**	**History of animal abuse**
Bradley	14	Caucasian	Male	ODD, RAD	No
Chris	7	Caucasian	Male	RAD, CD	No
Danny	9	Caucasian	Male	DBD, PTSD, Depression	No
Blake	15	Native American	Male	Depression, DBD	No
Lane	15	Caucasian	Male	RAD, CD	No
Duke	6	Native American	Male	RAD, DBD	No
Anna	10	Native American	Female	PTSD, MMR	No
Kirsten	7	Native American	Female	PTSD, RAD, PDD, MMR	No
Misti	8	Caucasian	Female	ADHD, RAD, DBD	Yes
Brandy	17	Native American	Female	Depression, ODD	No
Andrea	10	Caucasian	Female	ODD, RAD	No
³*Sarah*	13	Native American	Female	Depression, DBD	No
Zach	5	Caucasian	Male	PTSD, RAD,	Yes
Braden	12	Caucasian	Male	ODD, RAD	Yes

Note. Diagnoses are abbreviated as follows: Attention Deficit Disorder (ADHD); Conduct Disorder (CD); Disruptive Behavior Disorder (DBD); Oppositional Defiant Disorder (ODD); Pervasive Development Disorder (PDD); Reactive Attachment Disorder (RAD); and Moderate Mental Retardation (MMR).

size and power of a horse "demands that you confront it" and that interacting with them "forces whatever emotion you are feeling right to the surface" (p. 124). The accomplishment of tasks while working with horses creates confidence and can serve as a metaphor for dealing with a variety of life situations. Even mounting a horse can be stimulating and viewed as a success. Kersten (2003) added that horses are "proven to be versatile and dynamic assistants in therapy" (p. 17).

Each child was carefully matched by the riding instructor, Jim, with the most appropriate horse. Jim explained that each horse presents different characteristics and styles, so each participant needs to learn unique ways to work with their particular horse. For example, each horse has a preferred way to be prompted to trot and run. One horse responds to the use of a riding whip, another responds to a certain sound, while another is prompted by gently kicking the horse in a specific area. McCowen (1987) pointed out that the selection of a horse is pivotal to the success of any riding program, "second in importance only to the selection of the instructor, as together they make a working team" (p. 251). This is exhibited in a decision by the riding instructor considering one participant (all participant names and the riding instructor's name are pseudonyms):

I put her on that horse because, honestly, it was a gamble. That horse has a bad reputation of being stubborn. I figured he would sense how special she is and that maybe it would be a good pair. Turns out I was right. That horse, as you probably saw, responded well to her and always had his head and ears up. That's evidence of relationship.

And for another participant:

I paired her with a more docile horse. [Kirsten] is controlling and this horse is docile, but he isn't a push-over. I think the horse is more receptive to her. If you notice, she [Kirsten] started showing more affection toward her horse. It's all about the relationship.

Riding Sessions

Sessions were designed to facilitate a relationship between rider and horse. Jim said that the horse would replicate the participant's energy, which results in the participants learning to take responsibility for their own behavior.

During the initial session, participants were allowed a few minutes to get acquainted with their horse. This process allowed the participants to talk and share affection with their horse. Brushes were offered and participants were taught how to groom a horse. This interaction was designed to facilitate bonding between horse and rider. Next, participants were taught how to prepare to saddle the horse.

The next two sessions focused on participants practicing the basics of tack, and included more practice in grooming and preparing to saddle the horses. Jim began teaching participants the essential elements of riding, including how to maneuver the horse and prompt it to go and stop and move right and left. These initial sessions took place within a riding arena. To master the skill of maneuvering the horse, participants engaged in games such as horse basketball, red-light/green-light, and versions of Simon Says and Mother May I. When Jim felt confident in the riding ability of the participants, games were devised to practice how to trot and run the horse.

Eventually the riding sessions advanced outside the arena into trail riding. The instructor led these rides, but as participants demonstrated improved competency and behavior, they were selected to lead the group on rides through open trails. Participants had to agree on who should lead trail rides, which they discussed during the first few minutes of the session. The participants would ride to a specific place where they would stop to talk about what they had learned about riding and how they could apply what they had learned to daily activities. The sixth through the eighth sessions focused on trail riding and applying the riding lessons to life lessons.

The final two sessions allowed participants to talk more specifically about what they would take away from their experience. The final session allowed participants extra time after the trail ride to groom and talk privately to their horse. The processing group at the end of the final session focused on participants sharing what they had learned, what they will apply to their life, and how they felt about completing the program. Jim invited all participants to visit the stables in the future, and, if appropriate, to spend time as a volunteer grooming the horses.

Jim helped participants develop verbal and nonverbal communication skills as they worked to read messages from their horses. These messages may be communicated through facial expression, body movement, and vocalizing. This interaction also helped participants to develop communication skills that are necessary in developing and maintaining relationships (Corson & Corson, 1979; Levinson, 1978).

Table 1 lists Participant demographics including age, race, gender, diagnosis and whether the child has a history of animal abuse. Following is a summary of the experiences of 5 of the 11 children who completed the 10 sessions so the reader can get a sense of the impact of the program.

Bradley

Bradley, 14, said he was very excited to participate and had always wanted to learn to ride horses. During the first session, he hugged his horse and appeared focused on learning and completing tasks. Throughout the sessions, Bradley appeared serious, listened intently, and asked Jim to validate that he was completing skills accurately.

Though Bradley did well during the sessions, he continued to have struggles at home and in school. Bradley was involved in arguments and physical fights with his TFC sibling, who also participated in the riding program. During one riding session the instructor introduced the concept of "The Cowboy Way:"

If your horse trusts you then you are okay. It means you earn trust by trusting others. When you are fighting, violent, or bullying others, your horse will pick up on these characteristics and will have a hard time trusting you.

Jim encouraged participants to follow "The Cowboy Way" during the sessions, and at home and school. After this session, Bradley talked often about following "The Cowboy Way." He described this concept to a school counselor stating, "I told my counselor I was following The Cowboy Way and trying not to be a bully." Bradley's behavior outside of the sessions began to progress according to his TFC parents, and his school counselor. Improvements included a decrease in physical altercations, increased effort toward schoolwork, and a decrease in arguing with TFC parents. He did, however, continue to argue with his TFC sibling, who eventually left the TFC home.

Jim noticed that Bradley had difficulty with his anger: "I had to change horses because of his [Bradley's] anger affecting the horse. He [Bradley] agreed and told me that he had a lot to be angry about." Bradley said during the pre-interview, "I do not want to have to take so much medicine," and described himself as "quiet, sometimes a bully," and not having very many friends. Post-interview results revealed use of positive descriptive words and his personal goal to maintain his progress and "set a good example for little kids." Bradley stated during the post-interview that he felt different:

I am less angry and depressed. I think my horse makes me happy. [Jim] told me that he had to change horses with me because I was so angry it made my horses angry. That isn't fair. I shouldn't take my anger everywhere.

Andrea

Andrea, 10, is the participant who demonstrated the most positive change. All of her post-test scores improved. Andrea noted changes during her post-interview and her TFC mother exclaimed, "She is like a different child!"

At the first session, Andrea demonstrated affection toward her horse, and shared secrets by whispering into his ear. She worked diligently to learn skills and stayed focused. Andrea spent several hours trying to draw a picture of her horse. Her TFC mother reported

that when she would redirect Andrea's behavior, she would begin talking about her horse and what he would think about her actions. If Andrea received a reprimand, she was concerned if the riding instructor would be notified.

Jim also recognized changes in Andrea. He noticed that initially she isolated herself from the group and focused primarily on her horse. Eventually, Andrea began asking questions about horse's social behavior based on her observations:

She began asking questions about how horses make friends and if they feel sad if they have to leave their family. She really seemed to take an interest in the social groups of horses. She also began talking to the other participants about their horses and telling stories that she would make up about her horse.

During her post-interview, Andrea used positive descriptive words compared to ambivalent pre-interview responses. In the post-interview, she identified her goal as, "doing better and being nice to everyone." Andrea described the experience as transformative:

I am happy and don't want to be bad anymore. I think my horse will miss me but I know he would be really sad if I spent this much time with him and then started making bad choices again. He wants me to love myself and guess what? Now I do.

During the post-interview, her TFC mother said Andrea was no longer aggressive and would relate what she was learning from her horse to daily issues: "I was amazed at her ability to make such big changes, all from just riding a horse. I hope that wherever she goes from here, she will continue to work with horses."

Duke

Initially, Duke, 6, did not seem interested in learning the skills, and did not show affection toward his horse. He would direct his attention elsewhere by trying to talk with peers, or playing a game. Duke did not talk about his experience outside of the scheduled sessions, unless asked. However, during the third session, Jim asked how participants felt about their horse, if they wanted to change horses, and if they were dreaming about their horse. Duke raised his hand and stated he did not want to change horses and that he had dreams about riding his horse.

Jim noted that Duke was slow to develop a relationship with his horse:

> He seemed afraid of him but I noticed after the third session, he was petting him more. He also began paying closer attention to directions and even demonstrated a bit of competitiveness. I am not sure how he is doing at home or school, but it seems like the light has come on while he is here.

During the pre-interview, Duke had ambivalent responses and remarked, "I don't know," to questions about goals, and in describing himself and others. During the post-interview, Duke said he is funny and that his family and friends would say he is funny. He stated his goal is to do well in school and, "get all smiley faces." Duke said he liked his horse: "He makes me want to do better. I don't get in trouble as much as I used to. I made some friends too."

During the post-interview, his TFC mother stated she did not observe any major changes in Duke's behavior during his participation in the program except for a decrease in bed-wetting. Duke's TFC mother believed he enjoyed the program but did not learn anything from participating. Nevertheless, she expressed interest in allowing Duke to continue in the riding program.

Brandy

Brandy, a Native-American who was 17, followed all directions and asked questions about the skills they were learning. She also offered to help younger peers with grooming and other tack activities. Brandy would kiss her horse, rub his mane, and she could be seen petting his nose and talking to him while hugging his neck. This was significant since Brandy had difficulty demonstrating genuine affection.

Brandy had a history of sexually perpetrating behavior toward younger males. She has required re-direction in flirtations, and inappropriate behavior. She admitted during the pre-interview that she was more comfortable with physical relationships than "truly emotional ones."

Jim noted that Brandy improved on her tack and riding skills. He stated that

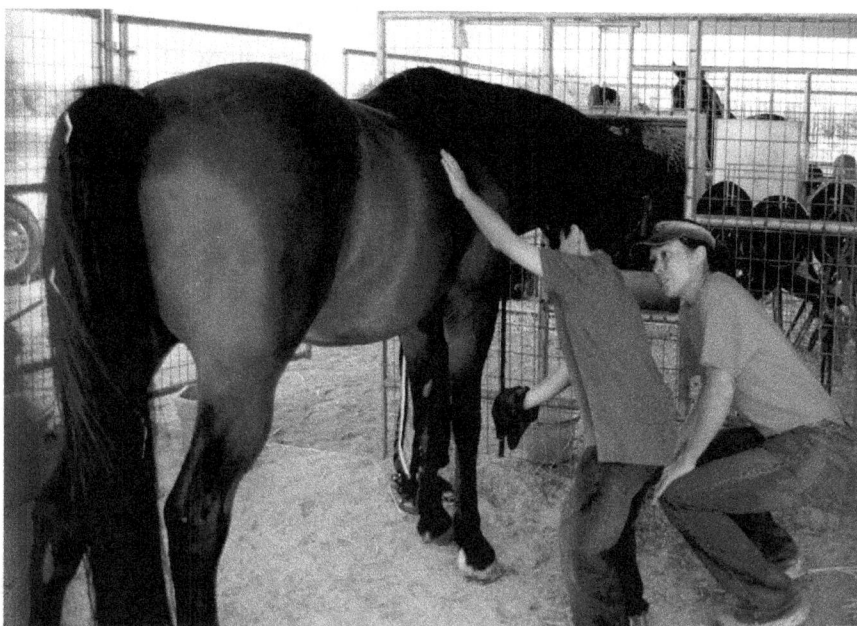

Note: Child is not a participant in the study.

Photo: Mariana Castro de Ali

by the fifth session, she started to share personal information and began asking questions that related to how horses bond with people. "She asked me if horses ever disliked people and for what reasons would they avoid someone."

Brandy's responses in her pre-interview revealed ambivalence, lack of goals, and a negative self-view. When asked about what she enjoyed doing in her spare time, Brandy stated working around the house. During her post-interview, Brandy stated that others would describe her as fun, and that she had goals to finish high school and attend college. During the post-interview, Brandy stated she enjoyed the riding program and "wish that all kids could do this." She described how when she was riding her horse, her problems "melted away." Brandy said, "I never knew a horse could make me feel that good about myself." She said she felt successful in this program and that she believed she lost weight because of participation.

Daily logs from her TFC parents revealed a decrease in problematic behavior as noted in fewer negative statements in the Comments section. Brandy's TFC mother noted in the post-interview that Brandy had fewer depressive symptoms and a notable decrease in statements of hopelessness while paying more attention to self-destructive behavior, including her eating habits. She also mentioned concerns that Brandy "still wants to care for everyone."

Anna

Anna, 10, quickly learned the fundamentals of riding as evidenced by her ability to perform skills without assistance by the third session. She was very affectionate toward her horse and would tell instructors that she did not need help with tack responsibilities. Anna was verbal during the sessions, talking primarily to her horse.

Her TFC parents noticed that Anna kept track of the days so that she would know what her day to ride was. Previously, they observed that Anna struggled with orientation to time and date. The instructor noted that Anna compared her ability to that of her peers.

During the pre-interview, Anna struggled with attention and focus. Questions had to be repeated on several occasions, and she often gave ambiguous responses. The post-interview demonstrated improved focus and ability to respond without hesitation. She identified goals to do well in school, and to listen to her parents. Anna talked incessantly about the riding program and stated she missed going to the sessions. She said she is "a good rider" and wanted to know if her horse missed her. Anna described feeling "related" to her horse and said that her horse was "never mean."

Due to Anna's apparent attachment to her horse, her TFC parents agreed to let Anna visit the stables and her horse at least once a week. Her TFC mother explained that her behavior was more compliant, she demonstrated a positive attitude, was less argumentative, and temper tantrums stopped during the weeks of the program. Her TFC father expressed, "We are so pleased with the results that we plan to let her continue in the program and we recommend it to others." Anna stated, "I love my horse and he teaches me to be good. I am a good rider and I wish I could have my own horse for when I feel sad and mad."

Summary of Results

Evaluation of the data indicated positive behavioral and emotional changes in participants that correlated with their completion of the therapeutic horseback-riding program. Participants described themselves as feeling happier, having more confidence, improved behavior, a desire to socialize with others, and described a sense of self-acceptance and responsibility. Some of the participants specifically identified their relationship with their horse as an important factor contributing to the positive changes they were experiencing.

Participants equally described feeling better about themselves and how others see them, as well as demonstrating affectionate behavior toward their horse. The older participants were more articulate about their changes while the younger peers characterized horse.

The TFC parents observed changes in the participant's behavior, attitude, confidence level, and efforts to interact with others. Some TFC parents were skeptical that the noted changes would be long term or were directly related to the horseback riding as opposed to other forms of positive incentive or reinforcement. However, other TFC parents were impressed with the changes they observed and were hoping to allow the children could continue riding. Post-interviews with TFC

parents indicated a decrease in conduct related issues as well as their opinion that participants demonstrated increased self-esteem and positive attitudes. Another parent described her TFC child, "I never heard him talk about feelings unless it was being mad. Now he will say things like proud, happy, and say that he is good at things It's kind of unbelievable the difference in his sense of self."

Findings of participants and TFC parents were consistent with Barwick (1986), who claimed that human-animal interaction promoted self-awareness and a relationship with the environment. Results support studies

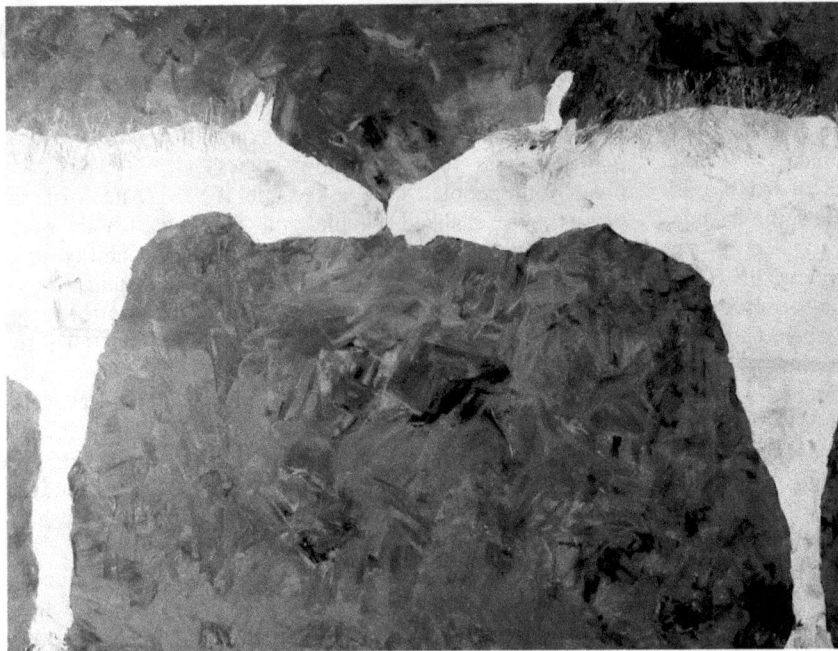

Art by Mariana Castro de Ali

and comments by Arkow (1984), Melson (2001), and Polsbuck (1997) that suggested a therapeutic relationship with animals is beneficial to psychological well-being.

Findings also support previous research that described the facilitative effects of AAT, human-animal interaction, and the human-animal bond (All, et al., 1999; Katcher & Wilkins, 1994; Melson, 1989). The results provided evidence that while interacting with an animal, a child may demonstrate improved attitude, bonding, self-discipline, independence, empathy, and ability to follow instructions, which may carry over into everyday life (All, et al., 1999).

Based on observations and comments by the participants themselves,

the reasons why this intervention produced positive results in self-concept and behavior issues related to the building of relationships. That is, the children were more socially active during participation and were in a socially accepting environment. Most participants seemed to share an interest in their horses, which naturally drew them together. As participants interacted with their horse, forms of socialization were stimulated. This may have redefined the participant's idea of what was possible for them to achieve if they dedicated themselves to learning. Riding, and essentially controlling aspects of the horse's movement, required the development of a relationship. Grandin and Johnson (2005) stated, "Real riding is a lot like ballroom dancing, or maybe figure skating in pairs. It's a relationship" (p. 5). Participant's self-esteem may have increased as they learned of their ability to positively interact and influence their horse. The participants demonstrated an increased desire to help one another as they performed various tasks with their horses. Nebbe (2000) explained that teaching children to treat animals with kindness and respect may result in similar behavior toward people. This tendency was evident with the participants as noted through increased socialization and improved relations with others as evidenced by observations of TFC parents and the riding instructor, as well as by comments by participants. Their participation boosted self-confidence by giving them success at learning to direct such a large animal. One child explained:

I believe animals are equal to human beings. At first I wasn't sure I wanted to do this, but I have learned a lot and have a lot more respect for animals, but I am still working on respecting and trusting people.

Findings paralleled Arkow (1984) and Triebenbacher (1998), who indicated that animals can improve socialization, bring enthusiasm to those who are withdrawn, improve confidence, and that attachment to animals is positively related to a child's self-esteem. As one participant stated, "I feel like myself when I am up there [on the horse]."

A critical point of this study is to mark improvement as a result of therapeutic horseback riding. As noted by findings on the post-assessment, dramatic changes were found in participant's behavior as recorded on the Conduct Disorder Scale. All 11 participants showed a decrease in negative conduct. This indicates that all TFC parents noted significant behavior changes in the participants since the pre-test, even though some TFC parents made comments in the interviews that they did not notice major changes. This is especially significant because criteria for placement in TFC include aggressive behavior and conduct that places the individual as a threat to self or others. These participants had a history of aggressive behavior, lack of respect and very low self-esteem often manifested through self-destructive behavior. During the study, there were no incidents of aggressive behavior by participants toward their horse or each other.

The statistical findings of the TSCS and the Piers-Harris 2 also supported the study with positive changes in self-concept as a result of the program with 90% of participants showing improved scores on post-tests indicating 95% confidence that results are due to therapeutic riding. This demonstrates that the participants changed the way they felt about themselves and how they believe others view them while building confidence. Though the numbers are compelling evidence of the positive effects of the riding program, we believe it is the participant's own words that dramatically support the nature and extent of findings that developing a relationship with a horse can be a catalyst for change. Through their own individualized experience, participants identified how they had changed.

All 11 participants who completed the study demonstrated affection toward their horse even though 8 had no previous history of this type of behavior. Participants may have felt more comfortable demonstrating affection toward their horse than another person. This relationship helped them learn trust, practice mutual respect, and develop a sense of loyalty. This response is of paramount importance to this study because 7 participants had experienced symptoms of Reactive Attachment Disorder, which includes identifying traits of an inability to form bonds and the ability to demonstrate genuine affection. Participants were observed talking and whispering to their horse. Wilson's theory of biophilia explains "humans are predisposed to respond to friendly animal as sentinels of safety and partners in dialogue," (Melson, 2001, p. 131)

Tucker (1997) proposed that participants would transform caring for the horses into caring for themselves. Six participants articulated changes in their behavior and their actions toward others because they were involved in the program. One participant said that her horse "makes me want to be good to other kids." Brandy associated an improvement in her physical health and desire to pay attention to her weight as a result of her riding experience. She exclaimed, "Being with my horse made me see myself." All, Loving, and Crane (1999) indicated that horseback riding can change a child's attitude toward touching and feeling and bonding as well as improvements in self-discipline, independence, attitude and understanding instruction.

Some TFC parents expressed amazement at the results and changes experienced by the participants. One TFC parent, after observing a riding session, stated, "I can't believe how attentive they all are to the instructor, to each other, and what they are doing. I couldn't get my kid to be that focused if I promised them candy!" Another TFC parent said, "This seems so natural, kids and horses together. They are all so gentle and deliberate in their actions with their horse. How can they be that way after all they have experienced and done?" Thematic content from TFC parent interviews supported change in participant's attitudes, respecting rules, and socializing with family.

A horse that is responsive to requests while being led or ridden may represent power to the rider (Leimer, 1997). Participants were able to identify themselves with a large horse which promoted increased self-confidence. One of the themes, Satisfaction, demonstrated that participants related a sense of self-satisfaction. Responses to post-interviews included the statements "I am fun," I am nice," "I am awesome," and "People like me."

Becker (2002) stated that horseback riding is beneficial for abuse victims because it helps them feel empowered. This resonates in comments by participants when speaking about riding their horse, "You have to be smart to do all that stuff." "I feel happy that I have found something I am good at." And one other participant stated, "When I ride Sonny, my problems melt away and I am free and strong."

Relationship qualities, such as trust, empathy, and companionship, can be developed and improved through working with horses (Lawrence, 1984). Often, children who have been abused, and experienced multiple placements, experience a loss of control. Children in these situations have typically been denied respect, or their feelings have not been acknowledged. One participant articulated his new understanding of past experiences when he stated, "horses don't judge you like people do. They don't care where I am from or what I have done." Another participant demonstrated new coping skills: "I need to be more like my horse and not blame my problems on my past and what my parents did."

Participants said they believed success was related to acceptance from their horse and a sense of companionship. Some participants described experiencing unconditional love and attachment to the horse without fear of what was expected of them. As one participant described, it did not matter to the horse if the child was unpopular at school, or that they were placed in TFC. The participants noted changes in their behaviors as well as in their comfort level in social situations. They improved in their ability to experience satisfaction and happiness. They recognized that they had increased self-esteem and acceptance as well as acceptance of others and of their circumstances.

Previous research indicated that children who interact with an animal may demonstrate psychological benefits. The purpose of this study was to evaluate the relationship of therapeutic horseback riding with children in therapeutic foster care. Results indicated that a therapeutic bond with a horse improved participant's self-concept. Additionally, the findings confirmed that participation in therapeutic horseback riding improved emotional and behavioral issues with a decrease in problematic conduct for children in TFC. Participants reported personal change in behavior, satisfaction, socialization, and acceptance. Participants of this study described the positive changes they experienced while participating in the therapeutic horseback riding program. TFC parents described positive changes in participant's behavior, attitude, and socialization.

The results of this study clearly support the use of animal-assisted therapy with TFC children. Therapeutic horseback riding is valuable with populations who struggle with relationships and have been non-responsive to other treatment interventions. Beck (2006) stated, "The term human-animal bond is a metaphor that is meant to capture not only the importance of our relationship with our pets but also the idea that it is a mutually beneficial relationship" (p. 10). Participants, as well as some of their TFC parents seemed to experience a paradigm shift as it related to their sense of value when they viewed themselves in the eyes of their horse. As Wilson (1984) stated, "Humanity is exalted not because we are so far above other living creatures, but because knowing them elevates the very concept of life" (p. 22).

NOTES

1. Randour (2000) identified the New Testament use of *psuche* as the Greek counterpart to *nephesh* (p. 108). This word is also synonymous with the word psyche (Encyclopedic Theosophical Glossary, 1990).

2. Initiative occurs in a preschool age child who begins to initiate or imitate activities and develops conscience. Industry is found in a school-aged child who tries to develop sense of self-worth by refining skills (Erikson, 1968).

3. Sarah, Zach, and Braden left the program before completion.

REFERENCES

All, A. C., Loving, G. L., & Crane, L. L. (1999). Animals, horseback riding, and implications of rehabilitation therapy. *Journal of Rehabilitation, 65*, 49-60.

Altschuler, E. L. (1999). Pet-facilitated therapy for posttraumatic stress disorder. *Annals of Clinical Psychiatry, 11*(1), 29-30.

Arkow, P. (1984). *Dynamic relationships in practice: Animals in the helping professions.* Alameda, CA: The Latham Foundation.

Ascione, F. R. (1992). Enhancing children's attitudes about the humane treatment of animals: generalization to human-directed empathy. *Anthrozoos, 5*, 176-191.

Ascione, F. R., & Weber, C. V. (1996). Children's attitudes about the humane treatment of animals and empathy: One year follow-up of a school-based intervention. *Anthrozoos, 9*, 188-195.

Barwick, S. (1986). Psychomotor therapy. In L. Burr (Ed.), *Therapy through movement.* Nottingham, England: Rehab Limited.

Beck, A. (2006, Summer). Tips for building and strengthening the human-animal bond. *Healthy Pet*, 10-11.

Beck, A., & Katcher, A. (1996) *Between pets and people: The importance of animal companionship.* Lafayette, IN: Purdue University Press.

Becker, M. (2002). *The healing power of pets: Harnessing the amazing ability of pets to make and keep people happy and healthy.* New York: Hyperion.

Bodmer, N. M., & Grob, A. (1996). Adolescents' well-being and daily hassles: A comparison between adolescents living in one-parent and two-parent families. *International Journal of Psychology, 31*, 39-48.

Corson, S., & Corson, E. (1979). Pets as mediators of therapy. In J. Masserman (Ed.), *Current Psychiatric Therapies* (pp. 195-205). New York: Grune & Stratton.

Corson, S., Corson, E., Gwynne, P., & Arnold, L. (1977). Pet dogs as nonverbal communication links in hospital psychiatry. *Comprehensive Psychiatry, 18*(1), 61-72.

Equine Assisted Growth and Learning Association (EAGALA). (2003). *Equine-assisted mental health resource handbook* (2003). Santaquin, UT: Author.

Erikson, E. (1968). *Identity: Youth and crisis.* New York: Norton.

Foster Family-Based Treatment Association (FFTA). (2001). *Annotations of research in treatment foster care.* Retrieved September 22, 2004, from the FFTA database.

Freud, S. (1994). *Interpretation of dreams.* (A. A. Brill, Trans.). New York: Barnes and Noble Books. (Original work published 1900)

Gonski, Y. A. (1985). The therapeutic utilization of canines in a child welfare setting. *Child and Adolescent Social Work Journal, 2*, 93-105.

Grandin, T., & Johnson, C. (2005). *Animals in translation: Using the mysteries of autism to decode animal behavior.* New York: Harcourt.

Granger, B. P., & Kogan, L. (2000). Animal-assisted therapy in specialized settings. In A. H. Fine (Ed.), *Handbook on animal-assisted therapy: Theoretical foundations and guidelines for practice* (pp. 213-236). San Diego, CA: U.S. Academic Press.

Hyland, R. (2000). *God's covenant with animals: A biblical basis for the humane treatment of animals.* New York: Lantern Books.

Jennings, L. B. (1997). Potential benefits of pet ownership in health promotion. *Journal of Holistic Nursing, 15*(4), 358-372.

Jorgenson, J. (1997). Therapeutic use of animals in health care. *Image: Journal of nursing scholarship, 29*(3), 249-254.

Katcher, A. H., Friedmann, E., Beck, A. M., & Lynch, J. J. (1983). Talking, looking, and blood pressure: Physiological consequences of interaction with the living environment. In A. J. Katcher & A. M. Beck (Eds.), *New perspectives on our lives with companion animals* (pp. 351-359). Philadelphia: University of Pennsylvania Press.

Katcher, A., & Wilkins, G. (1994). *The use of animal-assisted therapy and education with attention-deficit hyperactive and conduct disorders.* Paper presented at the 14th Annual Delta Society Conference, New York.

Kaufmann, M. (1997). Creature comforts: Animal-assisted activities in education and therapy. *Reaching Today's Youth, 1*(2), 27-31.

Kersten, G. (2003). More than horse play: Tips on how to investigate and choose effective therapeutic equine programs. In *Equine-assisted mental health resource handbook* (pp. 17-18). Equine Assisted Growth and Learning Association (EAGALA). Santaquin, UT: Author.

Lad, V. D. (2002). *Textbook of Ayurveda: Fundamental principles.* Albuquerque, NM: Ayurvedic Press.

Lawrence, E. A. (1984). Human relationships with horses. In R. K. Anderson, B. L. Hart & L. A. Hart (Eds.), *The pet connection: Its influence on our health and quality of life* (pp. 38-43) Minneapolis: University of Minnesota.

Leimer, G. (1997). Indication of remedial vaulting for anorexia nervosa. In B. T. Engel (Ed.), *Rehabilitation with the aid of a horse: A collection of studies* (pp. 35-54). Durango, CO: Barbara Engel Therapy Services.

Levinson, B. (1969). *Pet-oriented child psychotherapy.* Springfield, IL: Charles C. Thomas.

Levinson, B. (1978). Pets and personality development. *Psychological Reports, 42*, 1031-1038.

Levinson, B. (1997). *Pet-oriented child psychotherapy* (rev. ed.). Springfield, IL: Charles C. Thomas.

Masri, A. (1989). *Animals in Islam*. Petersfield, England: Athene Trust.

McCowen, L. (1987). Equestrian therapy: I can ride a horse. In P. Arkow (Ed.), *The loving bond: Companion animals in the helping professions* (pp. 237-256). Saratoga, CA: R & E Publishers.

McElroy, S. C. (1996). *Animals as teachers: True stories and reflections*. Troutdale, OR: New Sage Press.

McGaa, E. (1992). *Rainbow tribe: Ordinary people journeying on the red road*. San Francisco: Harper.

Melson, G. (2001). *Why the wild things are: Animals in the lives of children*. Cambridge, MA: Harvard University Press.

Melson, G. F. (1989). Studying children's attachment to their pets: A conceptual and methodological review. *Anthrozoos, 4*(2), 91-99.

National Foster Parent Association. (2000). *National foster care coalition: The end of foster care should never mean the end of caring*. Retrieved September 22, 2004, from http://www.nfpainc.org/.

Nebbe, L. (2000). Nature therapy. In A. H. Fine (Ed.), *Handbook on animal-assisted therapy: Theoretical foundations and guidelines for practice* (pp. 385-414). San Diego, CA: U.S. Academic Press.

North America Riding for the Handicapped Association (NARHA). (2000). *About NARHA: What is therapeutic riding?* Retrieved Nov 6, 2004, from http://www.narha.org/

Piaget, J. (1970). *The science of education and the psychology of the child*. New York: Grossman.

Polsbuck, L. R. (1997). *Animal-assisted therapy for children and adolescents with disabilities*. Proceedings of the 8th International Therapeutic Riding Congress, Levin, New Zealand.

Randour, M. L. (2000). *Animal grace: Entering a spiritual relationship with our fellow creatures*. Novato, CA: New World Library.

Ryan, R. (2002). *Shamanism and the psychology of C. G. Jung*. London: Vega.

Sams, J., & Carson, D. (1988). *Animal medicine cards*. New York: St. Martin's Press.

Scully, M. (2002). *Dominion: The power of men, the suffering of animals, and the call to mercy*. New York: St. Martin's Press.

Shepard, P. (1978). *Thinking animals: Animals and the development of human intelligence*. New York: The Viking Press.

Storm, H. (1972). *Seven arrows*. New York: Ballantine Books.

Sun Bear & Wabun Wind. (1992). *Black dawn and bright day: Indian prophecies for the millennium that reveal the fate of the Earth*. New York: Simon & Schuster.

Triebenbacher, S. L. (1998). The relationship between attachment to companion animals and self-esteem. In C. Wilson & D. Turner (Eds.), *Companion animals in human health* (pp. 135-148). Thousand Oaks, CA: Sage.

Tucker, S. (1997) Effects of equine facilitated therapy on self-concept, locus of control, impulsivity, and hopelessness in adolescent males. In B. T. Engel (Ed.), *Rehabilitation with the aid of a horse: A collection of studies* (pp. 207-220). Durango, CO: Barbara Engel Therapy Services.

Wilson, E. (1984). *Biophilia: The human bond with other species*. Cambridge, MA: Harvard University Press.

THE FLIGHT OF GEESE

So long ago
The geese took flight
Winging their way across the sky.
We who were in the garden
Heard that faint flapping
And the honking
Of the south bound seekers
Speaking of a distant land.

The sky is gray now.
Clouds mount in the north.
There will be snow
Though no one knows just when.

In the quiet of my room
I still hear the lingering echo
Of the flapping and the honking
Understanding now
That urgent language
Pressing onward
Ever southward
Homeward to the quiet land.

-- Michael Sheffield

Art by Mariana Castro de Ali

Creativity and Intention in Evolution

Albert Low

This year will see the bicentennial anniversary of Charles Darwin's birth; he was born on the 12th Feb 1809. In the same year, the 150th anniversary of the publication of *The Origin of Species* will also be celebrated. Darwin has now taken his place as one of the great scientific innovators of all time and has changed for ever the way we see ourselves, and our place in the universe. Even those who hold to the biblical account of creation and see Darwin's theory as a profound error can no longer take for granted that their beliefs are beyond question. Yet, the debate between the Creationists and the neo-Darwinians continues in full fury. One outcome of this has been that Darwin's theory has become entrenched as a dogma, defended by evangelical apologists, and because of the distortions introduced in this defense it is no longer a reasonable account of how human beings have evolved from earlier life forms.

While extraordinary progress has been made in the field of genetics, and while we are gradually beginning to understand the mechanisms by which hereditary characteristics are passed on, Darwin's theory itself has become ossified, resisting change and it remains more or less as Darwin originally wrote it down. Michael Shermer in his book *Why Darwin Matters* tells us that according to the famous biologist Ernst Meyer "five general tenets of evolutionary theory have been discovered in the years since Darwin published his revolutionary book" (Shermer, 2006, p. 6). Yet all five are intrinsic to Darwin's theory, and cannot be

Albert Low, LLD is the teacher and director of the Montreal Zen Center. He has authored thirteen books, some of which have been translated into French, Spanish, Portuguese and German. *The Origin of Human Nature: a Zen Buddhist Looks at Evolution* (Sussex Academic Press, 2008) and *Conflict and Creativity at Work: The Human Roots of Corporate Life* (Sussex Academic Press, 2008) are his latest publications. Before taking up practicing and teaching Zen full time he was an executive in a large utility in South West Ontario.

considered to be discoveries made since Darwin published his book. The lack of any real development in Darwin's theory is all the more surprising because according to the 2004 Gallup poll almost 90 percent of Americans polled rejected the neo-Darwinian solution to the mystery of life. Only 12 percent agreed with it. Fifty percent believed that God created the earth and all life on earth according to the way described by Genesis.

Darwin's theory has the simplicity and elegance worthy of a great theory: organisms have evolved. The changes leading to evolution have arisen through chance and random mutation. Because of natural selection, these changes have allowed some organisms to become better adapted to their environment than others. Those that are better adapted have tended to survive in greater numbers, and they have been likely to transmit their characteristics to the next generation. The idea that all life gradually evolved from a common ancestry is like a beautiful symphony evolving from the simplest of themes. One cannot help thinking that because this idea is so beautiful, so utterly simple, it must be true.

Darwin's original theory allowed for the possibility that influences other than chance and natural selection modify species. He protested, in the last edition of *The Origin of Species,* "I place in a most conspicuous position — namely at the close of the introduction — the following words: 'I am convinced that natural selection has been the main but not the exclusive means of modification.' This has been of no avail. Great is the power of steady misrepresentation" (Darwin, 1859). And one hundred and fifty years later, it is still of no avail. According to neo-Darwinian dogma, random mutation modified by natural selection is not *one* of the ways species have been modified: it is the *only* way.

Darwin, in his *Descent of Man,* offered one alternative to natural selection. This alternative was sexual selection, but for over a hundred years scientists ignored the idea. It became respectable again when an Israeli biolo-

gist, Amotz Zahavi, proposed the "handicap principle." The peacock's tail had caused evolutionists much consternation. The prevailing idea had been that all changes contributed in some way to the survival of the organism in which the change occurred. Yet the peacock's tail was cumbersome and made flight almost impossible for the bird, and so appeared to be a handicap, rather than an aid, in the struggle for survival. Zahavi's theory was that the tail is a "sexual ornament," and that sexual ornaments indicate the fitness of their bearers. The peacock has to devote a lot of energy to grow and maintain the tail, to say nothing of the energy that it takes to carry it around and to display it. An unfit peacock is unable to bear the cost that this entails and so cannot compete with a fit peacock in gaining the attention of a peahen. Hence he will be unable to pass on his genes to posterity.

A plethora of variations of and improvements to this theory have been suggested, but almost all of these have been linked to a mechanistic interpretation of genetic inheritance, and so the mechanistic/materialistic view of evolution has generally prevailed. The fascination with genes and the belief that they are in some way the sole key to understanding human evolution and development grips the scientific community.

Why has Darwin's theory remained frozen? Why have his protestations been of no avail? Why have influences other than 'natural selection' been resisted so strongly by mainstream scientists? Why has sexual selection only become truly respectable since it has been shown to be amenable to mathematical investigation and mechanical interpretation?

In the first place neo-Darwinians assume that the 'science' that has made possible the remarkable revolution in the way we think and so see the world that Isaac Newton and his successors have bequeathed to us, and which has given us technological mastery of the world, is an adequate science for investigating the mystery of life. A second questionable assumption is that classical logic, which is intrinsic to that science, is an adequate logic for this kind of investigation. These two assumptions have led to the conclusion that living organisms are but complicated machines and that evolution can only be understood as a succession of causes and their effects and that changes in the direction of evolution are initiated by random chance modified by natural selection.

During the sixties and seventies, when I was still an executive, management theorists debated the 'real' reason for a company's existence. Some said that a company was in business simply in order to make a profit for the shareholder. A management theorist, Earnest Dale, was a leader of this school of thought. Some said that the company was there to serve the market. Management guru, Peter Drucker, advocated this line of thought. Others again claimed that the company was there to serve the interests of the technocrat; John Galbraith held this view. Each school marshaled excellent logical arguments in favor of its position. None could logically refute the other. A fourth theorist, Wilfred Brown pointed out that all three -- the shareholders, the market and the employees – had equally the potential to close the company down, and so a company was in business in the interests of all three. In view of this, instead of a univalent theory that classical logic demands, a multivalent or systems theory was necessary. In *Zen and Creative Management* I pointed out that these three, shareholders, market and employees, make up a field out of which the product of the company emerges.

A similar kind of argument could be made in favor of a field out of which organisms emerge. The three dimensions of this field would be: natural selection, sexual selection and *creative selection*. The force that provides the impetus to evolve would be the struggle to survive. Darwin, and more recently biologist Geoffrey Miller, have given cogent reasons for the validity of the theory of sexual selection. In the *Origin of Human Nature* (Low, 2008) I argued

that creative selection too might well play a part in evolution.

The mechanical theory of evolution by its very nature excludes creativity. The idea of a machine being creative is absurd. Creativity is intentional and gives rise to novelty; a machine reacts automatically, and only according to the way that it has been designed. Creativity requires consciousness, but the expression 'mechanical' is used to indicate the very antithesis of conscious. The idea that we are nothing but machines is so deeply entrenched in modern thinking that to advocate the influence of creativity in life and evolution will immediately be dubbed "unscientific." The discovery of the DNA code seems to have confirmed that characteristics are transmitted only by way of the genes. With the recent success in mapping the human genome, and of genetic engineering generally, scientists now take it for granted that only a material solution holds promise of resolving the enigmas of the mind and of human existence. Cloning, stem cell research, organ transplants, cyborgs, genetic engineering, and most important of all the development of computers, give us a view of the world in which we, and all living organisms as well, are but complicated machines.

The development of the computer has led scientists to an even firmer conviction that we are but machines, because, in the way we think, the line between the human and the mechanical gets evermore vague. We are now 'switched on,' 'programmed,' have 'hardware' for brains and 'software' for minds. Even Al Gore in his book *Assault on Reason* continues the assault

on reason by saying things like "we have to absorb vast amounts of culture into the 'operating system' of our brains," (Gore, 2007, p. *52.*) and "our capacity for fear," which he tells us is turned on and off, 'is "hardwired" into the brain." (Gore, 2007, p. 28) Artificial Intelligence researchers talk about artificial intelligence and claim that computers will soon replace human beings in fields that so far have been our preserve. The physicist, Frank Tipler, assures us that it will not be long before it will be racist not to see machines as humans.

There is nothing wrong with using metaphors to help communicate ideas. Poets in all cultures and of all ages have done this. For Shakespeare, as an example, "All the world's a stage." To look upon the world as a machine, or the mind as a computer, can help when thinking about the world or the mind. However, although to talk of the cheeks of my beloved as roses is all very well, if I start fertilizing those cheeks to keep them young I'm likely to run into trouble. While a metaphor declares, "this is that" it declares, at the same time, "this is not that." Some value may be gained in likening a body to a machine and a mind to a computer, provided we keep squarely before us the truth that neither is the case.

A most obvious difference is that the operations of a machine and of a computer occur according to a string of causes and effects: this happens and this is the consequence, which in turn becomes the cause leading to a new effect. While this sequence can also occur in the body/mind, nevertheless the body/mind is capable of *spontaneous, intentional activity*. That this is so, that intention as well as cause, effect sequences are involved in living activity and its evolution, is, as I will show in a moment, borne out by Darwin's own theory of evolution. Why this is so important for us at the moment is that intention is an essential element in creativity. If, as I suggest in *The Origin of Human Nature*, evolution has creativity as a key component, or, better still, evolution is slow motion creativity, then I must

Art by Mariana Castro de Ali

first establish that intention plays a key role in that evolution.

STRUGGLE FOR EXISTENCE

Darwin's theory of evolution is based upon the notion of natural selection with its equally important counterpart: the struggle for existence. One could say that natural selection and the struggle for existence together provide the keystone of his whole edifice. Let us remember the theory again. Changes leading to evolution have arisen through chance and random mutation. Because of natural selection, these

I have said that the ideas of a struggle for existence and of natural selection make up the keystone of the Darwinian structure. Unfortunately the word 'struggle' is not quite as innocuous as it may seem. On the contrary, Darwin uses it in a very ambiguous way. This ambiguity of expression, and the misuse that neo-Darwinians have made of it with their mechanistic dogma, has been the main reason why the vitality has been drained out of his theory leaving an empty shell in its place. A careful reading of what Darwin has to say will show that draining the theory of evolution of vitality, and in particular of intentionality, is not just unwarranted; it is a corruption of the

and including (which is more important) not only the life of the individual, but success in leaving progeny.

I have emphasized 'in a large and metaphorical sense' because this part of Darwin's statement has been ignored by almost everyone who has written anything about the theory. R. C. Lewontin, the Alexander Agassiz Research Professor at Harvard, protests (1991, p.83), "Modern biology has become completely committed to the view that organisms are nothing but the battle grounds between the outside forces and the inside forces. *Organisms are the passive consequences of external and internal activities beyond their control*" (my emphasis) In a fictional letter to Darwin, The British geneticist Gabriel Dover of Leeds University specifically says (2001, p.9), "natural selection is not an 'active process' like artificial selection. . . [it] is *a passive outcome* of the particular interactions between prevailing ecological conditions and a particular set of genetically unique individuals." (again, my emphasis.)

> Unfortunately the word 'struggle' is not quite as innocuous as it may seem. On the contrary, Darwin uses it in a very ambiguous way.

changes have allowed some organisms to become better adapted to their environment than others have. Those that survive reproduce and pass on their characteristics to the progeny.

We could use the metaphor of a sieve. Natural selection is a sieve that 'sieves out' the 'unfit.' Suppose that you want to have organisms of a certain size or above. You put organisms in the sieve, shake it and those that are smaller than that size selected pass through the sieve to oblivion. Now, suppose you want large round organisms only. You pass the large organisms through the sieve and only large round organisms will remain. Now you only want green, round, large organisms. In this way, theoretically, natural selection could operate over millions of years with sieves of all kinds operating in series and parallel, producing all the species that we now discover around us, as well as all those that have eventually passed through to extinction. In such a model no intention is necessary. That natural selection "has no purpose in mind does not plan for the future....has no vision, no foresight, no sight at all," and that it is a "blind, unconscious, automatic process," (Dawkins, 1988, p. 5) is the essence of the *neo-Darwinian theory* of evolution. But *Darwin's theory* points in quite another direction, as we shall see.

theory.

Darwin (2004, p.74) writes about the struggle for existence in Chapter 3 of his book *The Origin of Species.* The first paragraph is quite clear and unambiguous: it stresses the importance of the idea expressed by the phrase 'the struggle for existence.' Let me quote at length:

All organic beings are exposed to severe competition. . . . Nothing is easier than to admit in words the truth of the universal struggle for life, or more difficult — at least I have found it so — than constantly to bear this conclusion in mind. *Yet unless it be thoroughly engrained in the mind, I am convinced that the whole economy of nature, with every fact on distribution, rarity, abundance, extinction, and variation, will be dimly seen or quite misunderstood.*

So far this is a very clear, unambiguous statement about the importance of the idea 'struggle for existence.' I have italicized the sentence that shows how important Darwin felt the idea to be. But he goes on to say (2004, p.75),

I should premise that I use the term 'struggle for existence' *in a large and metaphorical sense,* including dependence of one being on another,

Yet, that Darwin saw things quite differently is quite obvious if we continue our reading of him. By using the word struggle in a metaphoric sense, he says life is a struggle, and that it is not a struggle. He does this in the following way (2004, p.75), "Two canine animals in a time of dearth, *may be truly said* to struggle with each other which will get food and live. But a plant on the edge of a desert is said to struggle for life against the drought, though *more properly* it should be said to be dependent on the moisture." I have emphasized two phrases: 'may be truly said,' and 'more properly.'

The struggle for survival is basic to his whole theory. Yet, in spite of the beauty of his prose and clarity of thought, he is ambiguous. He tells us that he will use the term 'struggle for existence' 'in a large and metaphorical sense.' It is a struggle because two dogs 'may be truly said to struggle'; it is not a struggle because 'more properly' it should be said that a plant is dependent on the moisture. In other words he conflates two entirely different meanings under the one term: struggle. Darwin is convinced that, unless the struggle for existence "be thoroughly engrained in the mind . . . the whole economy of nature . . . will be dimly seen or quite misunderstood." Only the metaphorical struggle to survive has been thoroughly ingrained in the mind of the neo- Darwinians, and so they have only "dimly seen or quite misunderstood . . . the whole economy of nature, with every fact on distribution, rarity, abundance, extinction, and variation."

When I likened natural selection to a sieve I was referring to the struggle for existence in a purely metaphorical way. Those organisms that stay in the sieve survive yet they did nothing of themselves to achieve this. They just happened to be the right size and so stayed in the sieve. Let us say that an earthquake strikes a city and thousands die: the survivors mostly do nothing to survive. They just happen to be in the right place. A severe drought occurs. Some plants happen to be fortunate and are rooted near an underground well. The rest die of thirst. These are examples of the neo-Darwinian idea of the struggle to survive. As Dover said above, "Evolution is not an 'active process' like artificial selection . . . it is a passive outcome of the particular interactions between prevailing ecological conditions and a particular set of genetically unique individuals."

Darwin used a fight between two dogs to show what he truly meant by the expression 'struggle to survive.' One of the chief factors that determine whether the dog is going to survive is its determination to win. The drive to dominate, to be the alpha male, is a feature of human as well as wild life, and the struggle is not simply a struggle for food and sex, it is also an expression of what Nietzsche called the 'will to power.' Will to power, the will to dominate, is a driving force at all levels of life and makes possible the true struggle for existence, rather than the metaphorical struggle. This means that another form of struggle is possible other than the metaphorical struggle that is the sole interest of the neo-Darwinians. I will call it *active struggle* of which intention and the will to power are aspects. This struggle is quite different from metaphorical struggle.

Another aspect of active struggle is illustrated by a well-known experiment conducted by a gestalt ethologist, Wolfgang Köhler. He put some bananas outside the cage of a chimpanzee and just out of her reach. He put a stick that she could reach close by the cage.

When the chimp became hungry she saw the bananas and struggled to reach them by stretching her arm through the bars of the cage. She could not get them. After some frustrating moments she was able to perceive the gestalt, hunger-bananas-distance-stick. She pulled the bananas into the cage with a stick.

We can see then that active struggle is not only intentional, it is also intelligent. The conclusion that has been drawn from this experiment, and accepted by much of the scientific community, is that the chimp perceived a gestalt, the sudden appearance of the whole: hunger-bananas-distance-stick-satisfied hunger. The perception of a gestalt in a field that is apparently disconnected and random is a creative and intelligent act. The chimpanzee used intelligence and creativity. This means that intelligence and creativity, as well as volition, may contribute to making active struggle possible.

We now no longer simply have an organism being modified by the environmental sieve. We now have intelligent, creative and dynamic organisms that are part of, and so modifying, the evolutionary sieve. Ernst Jantsch says in his book *The Self-Evolving Universe* (1980, p.8), "Evolution is open not only with respect to its products, but also to the rules of the game it develops. The result of this openness is the self-transcendence of evolution in a 'metaevolution,' the evolution of evolutionary mechanisms and principles."

When two dogs fight to determine who will survive, the qualities that enabled the dog to be victorious now form part of the sieve and so the evolutionary mechanisms evolve. The qualities of the victorious dog 'sieved out' the defeated dog. The victorious dog won by strength, agility, speed and sharp teeth, all of which may have been evolved through successive metaphorical struggles. But also greater determination, stealth, cunning, intelligence were involved. These will now become part of the sieve that the defeated dog passed through to extinction. Cunning, stealth, intelligence, these are all creative; determination is the opposite of passivity. Kohler's chimp used cunning and intelligence when getting the bananas. Future animals when pitted against animals of superior determination, intelligence, creativity, cunning, or stealth will have to pass the test of determination, intelligence, creativity,

cunning or stealth to survive. But, because the more determined and intelligent will survive in greater numbers than the less determined and less intelligent, those that survive will raise the determination and intelligence threshold of the sieve. As the determination, intelligence, creativity and other such qualities of animals evolve, the sieve will evolve also, it will become ever more demanding, requiring higher and higher levels of determination and intelligence to survive.

Now that determination, intelligence, creativity, cunning and stealth are part of the evolutionary sieve, evolution is no longer the result of blind chance alone. Determination, intelligence, and the other qualities, now guide evolution as well as blind chance. That this is so, that the influence of intelligence becomes more important as the organism becomes more evolved, runs counter to most modern theories of evolution. To return once more to Dover's quote, he says, "Natural selection is not an 'active process' like artificial selection." Yet, on the contrary, active struggle is very similar to artificial selection. Because determination, creativity, intelligence, and judgment, are all parts of the evolutionary sieve, the selective process itself becomes active and intelligent.

Theories of evolution have the concept of the 'arms race.' For example, as prey become more swift of foot, so their swiftness selects out the less swift predators for extinction. These are unable to keep up with the prey and so starve. This means that the swiftness of the prey selectively breeds fast predators. But fast predators selectively breed fast prey.

The evolution of creative intelligence is the basic arms race, and eventually, with the advent of human beings, becomes the most important element in the evolutionary sieve. Creative intelligence is the most essential ingredient in both prey (to avoid the predator) and predator (to capture the prey). Intelligent and creative prey breed intelligent and creative predators, and intelligent and creative predators breed intelligent and creative prey.

Let us remember what Darwin said about active struggle: "two dogs fighting over food in time of dearth," may be truly said to be a struggle, but that metaphorical struggle, "a plant on the edge of a desert," is not so much a struggle and should more properly be

Uniqueness, Mariana Castro de Ali

said to be a dependency on the moisture. He exhorts us to remember the struggle to exist as a vital factor in evolution. In general, scientists have only kept in mind metaphorical struggle, which is not truly a struggle, and have ignored active struggle. They do this because the notion of metaphorical struggle supports a mechanistic theory of evolution, while the notion of active struggle negates such a theory. Intention, not causation or accident, powers this kind of struggle.

Creativity and intelligence form part of the evolutionary sieve. We cannot therefore simply speak of 'natural selection.' Evolution is not only intentional; it is also intelligent and creative. These, intelligence and creativity, do not act in an arbitrary way; they have to wait until the right circumstances are present. The tree of evolution may branch out and modifications of species or new species arise, but this is not because of foresight or because designs or decisions are made in advance; it is because the situation comes to demand it. Only very recently, and only in some modern art, has creativity come to be regarded as the expression of the arbitrary, the 'original', the different, and idiosyncratic.

While some scientists are doing all that they can to prove that human beings are simply machines, ironically others are doing all they can to prove that machines are humans and, eventually, their superiors. Frank Tipler, (1994) in his book, *The Physics Of Immortality: Modern Cosmology, God and the Resurrection of the Dead,* has calculated the complexity of the human brain in units called flops and, on the basis of this, has estimated that, at the present rate of growth in the complexity of computers, a mere seven years is

all that is necessary before we have machines complex enough for us to consider them to be, not just machines, but persons as well.

One would have hoped that he would have made his prediction with his tongue firmly in his cheek, but no, he claims the book to be a serious one, it has an appendix of about 120 pages of erudite formulae for the scientist, and it attempts to show that machines are to be our saviors. These intelligent machines will "enhance our well being, even if they are our superiors in every way. Without the help of intelligent machines the human race is doomed. With their help we can and will survive forever." (Tipler, 1994, p.86) To reject such an idea, "to regard the creation of such people - I call intelligent robots people because that is what they are, is racism." (Tipler, 1994, p. 86) He defined racism (1994, p.20) as "a belief in the inherent superiority of any group of intelligent beings." Presumably politeness would require that in our conversations with the machines we would address them as "You." Incidentally he made this prediction fourteen years ago and I've yet to call my computer "Sir."

GOAL SEEKING PROGRAMS?

Even so, with the advent of the computer the neo-Darwinian has a convenient way by which to side step the intentional and creative activity of organisms. Ernst Mayr (Mayr, 1988) was one of the first to take this route and he developed, in order to show that seemingly intentional activity is after all explainable in purely mechanistic materialistic terms, a strategy that he called *teleonomy.* Mayr was one of twentieth century's leading evolutionary biologists, and he is considered to

have invented the modern philosophy of evolutionary biology. So what he says must be taken seriously.

To point up the problem of intention Mayr used two quite opposing statements to describe a single activity: the turtle leaves the sea *and* lays its eggs; the turtle leaves the sea *in order* to lays its eggs. These are mutually exclusive because the first implies a purely mechanical activity explained by the principle of causation; the second implies intention of some kind. He said that scientists whose main concern was the evolution of organisms preferred the first way of describing the activity; scientists in the field studying the activity itself preferred the second way. He was a mechanist and so was committed to the first of these ways of describing the turtle's behavior, but he had the integrity to realize that a great deal would be lost if he discarded the second way. Most theorists, both those in the field and those in the laboratory, prefer simply to ignore the problem.

The problem is simply stated: how to account for what appears to be intentional behavior within a mechanistic/materialistic theory. To solve the problem Mayr tells us that the turtle is programmed by evolution to leave the sea and lay its eggs. Programmed behavior, or what he calls *teleonomic* processes, he states have a number of characteristics: they are directed towards attaining a goal and this goal-directness is the function of the program; they imply a dynamic process rather than a static condition; this dynamic process has two components: a program to guide it, and some end point or goal, *which is foreseen* in the program that regulates the behavior. Natural selection produces, and variations adjust, each particular program in ways beneficial to the survival of the organism.

So that no one will convict him of heresy because he introduces intention, he emphasizes that a program is material, that it exists prior to the initiation of the teleonomic process, and that it is consistent with a causal explanation. Not only this, "a teleonomic explanation is in no way in conflict with the laws of physics and chemistry." (Mayr, 1988, p.52)Although he claims that a program is material, he defines a program as "coded or prearranged *information* that controls a process (or behavior) leading toward a given end." (Mayr, 1988, p.52) (My italics)

He assures us that organisms are no different from man-made machines, and he explains that he chose his definition of a program deliberately to show the mechanistic nature of organisms. "One might overlook the mechanistic nature if one were to make a distinction between what seems to be 'purposive' behavior in organisms from man made machines." (Mayr, 1988, p.52) The truly characteristic aspect of goal seeking behavior according to Mayr is not "that mechanisms exist which improve the precision with which a goal is reached," but rather that "mechanisms exist which initiate, i.e. cause this goal seeking" (Mayr, 1988, p. 46).

I appreciate that Mayr was writing long before the recent developments in genetic research took place, and before the new science of 'Evo Devo' was developed. I have not introduced his theory of teleonomy for its current importance in evolutionary science, but to show the lengths that even celebrated thinkers will go to remain within the mechanistic/ materialistic dogma. His theory moreover gives the general outline of any mechanistic theory based upon the notion of programming no matter how sophisticated it might be.

Let us then consider Mayr's theory carefully as by doing so we can see the fallacies of this kind of reasoning. Mayr tells us that teleonomic processes are based upon programs. Mayr tries to make both programs and machines consistent with a material, causal explanation. He wants to make the programs consistent with the principle of causation because he says that one cannot draw a line and say organisms are purposeful and machines are mechanistic.

But, although the program is inscribed on some material, the program cannot therefore be said to be material. A program is not only the material on which is it inscribed; it is also a code. When I buy a program I buy a DVD; not long ago I bought a CD. Before that the program was put on a floppy disc; yet again before that it was punched onto cards. Before it was put on to any of these it was formed in the mind of the programmer. DVD, CD, floppy or card, all are material. In this way the program is material, and material that obeys the laws of physics and has had its own evolution. But, as I say, the program is also a code, and a code is not material. As far as the code in which the program is written is concerned, it does not matter what kind of material is used on which to inscribe it. The code is not material; it is 'mental,' whatever that might mean. The language in which the code is written is an offshoot of written language, which in turn is an offshoot of spoken language, and so has its own long evolution that is quite distinct from the material on which it is written.

Geneticists also conflate the material and the 'mental,' and reduce them both to the material. The DNA code is 'written' on molecules, which are matter. Even so, just as the computer program is written on material things but is not material, so the DNA code is written on molecules, but it isn't the molecules. Molecules are what the code is recorded on. The CD, floppy, and molecules obey physical laws. These must be thought about in one way; the program is subject to semiotic controls and these must be thought about in an entirely different way. Semiotics is the study of how meaning is made and understood. But Mayr is saying that *the code is subject to the same physical laws as the material on which it is inscribed.*

Mayr's programs, moreover, are blatantly teleological. He says that teleonomic processes are directed towards attaining a goal, which is foreseen in the program that guides them. Whether a 'mind' or a 'program' foresees the goal, and directs the organism to attaining it, the result is still teleological. Mayr moreover says a mechanism exists which initiates goal-seeking behavior. A program, either in its material aspect or in its semiotic, does not, and cannot, initiate goal-seeking behavior. Programs are tools that may improve the precision, speed, or accuracy by which a goal is realized, but intention, not tools, gives rise to what could be described as 'goal seeking' behavior. No amount of research into programming is going to change that fact.

A program is an extension of the programmer's intention. For example, s/he writes a program 'with the intention that,' when s/he presses a button on the computer, a printer in the next room will begin to print. If s/he does not have that intention s/he will not write that program. Furthermore the intention guides the programmer in everything s/he does including checking whether it functions as it should. If it does not, the programmer will trouble shoot the program, and this trouble shooting will be guided by his/her intention and, if necessary, s/he will write another program and this again will be guided by his/her intention.

One can say that getting the printer to print is the 'goal' of the programmer, if one likes. But this is just a way of talking. In the description that I gave of what happened I did not feel that it was necessary to use the word 'goal.' The word intention means goal oriented but that does not mean the intention and the goal are two and separate. When a composer writes a piece of music s/he may write a melody. But the melody is not the goal of writing the music. The programmer does not have a goal of writing the program nor does s/he need to have an image of a printer being turned on as s/he writes the program.

Moreover a 'goal' has no bearing on the way either the program or the printer will operate. The programmer's intention on the other hand does determine the way the program, and so the printer, *will* operate. I have emphasized the word 'will' because the 'goal,' that is the outcome of the intention, is in the future. But this future is not the future in time, but the future in sequence: first this, then that. Nothing lies in the future. The intention creates the future. The programmer could just as well go through to the next room, press a button on the printer with the intention that the printer should begin to print. By doing this s/he simply bypasses the program. The program just makes it easier for the programmer to carry out his intention. Whether s/he does bypass the program or whether s/he writes the program makes no difference to the intention; it remains the same.

After the program has been written and installed anyone can come along and press the same button and print a page. Someone might prefer to say that the printing is 'automatic,' meaning mechanical. This is true of the activity of the printer; it is entirely mechanical: this wheel turns and lifts that lever which turns on that circuit and so on. Another person might want to say that the program prints the page. Yet it is the programmer's intention that does the printing, coded as the program, and inscribed on the DVD though it may be. The hardware of the computer and the printer is necessary, but it too operates according to the intention of those who designed and manufactured it.

Even so one would not examine either the machinery of the printer for the intention of the engineer who designed it, or the CD of the program in the hope of finding the programmer's intention lurking in it like some ghost in the machine. But, without the intentions of the programmer and the printer's designer, the printer will not print.

simulate a purposeless evolution. Whitehead (1929, p. 26) points out the irony of this when he says, "Scientists animated by the purpose of proving they are purposeless, constitute an interesting subject for study." If a particular formula for proving that evolution is possible without purpose does not give the desired result it is refined, improved upon or rejected and another is sought. Thus, built into the program, is the scientist's purpose. By 'built in' I do not mean that one will find it in the binary logic of the program, but that the sequence and pattern of this program embodies the scientist's purpose.

The claim that *élan vital* is not necessary in the simulated evolution of species is refuted by the fact that if a power failure occurs the evolution stops and, unless an automatic 'save' has been installed into the program, all evolution would be lost. In other words the electric current flowing from positive to negative gives the thrust to the simulated evolution. Another way of

have, as a chess master has, an intuitive understanding of the strategies they use, so in the same way within the working of these evolutionary programs, no creativity is involved.

Perhaps, after all, evolution does not require creativity, and perhaps the chess master does not need to understand the moves s/he make in an intuitive way, but these programs can do nothing to resolve the question. All that they can do is to pose it in a newer and more interesting way. Indeed from what we have been saying it would seem that a kind of Gödel's law could be proposed: one cannot consciously and intentionally prove the nonexistence of consciousness and intention.

A car is also 'programmed.' The parts of a car are assembled in a certain way in order that when a key is turned in the ignition the engine of the car will start to run. The structure of a car and its program are the same. A computer differs from a car because, although it too is programmed in a certain way so that when a key is turned or button pressed the computer begins to run, a program other than its structure is necessary.

One could say that a clock is programmed to tell the time. Telling the time is the purpose of the clock. But, of course, the clock does not tell the time, nor does the clock have the purpose; the person who uses the clock, has the purpose and tells the time. Whoever invented the clock did so because s/he intended to tell the time, or s/he intended that when other people intended to do so they could look at his clock. The purpose of a computer could be said to be to process information. But, again, the computer does not process information; the person using the computer does so, but finds it expedient to use the computer to help in doing this.

Even the computer in a guided missile does not process information; the programmer who programmed it does so. This is also true of programs that can learn as they go that are built into robots. The robot neither processes information nor is it intelligent. The programmer uses arcane mathematics that has taken millions of human beings working for millennia to develop, and more recently the programming language, with which s/he codes his intention so that a robot *appears* to be processing information and acting in an intelligent way.

> So if one denies that an organism is intentional, they still have the problem of how to account for what appears to be intentional behavior within a mechanistic/materialistic theory.

Recently scientists have written computer programs to simulate evolution. Their intention has been to show how, within a few parameters built into a program, forms or structures evolve, compete with others, mate and procreate. The success of the programs have led these scientists to claim they have demonstrated that the evolution of life forms involves no *deus ex machina*, no *élan vital*, no purpose or intention. Evolution 'just happens' once the preliminary and simple limits have been imposed. The irony is, however, that these programs demonstrate quite the opposite.

The claim that evolution does not need a *deus ex machina* is refuted by the presence of the programmer. The programmer is the *deus ex machina* and chooses among a vast variety of highly sophisticated mathematical formulae in order to find the appropriate one to establish the necessary initial parameters. The claim that intention or purpose is not necessary is refuted by the scientist's own purpose which is to

putting this is that time, or *durée*, or a dynamic unity, is given by the current, which makes evolution possible.

Finally the simulated evolution of the species does not proceed 'ex nihilo'. On the contrary the computer itself simulates a highly sophisticated cosmic gel or cosmic soup in which the new 'life forms' crystallize out. One only has to touch the innards of a computer inadvertently and again evolution crashes to a halt. This inadvertent touch is perhaps a metaphor for a slight change in the environment within which life forms arise and within which they can be destroyed.

Thus far from proving what s/he sets out to prove -- that the evolution of life forms is a purely materialistic, purposeless and valueless affair -- the scientist, by creating his/her ingenious programs, proves just the opposite. Furthermore, the forms generated are not material forms at all, but purely symbolic forms, animated mathematical formulae with interesting graphics. Just as chess playing programs do not

The two behaviors, that of a machine and that of an organism, do not form a continuous gradient as Mayr would have us believe. But the break in continuity does not occur because the machine is mechanical and the organism intentional. A steam engine and an organism both use three 'energies' in their activities: caloric, electrical and intentional. The difference between them is that intention is extrinsic to the engine and is built into it by the designer, but intention is intrinsic to the organism. The origin of the intention of a machine comes from outside the machine; it comes from the machine's designer. The origin of the intention of an organism is the organism itself.

Said slightly differently: a structure that has intention as one of its dimensions, (an organism) is different to a structure which has the dimension of intention added to it (a machine). This distinction is very important and one that Mayr overlooks. The programmer's intention is essential for the creation of the program, no matter how sophisticated that program happens to be, although the intention cannot be found by examining the program. With an organism the intention is intrinsic to it.

When he was describing the teleonomic process above, Mayr said, "A teleonomic process depends upon some end point or goal, which is foreseen in the program that regulates the behavior." In a program this end point or goal is not 'foreseen' in the intention of the programmer. 'Foreseeing' is a way of describing intention. In the same way, an organism does not have a fixed and determined goal that it foresees. The 'goal' changes constantly according to the changing circumstances of which the organism is a part. One could say that just as intention is purposeful without having any fixed purpose, so an organism is goal oriented without having a fixed goal.

In spite of all that he says, Mayr leaves the most important question of all unanswered: "How does a program direct a given teleonomic activity and how does it cause goal seeking behavior?" Mayr (1988, p. 49)in truth replies, "Alas all the biologist can tell us is that the study of the operation of programs is the most difficult area of biology." One reason for this is, "the number of qualitatively different cells in a higher organism almost surely exceeds a billion." "Indeed", he also says,

"it must be admitted that the concept of a program is so new that the diversity of meanings of the term has not yet been fully explored." Mayr is saying that he is not quite sure what a program is and how it does what it does, but nevertheless he is sure it does it. So if one denies that an organism is intentional, they still have the problem of how to account for what appears to be intentional behavior within a mechanistic/materialistic theory.

A serious objection could be made to all that I have said. Someone might well challenge me and ask, "You speak of evolution as intentional, intelligent and creative. You speak of the programmer as the *deus ex machina*. Are you therefore introducing some kind of god into the evolutionary process? If not who is it that is creative, intelligent and acts intentionally?" Undoubtedly this is a serious objection. What, above all, has raised the ire of scientists when confronted with this new craze for Intelligent Design is the idea that God is the designer.

However, the question can only be answered by another question, "Are you sure that 'someone' an 'agent' or 'self' or 'God' has to be involved? In the West, most of us are quite sure that a 'self' of some kind is involved in deciding what to do, in thinking, in creating... indeed in all our activities. But is it? Is a 'self' involved? Presumably you have been reading what I have written so far; but what self was involved? It is true that I say *you* were reading it and that *I* am writing it, but do I use 'you' and 'I' simply because our language demands a personal pronoun of some kind?

With our current logic either someone is doing all this or no-one is doing all this. We cannot say both someone and no-one is doing it, any more than our logic allows us to say that a particle is both a wave and not a wave. Yet a celebrated master of Zen, a discipline that I have practiced now for more than forty-five years, assures us that "True self is no-self." This no-self to which the master refers transcends the mind and body, the repository of what we normally consider to be the self.

Perhaps we should be clear on what I mean by 'transcends.' When you go to the movies you experience a variety of situations – love and hate, war and peace, action and drama depending on the plot and script of the movie. At the end of the movie all that is left on the

screen is a white light. What you saw throughout the whole movie was a series of modifications of that white light, even though you were not in the least of aware of the light itself. The light *transcended* the images. In the same way all that you experience is a modification of what the Zen master Hakuin is calling No-Self.

In case one feels that this is too fanciful, Hakuin's true Self has much in common with the physicist, David Bohm's, 'Implicate Order' as well as Emmanuel Kant's noumenon. In his book, *Wholeness and the Implicate Order,* Bohm (1980, p. 11) talks of *Undivided Wholeness in Flowing Movement* and says, "Definable forms and shapes, some stable and some unstable, can be abstracted from the universal flux. In this flow, mind and matter are not separate substances. Rather, they are different aspects of one whole and unbroken movement." Kant also opined,

We can propound the transcendental hypothesis that all life is really noumenal only, not subject at all to temporal changes - neither beginning nor ending in death; that the life of change and birth and death is phenomenal only - a mere representation, through the senses, of a purely spiritual life - that the whole world of sense is only a picture hovering before us, formed by our present mode of knowledge - a dream lacking any objective reality in itself. (de Nicolas, 1976, pp. 240-1)

Hakuin's true Self is a very ancient idea that had its inception in the Vedic era. According to Vedic Hymns, "Divine and human forms of expression reflect in [their] own way that transcendent, hidden, unified principle of harmony and order that supports and directs the movements of all things" (Mahony, 1998, p. 1). Tibetan Buddhism expresses No–self thus, "That fundamental pervasive, unified, holistic process whose highly energized dynamics set up the variety of sub-processes and their associated structures." The name that the Tibetans give to this dynamism is the Ground (*gzhi*), and it "is the ground and reason for everything...[it is] thoroughly dynamic ...[and] responsible for the variety of structures, things, and experiences that are said to make up Reality" (Guenther, 1984, p. 5).

As long as we insist, as do the neo-Darwinians, that we must stay within the Newtonian worldview, and that to investigate the mind and life forms we must use the tools that have been developed to investigate the material world, we will never be able to make sense of Hakuin or of David Bohm, nor shall we ever be able to escape from the prison of mechanism. As Westerners we are relative newcomers to the study of consciousness, life and intention, and we should perhaps be prepared to adopt new methods, new logic and an entirely new worldview in order to make headway with this study. And how do we begin? The British biologist T. H. Huxley, also known as Darwin's Bulldog due to his vigorous defense and advocacy of Darwin's theory, gives the simplest answer, an answer that is in complete accord with the Zen Buddhist tradition:

Science seems to teach in the highest and strongest manner the great truth which is embodied in the Christian concept of entire surrender to the will of God. Sit down before every fact as a little child, be prepared to give up every preconceived notion, follow humbly wherever and to whatever abysses nature leads, or you will learn nothing. I have only begun to learn content and peace of mind since I have resolved at all risks to do this (Gould, 1999, p. 40).

REFERENCES

Bohm, D. (1980). *Wholeness and the implicate order.* London: Routledge and Kegan Paul.

Darwin, C. (2004). *The origin of species.* London: The Collector's Library.

Darwin, C. (1859). *The origin of species.* Last sentence of the Introduction. Available from http://www.talkorigins.org/faqs/origin.html.

Dawkins, R. (1988). *The blind watchmaker.* Harmondsworth: Penguin.

de Nicolás, A. T. (1976). *Meditations through the Rg Veda: four dimensional man.* New York: Nicolas Hay.

Dover, G. (2001). *Dear Mr. Darwin.* London: Phoenix.

Gore, A. (2007). *Assault on reason.* New York: Penguin Group.

Gould, S. J. (1999). Rocks of ages: science and religion in the fullness of life. New York: Ballantine Books.

Guenther, H. (1984). *Matrix of mystery.* Boulder and London: Shambhala.

Jantsch, E. E. (1980). *The self-organizing universe: scientific and human implications of the emerging paradigm of evolution.* Oxford: Pergamon Press.

Lewontin, R. C. (1991). *Biology as ideology: the doctrine of DNA.* Concord: House of Anansi Press.

Low, A. (2008). *Origin of human nature: a Zen Buddhist looks at evolution.* Brighton and Portland: Sussex Academic Press.

Mahony, W. K. (1998). *The artful universe.* New York: State University of New York Press.

Mayr, E. (1988). Towards a new philosophy of biology: observations of an evolutionist. Cambridge, MA: Harvard University Press.

Shermer, M. (2006). *Why Darwin matters.* New York: Henry Holt and Co.

Tipler F. J. (1994). *The physics of immortality: modern cosmology, God and the resurrection of the dead.* New York: Anchor Doubleday Books.

Whitehead, A N. (1929). *The function of reason.* Princeton: Princeton University

Art by Mariana Castro de Ali

EARLY WINTER

Summer has melted golden
Lying in brown softness of the earth.
Now silent winter moves among the hills.
The blue heron steps noiselessly
Through the snow.
On the inlet's bank
Trees stand motionless
Waiting to begin their dialogue
With the wind.

-- Michael Sheffield